Spain
History

13⁵⁰

The
Rise and Fall
of
Paradise

The
Rise and Fall
of
Paradise

ELMER BENDINER

G. P. PUTNAM'S SONS
NEW YORK

The author gratefully acknowledges permission from the following sources to use material in their control: Frank Cass &
Co Ltd for material from *Spanish Islam* by Reinhardt Dozy,
copyright © 1913 by Frank Cass & Co Ltd. David Goldstein
for material from *Hebrew Poems from Spain* by David Goldstein,
copyright © 1965 by David Goldstein. The Jewish Publication
Society of America for material from *The Jews of Moslem Spain*
by Eliiyahu Ashtor, translated by Aaron Klein and Jenny
Machlowitz Klein, copyright © 1973 by The Jewish Publication Society of America.

This book is set in 11 point Baskerville

Library of Congress Cataloging in Publication Data

Bendiner, Elmer.
The rise and fall of paradise.

1. Andalusia (Spain)—History.   2. Arabs—Spain—
Andalusia—History.   3. Jews—Spain—Andalusia—
History.   I. Title.
DP302.A5B46   1983   946'.8   83-3351
ISBN 0-399-12857-3

PRINTED IN THE UNITED STATES OF AMERICA

To Esther, Jessica, Winnie, Paul and Gabrielle

Contents

1 Land of the Four Blessings   9
2 Arabs at the Gate   25
3 The Immigrant Emir   45
4 A Jewish Princedom   60
5 Ziryab Sets the Fashion   76
6 By Goat to China   98
7 Martyrs to a Tyranny of Smiles   116
8 The Luck of the Mountain Boy   130
9 The Palace of the Caliph's Lady   145
10 The Kidnaped Rabbi   169
11 Doctor and Diplomat   187
12 The Dictatorship of Dogma   210
   Bibliographical Note   245
   Index   251

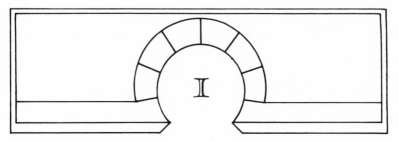

Land of the Four Blessings

"There are no Jews in Spain," says the bearded young Spaniard who sports on each cuff link a blue-and-green enameled Star of David.

We are driving—five of us—in a diminutive, rattling Volkswagen Rabbit from Lucena, a pleasant but scarcely distinguished town, to Cordoba, some thirty miles north.

Lucena has shrunk dramatically in size and glory from what it was a thousand years ago when it was celebrated as a Jewish metropolis, much enriched by the prestige of its scholars and the skill of its doctors. Students traveled for months or even years to find at the feet of its sages healing, wisdom or perhaps merely a reputation for strenuous piety. And young wild men were brought down from the forests along the Rhine and Danube or up from Africa to Lucena's surgeons to be expertly castrated and so launched, by biological correction, upon careers of glittering promise as eunuchs, close to the seat of power in the court of the Caliph of Cordoba.

Of course, Lucena was also a city of Jewish masons, plumbers, farmers, grocers, butchers, lute players, navigators, poets and saloon keepers. That was a millennium ago.

Now there are no Jews, says the man with the Davidian cuff links. There are only the Christian descendants of Jews. Nor are there any Arabs or Berbers, though the radio in the Volkswagen sings in a minor key that would befit a mosque, if not a synagogue. And the names of the rivers, mountains and towns on our route roll off the tongue like an Arabian chant.

In the VW we bounce past groves of gray-green olive trees, their trunks carved and twisted as if by an artist tormenting the truth out of a landscape. We rattle over the Roman bridge at Cordoba where Jews once took their Arab saviors by the hand.

Up front in our rattletrap are two young artists. Behind sits our friend with the interesting cuff links—teacher, student and editor with an eminent reputation in his native Lucena. (A bartender had readily pointed out his house and dispatched a customer to fetch him for us.) With him are Esther and I, intruding with our questions as we pass through the Spain of our time on our way to the tenth century.

Of course it is not strictly true that there are no Jews in Spain. In some cities there are even synagogues, aside from those that serve as museums. But the Jews who use them are newly arrived, not the descendants of the Jews of al-Andalus, that strange kingdom of a thousand years ago. Our friend, born of a proper Catholic family, knows that he is descended—on his mother's side undoubtedly and perhaps on his father's side as well—from the old Jews of al-Andalus. He and we are in search of the ghosts of Arabs and Jews who lit up this corner of Europe in a dress rehearsal for the Renaissance.

Why are these young Spaniards so fascinated by the long-dead inhabitants of their town? The truth is that the old ghosts have never been properly exorcised. They are visible every week in Lucena. "Walk down our streets on a Saturday," suggests the man with the cuff links. "You will see every apartment, every house and every patio in a whirl of conspicuous housewifery. Women are sweeping and mopping and shopping."

"On a Saturday?"

Obviously, I remark, these are not Jewish ghosts. He chuckles. Quite the contrary, he insists. He finds in this pattern of demoniacal Saturday housecleaning a reflection of a lingering worry concerning the long-vanished, ever-present Holy Office of the Inquisition. Those fifteenth-century Spanish Jews who chose baptism rather than permanent exile from a home they had known since the fall of the Temple in Jerusalem were closely watched. The penalty for a convert's relapse into Jewishness was spectacularly fatal.

Many of these New Christians had the effrontery to rise in Christendom. Many of them married into the aristocratic families of Spain. Some entered the Church rather more enthusiastically than had been expected. They became priests, bishops, archbishops, even inquisitors. Old Christians tended to suspect this adaptability and thought it smelled of fraud, even of blasphemy. Their outrage may have been whetted by envy, but in any case the search for lapses was undertaken with a zeal that promoted spying, carping, informing and the deft manipulation of evidence.

Among the many tests applied to the convert was his willingness to shift the Sabbath from Saturday to Sunday. This was an acid test, because to a Jew the Sabbath was holier and earthier, closer to home than were any of the grander holidays, fasts and feasts. On Saturdays, then, the vigilant Old Christians would watch their new brethren to see whether by a word, a sign, a look, a bath, the barest reluctance to work, to buy or to sell, they might betray a hankering after the ways of the old Sabbath.

The fifteenth-century inhabitants of Lucena, seeking to seem above suspicion, made Saturday their day of conspicuous, noisy housecleaning, and the habit is still with them. But do not Spanish Christians put their houses in order before Sunday? "Perhaps, perhaps, but never with such passion," our student friends assure us.

There must be more tangible, audible, visible ghosts than the paradoxical housewives of Lucena. We hear them perhaps in that flamenco processional—a saeta—that is based on the theme of the Jewish lament, Kol Nidre. Arab ghosts are almost visible in the baroque bell tower of the Mezquita of Cordoba, within whose squared-off masonry a minaret is said to be entombed. The airy structure from which muezzins once called the faithful to prayer proved too delicate to last, they say. It tottered dangerously during a simultaneous earthquake and hurricane in the sixteenth century and was set within these walls like a saint's bones in a sarcophagus.

We climb the tower stairway until we are on the level where great bronze bells hang in their yokes. We look down at orange trees regimented in close-order drill in the patio. We tease our minds with the thought that when the Mezquita was in its glory there were no orange trees in Spain, though some travelers might have seen them grow in North Africa. Whatever the Arabs planted—cypress or perhaps the ubiquitous olive—they were not oranges, and the trees probably were less squared-off and disciplined than they are now. No fountains play in the garden where once the faithful performed their ablutions before they prayed. (It is unfortunate, for the tinkling of the waters must have been musical. Also, if they were now bubbling up beneath the trees, young tourists in shorts and tee-shirts would not have to eat their bread and cheese dry.)

We look beyond the grove to the Mezquita itself, where astonishingly, amid the swelling domes that recall the pink-white roofs of Fez, there rears up an incongruous Gothic cathedral, complete with one-and-a-half flying buttresses and a collection of ramps and ogival arches. This one-time mosque, reconstructed to Christian purposes, is neither Moslem nor Christian. It is a chimera—half horse, half fish.

Like some organic creature, the Mezquita has grown here and shrunk there, developed warts, suffered amputations and other catastrophes both natural and strange. In its heyday it was the center of Moslem Spain. A Moslem can pray without a mosque. He merely spreads a little rug, if he is meticulous, turns himself toward Mecca and touches his forehead to the ground while reciting the prescribed formulae. He does this five times a day. But the Mezquita of Cordoba was more than a place where one might or might not go to pray. It was a center for obligatory political, bureaucratic, and social as well as religious participation. The Caliph came on Fridays not only to lead the prayers but also to gauge the state of mind of his restive and ambitious clans. Perhaps he came also because the Mezquita was high art and he fancied himself an artist as well as a ruler.

In the cool twilight of the Mezquita's interior we are sur-rounded by a miscellany of ghosts of diverse centuries, places and creeds. Topping the dimly seen marble columns are capi-tals of Byzantine, Persian, Roman, Greek and Syrian inspira-tion, some of them salvaged from ruins that were ancient when the Moslems found them. Above the columns soar a forest of interweaving arches—Arabic forms modified by Andalusian fantasy—rising into the gloom. It is dark because the Christians have walled in the once-open mosque, the better to hold the mysteries of the church.

In a clearing lit by a skylight that sends down a dust-filled radiance in a cliché of ecclesiastical art, the cathedral emerges from the twilight. Saint upon saint, in burnished gold or deep mahogany, clash brazenly with oriental arches and alabaster beehives of intricate geometry.

A cleaning woman, trussed like a haystack in voluminous apron and skirts, sends spirals of dust whirling upwards into the light. A cat leaps from a baptismal font and scurries down the shadowy Islamic naves. These are lit by exploding photo flashes, which warn a guard of the approach of a covey of tour-ists. He throws a switch and thus illuminates the Mirhab, that shrine without the form or face of God or saint. It is pure light blazing on great alabaster conches, on niches and domes of fiery purples, greens and gold, on roseate stone where tendrils twine with the shapes of fern and mingle with abstract patterns of squares, triangles and the ornate Arabic letters embodying the name of "Allah, the Merciful, the Clement . . ."

We shall return to this Mezquita when it was a mosque, when the light streamed in from the unwalled patio or when, on some holiday evening, fourteen hundred oil lamps shone in the Mirhab alone and countless torches, resting in sconces along the pillars, lit the marble and stone.

We look elsewhere for signs of that astonishing tenth century. Around the corner from the driveway that leads to the garage of the Maimonides Hotel is a shop that displays the customary tourists' assortment of fribbles. From that corner arching over to the shuttered windows of the first floor of the hotel there stood a gate a thousand years ago—the gate of the Jews. The streets behind it meander as if following a brook across a meadow. Here and there lanes empty into plazuelas named after Judah Halevi or Maimonides or other Jews, Arabs, Crusaders or Romans. The houses, sparkling white in the Andalusian sun, their windows filled with flowers and their wrought-iron gates topped by aristocratic crests, are all too new for our purposes. The houses we seek followed those same twisting streets but almost all were razed in the pitiless convulsion that toppled the urbane culture of Arabs, Jews and Arabized Christians.

We must try to discern among the passersby another, more ghostly crowd of slippered, white-robed men and women. We must try to find in the rhythmic clapping of hands that resounds from the bars a more ancient sound of mules clicking their hooves on cobbled streets. There would be the odors of lamb, mixed perhaps with the medieval stench of an open sewer.

If we stand at the western gate we are aware of roaring boulevards, of trees that seem too young, of a Victorian elegance in bars and hotels. Beyond these lie meadowland and farm, rocks and olive groves. In the tenth century all that was part of an exuberant city, running at least four miles in all directions from what is now the edge of town. Houses crowded on one another all the way to the sumptuous palace that was named by the first Caliph of Cordoba for his wife among wives, his love among loves, Zahra.

Then Cordoba was a metropolis of a million people. There had to be that many at least (though there were few cities in the world with a tenth of that number) because tenth-century observers counting Cordoba's buildings came up with this estimate: 213,077 houses of the middle and lower classes; 60,300 villas for the rich; 80,455 tents, mainly for commercial use, and 1,600 mosques. They did not count the thousands of bath houses or synagogues or churches or the little stalls that were rented by tradesmen. The glory has faded in the last thousand years and Cordoba now holds barely 215,000 people and is the shadow of a shade.

Here we stand, then, beyond the gates of modern Cordoba. The level ground is ideal for a farmers' market and it is strategically placed for business. The roads from Seville in the west, Granada in the east and Algeciras in the south meet here at Cordoba on the Guadalquivir. The twentieth-century road carries only a modest trickle of trucks, buses and cars with, here and there, a few black-goggled young men racing motorcycles.

Viewed a millennium ago those same roads—built by the Romans to tie together this imperial outpost—present a richer traffic. Farmers drive their cattle, which often perversely block the river of white-clad travelers hurrying on foot or on mule to Cordoba. There are few crossroads markets on the plains of al-Andalus, of the sort that in other parts of the world serve to motivate a burgeoning village life. Great cities, not small towns, lure buyers and sellers along with lawyers, bureaucrats, poets and politicians. They readily take to the road, although the 150-mile trip from Algeciras, for example, consumes a week or more.

Some travel alone and some go in mule trains. The animals and their gear may be rented from private companies that offer, for one low price, a total package including not only mules, saddles and harness, along with sumpter beasts complete with straw baskets to hold the baggage, but also armed guards to watch over the rented property and the travelers. Bed and breakfast can be had at reasonable prices in well-spaced inns along the route. These are profitably managed by Christians who look like blue-eyed Arabs. There are Christian monasteries as well in this Arab world and these are often recommended for moderately priced accommodations. They offer no private rooms but a modest dormitory and good wine. Innkeeping is a service that custom seems to have reserved for Christians.

These innkeepers wear Arab clothes and speak a fluent Arabic though they come from the north, which is thought to be a land of barbarians. They practice their religion with a tactful modesty and never proselytize. They have no zeal for martyrdom, the Moslems note with gratitude. Only a few generations earlier a ghastly death was the ambition of a band of Christian men and women. They energetically sought a hideous and correspondingly glorious fate by defaming the Prophet himself in the public squares. They were executed regretfully but nonetheless thoroughly by the sword or on the cross. For weeks their heads disfigured the spikes at the palace gates.

Standing here at the side of the road just beyond those gates it is not possible to distinguish Arab from Christian from Jew. Even men and women dress alike, it seems, except that the men go bareheaded or, in inclement weather, put on a close-fitting felt hat, while the women wrap their hair in kerchiefs and let transparent veils fall in front of their faces. These often dangle coquettishly below the neck. The veil, as a religious necessity, is somewhat out of fashion now, as the mullahs sadly point out in their prophecies of doom.

Class differences are obvious. Here and there the sea of white is broken by a scarlet cloak draped from the shoulders of a man of means. A turban signifies a judge or lawyer, though other gentlemen at court are beginning to wear it as a mark of high fashion. In the spring tunics and skirts blossom in brightly colored silk. Summer and winter are seasons for white.

The complexion of the travelers varies from Sudanese black to Frankish pink with every shade of brown in between. One cannot find in skin color a clue to class—for in al-Andalus blacks may be free and whites may be slaves. To the naked eye slaves look as free as their owners unless their owners are rich enough and gauche enough to dazzle the people around them with fancy scarves and mantles, pendants and rings.

The traffic curls on to the level ground outside the wall of the Juderia. One must stand a little away from the wall because the city garbage collectors have made huge, malodorous hillocks of what they pick up from the streets. The field is covered with tents, jammed close together, leaving only winding labyrinths between them. There is an apparent chaos but an underlying order. The Caliph's bureaucrats have regulated the markets down to the last detail, assuring the buyer that he will get fair weight in the scales, that no bad figs will be buried beneath the good in prepared packages, that the milk will not have been watered, that he will find no spurious diamonds, spavined mules or sick slaves.

Each trade must stick to its own area, and under the law the leader of each guild is held responsible for the infractions of its members. Every craftsman must be a member of a guild, for al-Andalus is held together by meticulous regulations, enforced by inspectors and the inspectors of inspectors.

Weavers, potters, shoemakers, ironmongers, coppersmiths, rice dealers, olive oil sellers, herbalists, stone workers, jewelers—each trade or craft has its own street, lane or alley. Secondhand clothes dealers are permitted to wander throughout the market singing out their wares to whomever will buy.

And who buys at the market? Everyone from slaves, to the ladies of the royal harem, to Jewish vintners and exporters. These last shop at wholesalers', seeking to fill the holds of their ships that wait at Algeciras to sail to Venice or Tripoli or Constantinople or India or wherever their kin and connections make trade possible.

Food stalls are fragrant with plants, dried or fresh-cut, to be used in cooking or for the color they lend to cushions or curtains or drapes.

Elbowing through the throngs go the lute players, jugglers, acrobats, puppeteers, magicians, story-tellers and the players of chinescas, those tinkling bells dangling from multicolored tasseled staffs, making the happy sound that is said to ring out as the breeze passes pagodas in far-off Cathay. Entertainers gather around the taverns where wine is bought by the cup or the jug. Mullahs quote the Koran against drink, but this is not Damascus or Baghdad. This is the Caliphate of pleasure where piety is revered—in others. Ancient injunctions, ritually repeated by Moslem and Jew, against the graven image have little to do with the displays of carvings in the jewelry bazaars where graceful animals, alluring women and heroic men are sculpted in silver and gold.

Al-Andalus is also a country where taxes are needed to support a grand and costly civilization. Taverns yield revenue, as do the brothels that accommodate visitors far from the comforts of home. Such sins must be glossed over. Purse-snatchers and cheating tradesmen are another matter entirely. These criminals pay no taxes and there is therefore no need to indulge them in their vices. When caught the wretches no longer suffer the amputations and disfigurements prescribed by the Koran. (Such ideas are viewed with horror in fastidious Cordoba.) Capital punishment, however, is not uncommon. Executions offer the public not only justice but also a macabre thrill and a salutary feeling of superiority in virtue, canniness or luck over the hapless criminal. It is generally regarded as a moral entertainment.

High fashion is set in the workshops of Almería and Seville, but in the Cordoba market silks, brocades and damasks catch the eyes of women who can pay. These may be harlots or ladies of the court or women from the provinces who claim a kinship, however tenuous, with the Caliph. (His family tree sprouts innumerable twigs and all those perched thereon claim pensions, petty titles, stipends and other perquisites that give them the wherewithal for fancy shopping.) In these genteel markets wealthy women, without the veil, try on silk kerchiefs and run their fingers over crystal glassware. These are the latest products of Cordoban artistry and technology, turned out by the royal factories, which seem to promise no end of beauty, comfort and delight to the senses.

Things are constantly changing under the beneficent rule of Abd-er Rahman III, the first actual Caliph of Cordoba. His predecessors have always acknowledged, if only as a matter of form, the suzerainty of the Caliph of Damascus or Baghdad. Now Cordoba so outshines those ancient capitals that it would be ludicrous to make even a formal bow in their direction. The political critics in the taverns think Abd-er Rahman was right to declare his independence, though by assuming the Caliph's title he has moved some little distance from the people. Perhaps that, too, is right, they say, for what is proper for an emir is not necessarily proper for the Caliph.

What does it matter if the people do not see as much of their ruler as of their mullah or their barber? They see the glorious processions trotting on miles of carpeted streets to the royal palace at the end of the city. The life of the streets is uninterrupted theater.

And here is another sign of change, the genteel shoppers note. Only a few years ago the stalls sold the finest parchment in the world, made from the skins of Andalusian sheep or Saharan gazelles. There is still parchment being sold that is as fine as ever, but now most people are using the new paper that Cordoban technologists have made from flax.

Linen paper is showing up in the bookstalls. Handsomely calligraphed scrolls are attracting a greater public every year. Aside from the Koran and delicately illuminated Haggadoth, there are poems and romances and mathematical essays. Such scrolls have become high fashion in interior decor, and some of the rising business class, who pay extravagantly for a copy of a learned medical treatise paraphrased from the Greek by some Jewish doctor, leave it partly unrolled on a pillow where it gathers dust but sheds prestige.

The literary-scientific talk of the day is of just such a book being prepared by that singular favorite of the Caliph, the physician-poet-diplomat, the Jewish prince, Hasdai ibn Shaprut. They say he is collaborating with the monk Nicolas on a monumental translation of an ancient work, brought as a gift from the Eastern Emperor Constantine Porphyrogenitus. It is a copy of the *De Materia Medica* by Dioscorides. Who knows what these two will get out of it in subtle therapies and potions that even the Greeks have long forgotten? In any case the Caliph will love it and the court poets will sing of his wisdom in developing the nation's natural resources, which include the brains of Jewish scholars and Christian monks.

The market stalls of musical instruments do a brisker business than do the bookshops. There are for sale lutes, mandolas, drums and flutes of varying timbres, decoration and price. Those who cannot play an instrument see to it that their children or their wives are taught to play. The poor struggle on homemade pipes or sing their wailing melodies as they sip their rose-scented water at the end of the day.

The rich and almost rich and would-be rich must have music

for their parties, which proceed from food and drink to poetry and dance to the acrobatics of the bedroom. Someone, it seems, must warble or whistle or strum up to the final climactic act of man and woman or man and boy. In the cities of al-Andalus the poor people listen to music if they can, to poetry if they can't. Pious Moslems deplore all of it. Jews, and the more adaptable of the Christians, enjoy the secular life of this teeming, stimulating metropolis and keep their piety for their homes.

There are business people who do not hawk their wares like those flashy merchants who have just brought in the latest novelty in fashion—pants for women. A solemn dignity attends the shops of carpenters and bricklayers, men of importance in the community, who do more than saw wood and lay bricks. In their stalls, seated on pillows, they discuss the problems of creating, for example, a communal house to be built for a group of families in the Jewish manner, or a private palace, complete with baths and gardens. These are the architects of Cordoba. You will find them a little way apart from the market up the streets that wind away from the Mezquita toward the west and north.

The quality of this city, in its most shining century, is best seen, perhaps, in the slave market. There you have a sample of Divine Providence at work, arranging the social order of the world as at a gaming table. One may be a master one day and—if one is not related in some way to the Caliph—a slave the next. Slaves may rise to be slaveowners. Freemen may wish they were slaves. The color of one's complexion or the creed one follows does not define the difference between slavery and freedom.

Still, there is no doubt that color counts. Blacks, mainly Sudanese, are held apart in the market because they draw higher prices. Sudanese men tend to be tall and handsome, and the Caliph fancies them for his guard. They are the envy of the slave market and of poor freemen because they will be well fed and magnificently caparisoned in white tunics and red cloaks. They will ride not mules but Arabian horses, the pick of the breed-farms set up on the islands in the Guadalquivir below Seville. At the very worst they may be used as runners in the postal service. Sudanese men have a reputation for fleetness and fortitude, and are trusted to carry the messages of empire from the Caliph's palace to the farthest outpost in the north. A code of smoke signals can only carry the crudest messages and trained homing pigeons have just come into use but are not regarded as reliable.

Sudanese women are prized not only as concubines but also as promising material for the schools that have been patronized for a century or so in Cordoba. Here they learn how to entertain their masters and mistresses, not only in bed but also at breakfast and at dinner. They learn to make music and to dance but that is scarcely the beginning of their education. They are also given courses in astronomy, mathematics and medicine, as well as Greek, Roman and Arabic literature, so that they may be stimulating conversationalists as well as adepts in love.

Such schooling exemplifies a penchant the upper-class Cordobans seem to have for devising trouble for themselves. These women, often as educated as their masters, have come to exercise an extraordinary influence on the politics and culture of the time. The harem coup is an eventuality that princes fear.

Light-skinned slaves are confined in separate areas of the market, depending on whether they are Franks, Berbers, Gallegos or Slavs (a term that includes Frankish and Germanic tribes and the peoples east of them). The blue-eyed Germans are thought to make excellent house slaves. Slav women are considered attractive enough to fetch a good price. Many of the men, however, end up on small farms where they may spend years or perhaps a lifetime in back-breaking work. Still, their lot is not much worse than that of the free farmer who owns them and works beside them. Al-Andalus is made for city folk. Being sent to the galleys of the Royal Navy is likely to be a far more onerous fate, though there is always hope for liberation in battle or after it.

Some slaves undoubtedly have been kidnaped from their

homes, but these are a small proportion of the men and women brought to market. Most have been captured in wars or taken at sea by pirates. Even in the holiest of wars the Moslem soldier—who is expected to serve without pay if the mullahs declare the conflict to be truly sacred—is allowed a share of the loot. And the loot often includes prisoners.

A soldier can take his captives to market himself, but few want the trouble or the expense of feeding and caring for such perishable property on a long voyage. Most sell their prisoners to wholesalers.

There are many roads to emancipation. A man may send his slave into war as his proxy, and if the slave survives he is automatically freed. (The owner would have difficulty in any case retrieving him after a victory on a far-off battlefield.) The erstwhile slave might then have a slave or two of his own to sell. Those who serve the court have a rare opportunity, for the Caliph Abd-er Rahman III has learned to tap the talents of his slaves, whether eunuchs or not. He has pensioned off inept aristocrats among his officials in order to make room at the top for the captives. The policy has done wonders to improve the efficiency of the bureaucracy and the military. Generals and viziers frequently turn out to be ex-slaves these days.

Pious Moslems are supposed to free their Moslem slaves after a reasonable amount of work has been sweated out of them. The soldier or part-time pirate who captures a Jew is in luck. The Jewish community, whether in Cordoba or Lucena, Jaen or Seville, uses its own resources to ransom fellow-Jews and will pay particularly well for a rabbi or a poet with a religious reputation. (Cordoba has gained its most celebrated rabbi by ransoming him and his family after they were captured at sea along the coast of their native Italy.)

A woman slave is generally freed after giving her master a son. These manumitted slaves usually do not leave Cordoba but stay to ride the whirligig of fortune, buying and freeing slaves, falling again and perhaps rising once more.

The slave trade, like any other, is meticulously regulated, inspected and taxed. Doctors must be on hand at the market to examine the merchandise. (Midwives are assigned to check the women slaves in order to spare the doctors any temptation.) All purchase contracts must include a clinical assessment and a full list of body blemishes so as to establish a record in case a suit should develop among the highly litigious Cordobans. A proverb declares that "Jews spend their money at Passover, Moors at weddings and Christians in lawsuits," but actually the high-pitched clamor for civil justice rises from all sides.

There is no record that anyone—Arab, Jew or Christian—has seriously criticized the slave market. The laws are supposed to make it fair—at least for the buyer and seller. And is not slavery the way of the world? True, the Koran frowns upon the enslavement of Moslems; Jews do not countenance the holding of Jews in slavery—at least not beyond the seven-year term specified in Scripture—and Christians are dismayed at the sight of Christian slaves. But slavery itself is not called into question. (Actually Christians are continuously being embarrassed by the flood of Christian slaves who flee from Christian masters in the north. As soon as they reach Cordoba they rush to some Islamic judge and utter the magic formula that wins their instant emancipation: "There is but one God and Mohammed is his messenger.")

Al-Andalus is a country of innumerable laws, some mild and some onerous, but the Caliph's serene caprice is above all. As a corrective to tyranny there is only the influence of past history and of present advisers, or the assassin's knife. To correct the assassin's tyranny there is the headsman's sword. But grisly politics do not greatly trouble the high spirits of the time and place.

There is a legend, probably invented by a poet during a lazy afternoon in Cordoba, that characterizes this most paradoxical of countries: When Allah was furnishing the empty shell of the world, the legend has it, al-Andalus petitioned for five blessings—clear skies, a beautiful sea bountifully stocked with fish, trees hung with fruit, fair women and a just government. Allah granted all but the last wish, reasoning that if all the other blessings were given a proper government, al-Andalus might rival paradise.

If simple worldly justice is sometimes out of reach in al-Andalus—and it is not always so—the arts and delights of the world are readily at hand. A question stirs, not in the minds of the Andalusians but in that of the astonished visitor. How did this oriental bazaar of sensuous delights arise in medieval Europe? The answer involves the asking of other questions. Why did the Arabs and Berbers come out of the African desert and why did the Jews, those pre-Hispanic Spaniards, open the gates and offer them the keys to the kingdom?

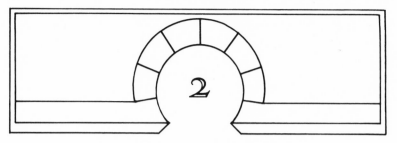

Arabs at the Gate

Sixth- and seventh-century Spain, before the Arabs and Berbers discovered it, was an invalid lapsing into terminal agony while strangers rummaged greedily through closets and under the bed to see what tattered glories or broken gods might still be put to use.

The old Roman middle classes had almost disappeared. Their remnants grumbled about ruinous taxes. Roads that once channeled the life-blood of this imperial outpost had fallen into disrepair. Sewers that had carried away the detritus of a sophisticated society had broken down. The resulting stench was driving the rich to their country villas.

Cities, which had been meant to copy Rome or Athens, had become the inheritance of the unemployed, who had to be maintained on a dole and supplied with parades, circuses, gladiatorial bloodshed and low-priced theater. (The critics called their theater little more than pornographic vaudeville.) When the unemployed were not amused they rioted.

Theatrical folk were regarded as so vital to the preservation of urban peace that they had to be kept at their essential jobs by force of law. Some tried to escape to other professions or to idleness and had to be brought back forcibly to the stage. Worse yet, their children were condemned to be actors, hack writers, singers, mimes or producers.

This caste system had been an experiment of the Emperor Diocletian, who three hundred years earlier tried to impose stability on chaos by ordaining that the occupation of a father should be followed by his children. The sons of soldiers would be soldiers; the sons of bakers would be bakers; and the sons of the rich would be rich. The idea was never followed to the last detail throughout the empire but it was still a force to hold together the fabric of society in this crumbling colony without a motherland.

Who, for example, would have paid for all these amusements if the middle class had not been chained to their responsibilities? At one time the curia had been a much-honored institution of the propertied classes. The cities were run by the curials, who were accustomed to be treated with a grave respect, like home-grown senators. Now those still listed on the property rolls as owning more than the twenty-five acres required in the definition of curials cursed their fate. They paid most of the taxes, they paid for relief of the poor, they paid for the mimes and gladiators, even for the whores, whether or not they enjoyed them. They had little left to live on and still less dignity. They could not sell their land without governmental permission, and in any case no one would be mad enough to buy a millstone to hang about his neck.

Some abandoned their fields to join the runaway actors, serfs and slaves in outlaw bands that peopled the woods. There they kept their freedom and harried those who stayed at their places and pretended that society was still viable.

The more comfortable ghosts of Roman civilization could still be found in some stately villas of the countryside. Patricians often wore the aristocratic title of senator though few had ever participated in that body, long since become archaic and impotent. They ate what was raised by their slaves and tenant farmers, drank their home-grown wines, relaxed in the summer under fans wafted by slaves, and warmed themselves in winter with wood that slaves cut from the forest. Their mosaic floors and fading frescoes were washed by the household staffs, but it had become almost impossible to find craftsmen capable of repairing the plumbing or the chipped masonry.

The Romans amused themselves by recalling their ancestors who had distinguished themselves in frontier fashion by subduing, in two hundred years of intermittent guerrilla warfare, the indigenous peninsulars. These were the semimythical Iberi whose genius for hit-and-run warfare was probably embellished by the Romans to make the conquest seem greater. The long-vanished frontier glories were inadequate anecdotal consolation. The empire builders, gone to seed, venerated the past while they consigned the present and the future to tearful, drunken damnation.

They were Romans in decline, some graceful, some tawdry, lolling in their baths, reading or remembering old verses and old gods. They played with dancing girls or boys, with statuettes, with tapestries and hangings brought back from the edges of the world at a time when barbaric people still accepted tutelage in civilization from the universally acknowledged masters of the art. Now there would be no more tapestries from quaint faraway places. Only one people of the past remained close at hand—the Jews.

Once the Jewish rebellion in Jerusalem had been suppressed and the Temple destroyed, Jews ceased to be the enemy. (The emperor Julian had even tried to restore the Temple, though more out of dislike for Christians than love for Jews.) In any case Jews had been welcomed in all parts of the empire as exotic but interesting and useful adjuncts. They enjoyed the dignities and privileges of a *religio licita*—a lawful religion. The title was a ticket to civilization. In Spain, where a million or more settled, they were farmers, navigators, doctors and merchant seamen. They traveled, wrote, performed their religious rituals, guarded the Torah and, on high holidays, sighed for the vanished Temple. They were allowed to follow their own laws for the most part, but in any case Jewish and Roman law shared a kindred logic. The Jews gave Caesar his due in taxes and lived in reasonable contentment under the protection of their erstwhile enemy. Culturally they stood apart, mistrusting the easy-going Hellenistic temptations of latter-day Roman society, but they relaxed in the toleration of the Roman state, which was traditionally extended to those subjects lucky enough to be impotent as well as useful.

Officially Romans were Christians. They became so almost

by royal fiat when Constantine found universal Christianity to be a solution to his problem of managing a huge, sprawling and disunited empire. Although the Church gloried in the official status it never fully trusted the pagan predilections of Roman aristocrats.

St. Augustine tried persuasively, but with apparently only indifferent success, to rally the patricians out of their nostalgia for the good old days of the empire. "Let us lead a good life and the times *are* good," he argued. "WE are the time. As WE are, so are the times." The difficulty with that approach was that the Romans, particularly what was left of them in the provinces, were being asked to incorporate themselves into the Augustinian, not the Augustan, "We." It was hard to forget Rome's glory, to forget its "mission," as the empire builders fancied it. And it was doubly hard to accept the uneasy present as a high road to glory when beyond the walls of the villas, in the torn and bleeding countryside and in the ravaged towns, the poor were being driven, in some shocking cases, to cannibalism.

On the other hand, missionaries and bishops had been received with almost passionate enthusiasm by the Germans and Slavs who encountered Christianity as they came out of the woods. The new faith was seen by them as the very essence of Roman civilization. As they admired the legend of Rome's might, the majesty of its law, the marvel of its architecture, its armor and its machinery of war, so did they take to the new God, jettisoning the old and ineffectual Teutonic pantheon.

These were strange converts, worshiping a novel, gentle god while they whooped through what was left of civilization, wearing animal skins, painting their faces, drinking, fighting, pillaging and raping. The Romans had long ceased to offer resistance. The fading succession of emperors had armed one tribe to beat another, only to find that the trusted ally was unwilling to relinquish the province or the city he was hired to save. A fifth-century country gentleman and literary dilettante, Sidonius Apollinaris, wrote to a friend: "You avoid wicked barbarians; I avoid even good ones."

While it is true that many patricians were content to eat their way to oblivion, tickling their palates with peacock eggs, there were some in the long twilight of Roman rule who experimented with asceticism, taking to heart the terrible strictures of St. Jerome. Still others advocated a down-to-earth brotherhood, acknowledging a kinship with slaves since all humanity was the captive of capricious fortune or an inscrutable god.

Mixed with such brotherly love was the old fear of the slaves' revenge. In earlier days, when those fears were raised in the Senate, it was proposed that slaves wear some distinctive piece of clothing so that they could be distinguished from free men. The motion was overwhelmingly defeated when the Cordoban Seneca warned, "The slaves might then take to counting *us.*"

As the patricians concentrated property in fewer and fewer hands they similarly concentrated the slaves. In some cases several thousand slaves and their families worked for a single master. At the dawn of the seventh century those slaves, many of them Germanic, were joining their kin, who had become the real masters of Spain.

The Suevi, for example, scorched the Galician earth in a sixty-year terror that ended only when the Visigoths ousted them. When the Visigothic tide went back over the mountains the Suevi resumed their enjoyment of Galicia and the Asturias. The Vandals came in from the Balearic Islands and laid waste the countryside around Cartegena until the Romans bribed them to take off for Africa. They later regretted that decision when North Africa showed signs of being Vandalized.

When the Visigoths were won over to Christianity, half a century before they crossed the Pyrenees, they followed the Arian doctrine, which cast doubt on the divinity of Jesus and stigmatized the concept of the Trinity as a dilution of strict monotheism. Hostilities between them and the Catholics were as fierce and bloody as only disagreements among holy men can be.

Spain was part of a vast battleground where Visigoths, Suevi, Basques and Franks fought one another, and where

Arian bishops and Catholic bishops cheerfully let their respective vicars profane their rivals' churches by stabling horses in the naves.

Some of the Visigothic kings, who succeeded one another with great rapidity, tried to curb the anarchy of outlaws, freebooters and extortionists disguised as tax collectors. They did not get far in their attempts at order because they were forever contending with fresh invasions or insurrections by hostile tribes. Pretexts for hostility were eagerly sought. Often they were found in marriages.

In one such instance King Amalaric, an Arian Christian, married a Frankish maiden named Clotilda who was obstinately Catholic. He nagged at her so relentlessly to allow herself to be converted that she complained to her powerful Gallic father, who launched hostilities at once. That war ended with the Visigoths driven forever out of Gaul and sealed inside Spain by the Pyrenees and the angry Franks. What happened to the stormy marriage of Clotilda and Amalaric is not known.

The Visigoths made Toledo their capital but their rule was spotty. Where their garrisons could sit on the lid of religious or political dissent the Visigothic king of the hour could be said to govern. For the most part loyalty to the regime was a bare formality in the windy anarchic spaces of the Spanish countryside.

It was in the year 587 that the hitherto staunch Arian, King Recared, ten months after his coronation, surprised Toledo by announcing that he had been converted to Catholicism. Some historians grant a modicum of importance to the role played by doctrinal arguments in the conversion of Recared. Others tend to think that his change of heart was a political maneuver. The Catholics had the money and the support of Byzantium—far away but still carrying the prestige of the Roman Empire. And most Christians in Spain were at least nominal Catholics.

Even more unifying than a common faith, however, is a common enemy. The likeliest common enemy, conveniently at hand, was the Jew.

If Catholics could not tolerate Arians they were unlikely to pass over the long-standing religious competition of the Jews.

Even under the Arian kings and bishops there had been laws branding marriage between Christian and Jew as simple adultery. (Jews would scarcely call that decree oppressive since, on the whole, they tended to agree with the notion.) Jews were also forbidden to own Christian slaves or to hold public office. All this might have been bothersome but, like most Visigothic laws, these were not widely obeyed. Jews continued to preside over their own courts, to practice their religion and to marry Christians.

The tendency to intermingle despite statutory restrictions is proven by the annual spate of new regulations designed to disrupt this lovemaking. One year, for example, it was decreed that all children of such intermarriages should be baptized. That regulation had to be reformulated and solemnly enunciated annually in succeeding years. The measure was unenforceable. Even when it was complied with as a formality it was ineffective, since a Christian conversion could not be assured by the application of blessed water to the head any more than circumcision could guarantee adherence to Judaism.

The situation grew more grim, however, with the coming of Sisebut to the throne of Toledo in 612. In the fourth year of his reign he summoned a council to hear new proposals concerning the Jews. By the end of 616, he declared, any Jew refusing baptism would be given one hundred lashes and, if he still proved stubborn, he was to be banished and all his property confiscated.

Sisebut claimed divine sanction because he had made himself an archbishop of sorts. Actually, although some churchmen eagerly assented to his decree, others, including that comparatively broad-minded humanist Isidore, archbishop of Seville, objected vehemently.

It is likely that Sisebut and his supporters were motivated, at least in part, by the prospect of confiscating the rather extensive farms run by Jews. In any case by the end of 616 some ninety thousand Jews had accepted baptism, but this is generally reckoned to have been a small fraction of the total Jewish population in Spain. Of the ninety thousand it is thought that many continued to lead Jewish lives in secret. Some left the country but most stayed on. Many continued to work their lands. After all, the Jews had a very long history of peaceful collaboration in Roman Spain. The persistence of old customs and old friendships tended to water down the effects of royal decrees.

A later council, organized by Isidore, moderated the anti-Jewish laws but in turn that moderation was repealed by still other angry councils of Toledo. In the end all Visigothic kings were to be sworn to the mission of stamping out Judaism. Terror now descended on the Jews of Spain, the people chosen by officialdom to demonstrate the power of monarchy and of the state Church.

Neither the unity of the Church nor the preoccupation with hounding Jews was enough to end the murderous wrangling of Visigothic nobles, kings and generals, however. Since kings were elected by a council, a crisis of succession occurred every time a king died. Sometimes the king named his successor, but that choice was not always honored. Often the old king was shuffled off his throne to death or dishonor before he could pronounce the name of his successor. In 680, when King Wamba was dethroned after an eight-year reign of unremitting warfare against power-hungry nobles, a politician named Erwig took the crown.

Erwig set about killing or banishing the friends of his predecessor in the time-honored way, and then aspired to a religious role by drafting a brand-new set of anti-Jewish laws. Again the Jews were given a year to have themselves baptized or face banishment, horrendous whip scourging and the humiliation of having their heads shaved. He was probably the first European leader to use the phrase *Judaeorum pestis*—a plague of Jews—and to call for their extermination.

After seven years, in which again the murderous laws proved generally unenforceable, Erwig died. He had chosen his son-in-law Egica to succeed him. However, as soon as he was crowned, Egica divorced his wife, the late king's daughter, and scuttled the fortunes of all relatives and friends of his predecessor. Then followed the usual uprisings of angry nobles, including the primate of Toledo, who hatched a conspiracy to assassinate the king and all his officials.

Vastly more important than any of these routine conspiracies was the attempted revolt of the Jews in 694. The Spanish Jews had planned it painstakingly with their fellow Jews across the straits in North Africa. There were then a good many Jews along the North African coast, including the descendants of those who had fled Jerusalem seven hundred years before, plus those who had gone into exile, goaded by Visigothic persecution, plus many Berbers from the Atlas Mountains who had been converted to Judaism.

It is impossible to reconstruct the complicated diplomatic and military preparations of that fateful year. In any case the Jews were betrayed by informers and the revolt crushed before it began. It was later charged, probably with considerable accuracy, that the Jews had planned to establish an independent state of their own in Spain. It would have been a clear and simple solution to their desperate plight.

After the collapse of the Jewish rebellion another council was summoned to Toledo to devise still more horrible schemes for extirpating Judaism from Spain. Jews were now seen as a major political danger. They would all henceforth be slaves, it was decreed. Their goods were declared confiscated. Jewish sons at the age of seven were to be given to Christian slavemasters who would raise them as Catholics and see that they married Catholics.

Still, what was thundered in Toledo echoed only faintly beyond the walls of the city. Some Jews died and some were converted and some lost their children, but most went on with their farm work and their marketing while kings and nobles were busy fighting one another. Coup and conspiracy followed with dizzying speed. Rebel nobles, when captured, were routinely tortured, blinded or put to death. Bishops conspired with this faction or that, and some went to their deaths in small partisan causes that loomed great for a season.

In 710 a rebellion tossed to the surface a king named Roderick, who would be assigned a major role in history although he was to play his principal scene, a short one, in the arms of a girl.

While Roderick was raging in the customary and bloody manner appropriate to the first year of a new administration, another political aspirant was struggling to hold his own as governor of a city in another part of the collapsing Roman Empire. That city was Ceuta, the "Pillar of Hercules" on the African shore at the gateway to Europe. Ever since Carthage fell the emperor in Constantinople had held on to the African continent by clutching at this forlorn fortress of Ceuta. Now, as the eighth century opened, the Romans lost their last African outpost. Arabs, trailing the green banners of Islam westward from Damascus, had taken Ceuta. They had swept through the ranks of the valiant but disorganized Berbers from the Rif and Atlas mountains. Those who survived the sword of Islam were quick to perceive the spiritual qualities of the Koran. Actually they tended to become more Moslem than the mullahs.

The westward push had been astonishingly successful but now the Arab armies were stopped by the Atlantic in the west and by the high Atlas range and the blazing deserts of Ifriquiya in the south. Across the straits from Ceuta, Spain looked inviting, but the Arabs were in no position to invade an unknown land where the logistics seemed risky. They would have to depend upon sea transport and their escape route, if needed, would be a bottleneck at Gibraltar. Spain looked like a nicely baited trap.

Musa ibn Nusair, who had brought off the conquest of Morocco, was not given to rashness. He was old and content with parading his supreme authority in front of the Berbers, whom he regarded as freshly rescued from godless barbarism. After he had taken Tangier and made it his headquarters Musa turned to Ceuta, which was commanded by a Christian Berber of the Ghumara tribe who had a long record as a canny politician. He had to be a Christian because the Roman bishops would never have allowed an unbeliever to govern even a remote garrison town.

He was probably called Yulyan but his name entered history

in a variety of transcriptions from the Arabic, such as Urban or Olman. Centuries after he was dead he came to be called Julian.

Whatever his name, he had maneuvered to maintain himself and Roman authority in Ceuta by dealing, not warring, with those at his gates. When the Arabs conquered the African shore and threatened Ceuta, Julian proceeded to negotiate as he had with the local tribesmen, though clearly with more circumspection. He readily surrendered in the name of Rome and acknowledged the suzerainty of the Caliph of Damascus. In return for this peaceful transition and his pledge of cooperation he persuaded the Arabs to let him continue to govern Ceuta with a measure of autonomy, to retain his standing in the Church, to keep his princely rank, and to practice his highly successful brand of diplomacy.

For some time he had had to dabble in Visigothic as well as Berber politics. He had played the game of backing the winning factions with remarkable success, thereby keeping his head on his shoulders. Complicating his position was the increasing number and diversity of Spanish exiles seeking refuge in Ceuta. Visigothic politicians out of office crowded into the port along with Jewish refugees.

Now, Julian—as we may as well call him for the sake of simplicity—had a daughter named Florinda. It had long been customary to send young men and women of wealth or aristocratic pretensions to school in the Visigothic capital of Toledo. There they would learn whatever courtly customs and ceremonies had been adopted by the Visigoths. They would also study religion under the churchmen who clustered about the court and who would probably teach them to read and write Latin as well.

Accordingly, Florinda, in full nubile bloom, was packed off to Toledo. Not long after she arrived she was bathing in the shallow Tagus River, which runs below the walls of the city, when Roderick, newly come to the Visigothic throne, spotted her, admired her and promptly took her. Whether it was seduction or rape is not known.

The distinction did not matter to her father, Julian, who, as soon as he heard the news, headed for Toledo even though the Tagus valley was then beset by chill winds, which were brutal to visitors up from Africa. He snatched his daughter from the court and brought her home vowing vengeance.

The Arab chiefs were not greatly moved by the deflowering of Florinda, but they were interested when Julian told them of the vast confusion that reigned in Visigothic Spain, of the frailty of the defenses and the boiling popular dissatisfaction. He tempted Musa: "Hasten to that country where the palaces are built of gold and silver, and those who dwell in them are like women, owing to the exuberance of their comforts and the abundance of their riches." Old Roman and Iberian families were tired of disorder and banditry, he reported. Every Visigothic noble had a grievance. Slaves and serfs were ready to rise. And the Jews, now desperate, would be natural and valuable allies.

Actually some Jews who had fled to Morocco were ready to return with an Arab army to rescue their families. There were also the Jews of North Africa who had been alerted by their Spanish kinfolk for the abortive revolution. Furthermore, Julian argued, the North African shore was now full of Islamicized Berbers, fully armed and constituting a political danger unless they had something to occupy their minds and hopes.

Musa still wondered why the Caliph of Damascus should be interested in a Spanish adventure. For an answer Julian presented a rough inventory of Spanish resources, including grain, wine, iron, gold and silver. There were enough rich cities and villas to delight any army or governor or Caliph, Julian suggested.

Musa was not about to decide on an invasion without careful consultation with Damascus. His scribes penned exhaustive reports to the Caliph and received in return a very cautious go-ahead for a reconnaissance expedition to probe the Visigothic defenses. The expedition was to be very limited and Musa was warned not to "expose Moslems to the perils of a storm at sea." The Arabs apparently had a cavalryman's horror of naval expeditions, even if only across the narrowest of straits.

The royal assent was enough for Julian, who transformed four coastal cargo ships to transport the troops. A Berber chief named Tarif ibn Malluk led three hundred foot soldiers and one hundred horsemen with their mounts on board the flotilla on a July morning in 710. They landed on the southernmost tip of the continent of Europe (a peninsula that is still called Tarifa) and joyfully paraded up and down the nearby Spanish coast. The booty picked up in this brief excursion seems to have been highly satisfactory although the only items recorded by historians are some very attractive girls who were carried home by the invaders. Musa was delighted with the consignment of Christian maidens delivered to his headquarters at Kairouan. He was moved to order a full reconnaissance expedition to be commanded by the governor of Tangier, Tarik ibn Ziyad. Some say Tarik was Berber but others insist he was Persian. (The Arabs commanded a multinational, multiracial army.) Julian was to go along as a political expert to steer Tarik through the Visigothic chaos.

Julian's four ships would shuttle back and forth across the straits to ferry the troops. Meanwhile Musa would launch a crash program of shipbuilding so that additional reinforcements might be sent for rescue or evacuation.

An army of seven thousand men, mostly Berbers, was assembled to fulfill the strictly limited reconnaissance mission. The spring of 711 was chosen because Roderick, the Visigothic king who had been so uncontrollably roused by the sight of Florinda, was having his hands full subduing fresh rebellions in the northern town of Pamplona.

In April or May (historians are not sure which) Tarik led his men onto the transports. While waiting for his army to assemble, Tarik pitched his tent on a steep slope and thereby gave it a name it has worn ever since, Jubal-Tarik (Gibraltar). He took Carteya and pitched camp on the site of what would soon be the port of Algeciras. That spot, he decided, would be his supply base, and he put Julian in charge while he led his little army inland.

Roderick, informed of the invasion, sped down to Cordoba,

once a modest Roman market town, now grown seedy under the Visigoths. There he gathered what legions he could for an offensive against the invaders. Tarik, obsessed with his instructions to take a minimum of risks, dug in along the coast expecting a full whooping Visigothic onslaught. He sent for reinforcements and some five thousand Berber infantrymen came over.

He had, then, some twelve thousand Moslems, mainly foot soldiers, and a handful of Visigothic exiles each seeking his own revenge. Allies began to flock into his camp. These included many of the discontented in Spain, but principally the Jews, who had been expecting and praying for such a deliverance. Now they offered to fight for it and some of them sparked local uprisings to pave the way for the Moslems.

When Roderick marched down from Cordoba his army looked fierce but the supporting wings of the advance were commanded by men who envied or loathed their king. The rank-and-file consisted mainly of serfs and slaves who had been offered as proxies by unenthusiastic landholders. A slave fighting to keep his master on top of him is likely sooner or later to see the absurdity of his situation. Many did and faded away into the woods. Their officers, confident that the invaders wanted nothing more than booty, hoped that they would take Roderick along with greater treasures, leaving the throne up for grabs. Many of the disaffected Visigothic nobles broke and ran as the first Berber or Jew stood his ground.

On July 19, 711, along the shores of the Barbate River, near where it flows into the sea at what is now Cape Trafalgar, the Moslems met what was left of the Visigothic army. Roderick was routed. He also disappeared from history at that point. No one knows whether he died in battle or went into hiding. Julian's celebration of his revenge for the ravishing of Florinda is a scene lost forever. Chronicles of that time usually neglect the interesting supernumeraries.

The combatants, who saw only their own small theater of war and were motivated by their private ambitions, could not have understood the grave and glorious significance of the encounter on the Barbate River. It was the prelude to eight hundred years of Arab-Jewish-Christian civilization in Spain.

Tarik, unmindful of his importance, as a key is careless of what goes on beyond the door it unlocks, was in a quandary. If he were to follow his orders he would have to return to Africa with a full reconnaissance report but it seemed to him that all Spain was opening to his touch. His army was growing every day. The booty picked up in Roderick's camp was delighting his troops, who had visions of more glittering loot to come. If he had given orders to fall back to Africa would they have followed him? In any case would he not go down in history as a colossal fool who failed to pick up an empire that lay at his feet?

He went on to Ecija and then dispatched a lieutenant with seven hundred horsemen to capture Cordoba. That city held out for three months and was finally taken only with the help of impatient Jews and dissident Christians within the walls. It is said that the Visigothic defenders were herded into a church and massacred. If so, that was the bloodiest hour of the entire Moslem conquest.

Tarik, himself, was proceeding that autumn toward the capital of Toledo. His advance guard was made up of Jews and Christians who had gone over to the invaders. The Christians were probably serfs who would eagerly join in the hosannahs to liberation.

The march on Toledo was a celebration. Long before the army reached the city the archbishop of Spain, Sindared, packed and left for Rome. When the primate was gone the assembled dukes, duchesses, generals, lieutenants, garrison and townspeople took to the hills in panic. It was a deserted city that greeted the celebrating army of Tarik. The booty left in the palaces and granaries exceeded even the luxuriant imaginations of Arabs and Berbers. Tarik contemplated pursuit of the Visigothic remnants but the spoils of victory had to be digested, winter was coming on and the mountains were more forbidding than anything so far encountered in this conquest that had been more like a walk in a garden than a war.

The Arabs, Berbers, Jews and Christian dissenters spent the

winter holed up in Toledo living amid the treasures gathered from Gaul and the Roman settlements by the lords and bishops of Visigothic Spain.

The governor of Ifriquiya, Tarik's superior, Musa ibn Nusair, was not happy on hearing that his reconnaissance party had conquered an empire. Such glories were for governors. He resented the younger man's success with all the rancor of a soldier who feels himself beginning to creak with age. He was well into his seventies.

Musa gathered an army of eighteen thousand men, mainly Arab horsemen, and crossed the straits in June of 712. With him was his son, Abdul Aziz, a dashing cavalier. Musa led his forces north, plucking cities along his route like grapes from a vine—Medina-Sidonia, Carmona, Alcalá de Guadaira, Seville. Everywhere the Visigothic garrisons fled. Everywhere Jews and others, whose lives had been corroded by brutality or chaos, rallied to Musa as to a new hope. Musa left Jews to garrison the cities while his Arab cavalry cantered through Spain, filling in the gaps left by Tarik.

Only Merida, where desperate Visigothic chiefs decided to make a last stand, offered serious resistance. The city withstood a siege all through the winter and spring of 713, then surrendered, spilling a fortune into the laps of the conquerors. The Moslems reveled in the treasure of palace and church but scrupulously left intact the possessions of the private citizens of Merida, even those who had fought bitterly to the last day of the siege. This was strange conduct in a country where men and women had traditionally fought to the end because they knew that losers in war do not usually survive except perhaps as slaves or beggars.

It is true that the Moslems instituted a poll tax on infidels, but along progressive lines. The rich paid four times the rate of the poor and twice that of the middle class. Women, children, monks, slaves, beggars, the blind and the sick were all exempt. Christians who embraced Islam were freed of all taxes, but such conversions were not encouraged. To the Arab governor, keeping taxpayers paying was vastly more important than harvesting the souls of infidels.

When at last the governor came to Toledo he seated himself on the throne as if he were at least an emperor. This show was designed to impress not only the new subjects of the Caliph but, in particular, Tarik. When that lieutenant formally handed over the treasures of Toledo to his superior, the governor is said to have struck him with a whip for disobeying orders. (If Musa had been truly disturbed he would have used not a whip but a scimitar.)

The governor immediately set about organizing Spain with delicate tact. He was eager to maintain peace, so vital to the flow of revenue. He minted money that bore his name in Latin along with a Latin translation of the holy Moslem formula extolling the one and only Allah. He made no effort to revolutionize the economic system but tried only to ameliorate its rigors. Taxes were lightened and people were no longer bound to their craft or their land, except for serfs. There was no attempt to seize property because the Arabs and Berbers, loaded with loot, had little interest in plowing. Farming was grubby work compared to the conqueror's trade.

The temporal power of the Church was utterly destroyed but the actual churches were left intact with the proviso that henceforth half of each sizeable cathedral must be set aside for use as a mosque. Such cohabitation of faiths seemed bizarre in a land where until recently Christian sectarians had self-righteously slaughtered one another. Never had the Jews known such toleration since the Romans abandoned their pantheon. All the laws afflicting Jews were repealed. Jews paid their taxes as did other infidels and felt themselves truly liberated. Their kinsmen from North Africa soon crossed the straits to taste the new freedom.

The tolerance of Musa recalled the genial characteristics of the Arabs before the advent of Mohammed imposed the dread certainties of dogma. Marthad, King of Yemen in the fourth century, summed up this enlightened policy: "I rule over persons, not over opinions. I require my subjects to submit to my authority, but their doctrines I leave to the judgment of God their creator."

Musa and Tarik, quickly reconciled to each other, completed

the conquest. They marched up the valley of the Douro toward the Asturias and Galicia, and northeastward to Barcelona. Three years had passed since Tarik had entered Spain. Musa had been sending handsomely calligraphed war bulletins to Damascus but now it was time to go to his Caliph in glory.

He left his son in command of Spain and set out with Tarik for Syria. They dallied along the way in Egypt and Palestine, gathering a magnificent entourage of Arab and Berber dignitaries, so that it was February 715 before they reached Damascus. As they neared the capital the old Caliph lay dying while his brother stood in the wings impatient to take over. The old Caliph sent word to Musa to hurry, but the Caliph-to-come ordered Musa to wait so that he might have a free hand with the Spanish treasures. Musa, nearing his eighties, chose to follow the commands of the dying Caliph rather than play politics with the one waiting to be proclaimed.

When the new administration took office Musa fell from favor, as he no doubt expected. Some historians say he died in prison. Tarik wisely chose an obscure, inglorious retirement in the Far East. And Abdul Aziz, the son Musa left behind in Spain, married Roderick's widow, a princess whom the Arabs called Ailo, a mispronunciation of her Visigothic name, Egilona.

For two years Abdul Aziz pursued the mild and canny policies laid down by his father. An example was the bloodless victory he scored in what is now Murcia. The region was then controlled by a Visigothic noble named Theodemir. A treaty, one of the few documents of the period that survive, testifies to the priority Arabs gave to sound business relations over ideological or religious supremacy. The treaty opens with the traditional formula: "In the name of Allah, the Clement, the Merciful . . . written by Abdul Aziz ibn Musa ibn Nusair, to Tudmir [an Arabization of Theodemir] ibn Abdush."

It then proceeds in straightforward fashion with the quid pro quo: "The latter [Theodemir] obtains peace and receives a pledge, guaranteed by Allah and His Prophet, that nothing in his situation or in that of his family will be changed; that his right of sovereignty will not be challenged; that his subjects will not be killed, nor taken into captivity; nor separated from their children or their wives; that they will not be troubled in the practice of their religion; that their churches will not be burned, nor plundered of religious objects; and that this guarantee will last as long as he satisfies the obligations imposed upon him.

"Peace is granted on condition of the surrender of the following seven cities: Orihuela, Baltane, Alicante, Mula, Vilena, Lorca and Ello. Moreover, he will not grant asylum to anyone fleeing from us or who is our enemy, neither will he wrong anyone to whom we have granted amnesty, nor will he keep secret information that may come to him concerning our enemies. He and each of his subjects must pay each year a personal tribute consisting of one dinar in currency, four bushels of wheat and four of barley, four measures of new wine, four of vinegar, two of honey, and two of oil. This tax will be reduced to half for slaves."

Abdul Aziz and Ailo, who became converted to Islam, not only governed royally but held a grand court in Seville. Some Arab chroniclers say that it was too grand. They suggest that Ailo had missed the royal pomp she knew as Roderick's Visigothic queen. They say she urged her husband to actually put on a crown, which, in an underling, is an act very close to treason. They say that she insisted on having the governor's subordinates prostrate themselves as in a royal presence. Perhaps she did or perhaps it was only the malicious report of an envious courtier designed to needle the new and nervous Caliph at Damascus. Perhaps the Caliph himself invented the tale as an excuse for reprisal, since he liked neither Musa nor Musa's son.

In any case, in March 716 an assassin found Abdul Aziz in a part of the church of San Rufina that had been turned into a mosque. The murderer drew his scimitar, decapitated the governor and brought his head to Damascus.

The murder was shocking but for the common people of newly conquered Spain it was only a shadow on a far-off mountain. So long as kings, princes and governors murdered only one another, the farmers, tradesmen and builders could go about their business, deploring the news but seeing no reason to take to the hills. The history of Moslem Spain thus opened with hosannahs of gratitude that bloodshed and scandal were at last confined to high places, allowing ordinary people to lead ordinary lives.

The Immigrant Emir

Arabs are forever turning from the world to heaven and back again, each time with a sigh of relief. Their history tends to zigzag. For a while it follows a sunny course favored by that part of the Arab character that is urbane, intellectual, aesthetic, sensuous, tolerant and commercial. Then abruptly it swings to an alternate phase: dogmatic, devout, puritanical, intolerant.

Before the coming of Mohammed the diverse peoples who lived in what is now Syria and Iraq wore their religion lightly, as if it were a gossamer rainbow. They made a kind of poetry out of it. Sometimes they prayed to their various pagan gods; at other times they threatened to reduce the ration of sacrifices and devotion if the deities continued to be stingy with their favors.

The Jews, though they were absolutely convinced of the correctness of their monotheistic tenets, rarely tried to force them on unbelievers. Dialogue between the two groups might have been strained at times but doctrinal wars do not usually break out when one side is characterized by a private austerity of spirit, and the other by a good-natured joie de vivre. Crusading zeal was alien to both.

Even after Mohammed emerged from his lonely moonlit vigils bearing messages from the One True God, many were unconvinced. For example, there was the seventh-century poet Tarafa ibn al-Abd, who wrote:

"My boon companions are noble youths whose faces shine as the stars. Each evening a singing girl attired in a striped robe and a tunic of saffron graces our company. Her vestment is open at the neck; without reproof amorous hands fondle her charms . . . my life is surrendered to wine and pleasures . . . but you, O Censor, who blame my passion for carousal and the fray, can you make me immortal? If in your wisdom you cannot ward off the fatal moment, suffer me to lavish all in enjoyment before Death has me in his clutches. . . . Tomorrow, harsh reprover, when you and I are dead, we shall see which of us two is consumed by burning thirst."

And women poets sang in counterpoint: "We are the daughters of the morning star; soft are the carpets we tread beneath our feet; our necks are adorned with pearls, and our tresses are perfumed with musk. The brave who confront the foe we will clasp to our bosoms, but the dastards who flee we will spurn; not for them our embraces!"

Wine, valor, love and the gorgeous cascade of words with which to celebrate the sensual glories of the world had quite seduced the Arabs before Mohammed announced himself with dread assurance as the Messenger of God. After the Prophet's death his apostles Abu Bakr and Khalid, whose ferocity frightened even Mohammed, wrote the divine message in a vocabulary of battle cries, blood and fire.

Interpretations of that message were somewhat ambiguous socially. The Prophet had proclaimed: "No more pride of birth! All men are Adam's children!" Simultaneously, however, he empowered the noble sheikhs to go on ruling as they had always done, with their lands and lordly prerogatives untouched by the democratic implications of the new gospel.

The nobles had only to take their pleasures more discreetly, while publicly extolling the high puritanical virtues. A delicious underground appreciation of the flesh persisted among the Arabs even though they prayed five times a day. High spirits, combined with a good business sense, thus continued in secret to nourish the puritan desert.

In the year 644 that secret spring threatened to burst to the surface in a flood. The Caliph of Damascus had been stabbed by a Christian, who was as convinced as the most pious mullah that he held the one and only Truth.

In the week that it took the Caliph to die that conscientious monarch pondered the method of succession, always a tricky passage. At last he hit upon a formula, but it was one that might have been designed for chaos. The six surviving companions of Mohammed were to meet and pick the next Caliph. After announcing this ruling to the waiting courtiers, the Caliph collapsed before the inevitably rancorous effects of his scheme could be felt.

The six elders wrangled for three days and then decided that the choice should be left to the one man who had already taken himself out of the running. That man thereupon announced that he would award the Caliphate to Othman of the Omayyad family, a wealthy clan much addicted to the merriment of life and the money that made it possible.

Othman's conversion to Islam had exemplified the Omayyad capacity to recognize the force of reality in matters of principle. He had fought the new creed until his forces were hopelessly outnumbered. Mohammed, it is said, then called upon Othman to acknowledge him as the "Messenger of God." Othman's answer was couched in the tentative manner of one who would prefer to discuss such matters over a glass of wine. "Pardon my candor," he is supposed to have said, "but I still feel some doubt upon that point."

Mohammed, having no appetite for such intellectual exercise, sent word: "Bear witness to the Prophet or your head falls." To the rational Othman this was a very telling argument.

Now, by a curious chain of circumstances, he was to be the Caliph, successor to Mohammed and devoted to his will. Othman began his administration in the time-honored way by distributing all the lucrative and prestigious posts to members of his family. The righteous indignation of other clans, excluded from power, broke into war.

Ultimately, the Omayyads were to lose the throne in Damascus and find another in Cordoba, but in the process thousands of heads were to roll in the deserts and mountains of Arabia. Moslems would be divided and subdivided into warring factions based on doctrine, territory, wealth, clan loyalties and personal vengeance in the manner of most righteous movements.

The Omayyads were competent politically and militarily and, what is more, endowed with a histrionic charm. Their enemies, however, viewed their worldly manners as verging on blasphemy. Indeed, they were not the most cunning politicians. For example, Othman appointed his half-brother Walid as a provincial governor, charged with suppressing revolts and converting vanquished rebels into taxpayers. Walid was very successful in subduing and pacifying Azerbaijan and Cyprus. However, after days of battle or bargaining he liked to spend his nights playing with dancing girls, drinking with friends, writing and reciting ribald poetry.

He was aware that as governor and commander he had religious as well as administrative duties but he could not always adjust his varying moods to his roles. On one occasion he broke up an all-night party when he heard the muezzin's call to morning prayer. He reeled into the mosque half-dressed and got through the four-minute prayer without excessive scandal. But then came a characteristically mischievous Omayyad gesture. Grinning boyishly the governor turned to the crowd of faithful and offered, with the sweeping generosity of a cheerful sot, to recite it all over again just to prove that, drunk or sober, he could pray with the best of them.

When the faithful began to pull up paving blocks from the mosque's floor to throw at the governor, he exited singing. Then the elders of the community reminded each other that Walid's father had once spat at the Prophet in the heat of a religious confrontation. Before Walid's father was condemned to have his head struck off, he asked, "Who will care for my children?" The Prophet is supposed to have answered: "The fire of Hell." After the incident in the mosque Walid was commonly referred to as "the child of Hell"—a horrendous name for so cheery and competent an administrator.

Regretfully Othman removed Walid from his post but even that concession did not appease the puritanical element. While piously reading the Koran to which he had come belatedly, for he was now in his eighties, Othman was assassinated. To mark the change of regimes, the pious assassins pillaged the treasury and cut off the fingers of Othman's wife, who had tried her best to defend the old Caliph.

Then the followers of the Prophet proceeded to tear one another apart. Clan fought clan and tribe fought tribe and each one belabored the other with sword and doctrine. The nomadic Kaisites of the north fought the Kalbites of Yemen. (These were quarrels between families.) The Prophet's widow, Aisha, fought the Prophet's son-in-law, Ali, who had seized the throne. (This was a conflict of political ambitions.) The Kaijites, fierce and fanatical, fought the Shi'ites. (This was a conflict of doctrine.)

In 692 the Omayyads emerged on top of this struggling heap of warlords and ideologues. The clan resumed their worldly ways, relishing the perquisites of power and regretting the necessary brutalities. They tried to organize the debris left by Greek and Roman civilizers. They thought they gave as good as they got, for example, bestowing a new gospel on the hitherto unenlightened Berbers of North Africa while taking from them their Merino sheep to make the fine white wool then fashionable in Damascus.

Along with tax collectors they sent out artists and architects, who built the Dome of the Rock in Jerusalem and left other gleaming testimonials to the good taste as well as the wealth of mighty monarchs. The Omayyads might have done more for art and scholarship but it was an uneasy time in which survival and a safe family succession took precedence over all else.

The Omayyad line, despite compromises, ran out with Marwan II, a soft and sensible man, reasonably efficient but too lightweight to sit upon the lid of such a bubbling pot. On November 28, 749, Abu al-Abbas stood in the great mosque of Kufa and raised a black flag, the standard of a new dynasty that would drive the Omayyads from Damascus. He also waved the bloody shirts of those whom the Omayyads had killed or deposed. A somber, sanctimonious man, he claimed to be the great-grandson of a first cousin of the Prophet himself. To publicize his holy ferocity he gave himself the sobriquet al-Saffah, meaning, "He who pours blood."

The blood-spiller drove Marwan II from Damascus, chased him across Syria, across Palestine and into Egypt where he cornered and killed that last hapless Omayyad Caliph of Damascus. The world of Arabs and Berbers then stood amazed when al-Saffah declared an amnesty for all other Omayyads. Some eighty of them gathered near Jaffa to receive their pardons and pay allegiance to the unexpectedly generous Abbasid dynasty. When they were assembled, however, all of them were slaughtered. A grandson of an Omayyad Caliph, with a hand and a foot cut off, was mounted on an ass and paraded through Syrian towns.

One of those Omayyads who had not trusted the promise of amnesty and perhaps had no taste for the grim Abbasids with their black banners was a twenty-year-old prince named Abd-er Rahman. His grandfather Hisham had been an Omayyad Caliph and his mother Rab had been a Berber captive in the royal harem. He was now a scion of an outcast family, many of whom had been massacred at Jaffa. He was set adrift in a bitter season, with apparently no taste for high intrigue or doctrinaire logic-chopping. For a man without talent as saint, soldier or conspirator it was useless to think of a political career.

Abd-er Rahman hid out in the countryside but he could scarcely have been inconspicuous, since he had with him two brothers, two sisters, a handful of loyal servants to manage the flight with dignity, and his four-year-old son Suleiman, barely sixteen years younger than himself. (The name of the boy's mother, a descendant of one of the companions of the Prophet and hence a distinguished lady of the court, has been lost to history.)

Inevitably Abbasid spies ferreted out the fugitive Omayyads. They had orders to kill only Abd-er Rahman and his elder brother Yahya, however. When they arrived at the Omayyad camp, Abd-er Rahman was off hunting and so they made do with Yahya. The assassins waited for Abd-er Rahman to return but the prince had been warned by his family retainer, Badr, an ingenious, practical, loyal and durable man who did much to shape the history of Spain, while thinking of himself as only the humble servant of his prince.

It was arranged, probably by Badr, that Abd-er Rahman and his younger brother, barely thirteen, would escape to a village on the shores of the Euphrates where in time the rest of the family would join them. They would then cross the Red Sea to Africa where it was hoped they all would live out their lives in modest but still royal obscurity with only a few chosen servants, some gems, gold and silks they had managed to pack in the flight from their past.

Badr and the two princes made it to the Euphrates where after some months the sisters and little Suleiman caught up with them. Abd-er Rahman was suffering from an eye disorder. (To this day eye disease is endemic in the area.) He was lying in a darkened room at midday when Suleiman ran in and buried his face in his father's shoulder. Abd-er Rahman looked up from the frightened boy and saw a group of horsemen galloping toward the house. Above them waved the black banners of the Abbasids. The boy remembered that when he last saw those ominous flags his uncle had been killed before his eyes.

Badr scooped up a supply of gold and rode off with Abd-er Rahman and his younger brother. They rode along the banks of the Euphrates until Abd-er Rahman found a man he thought he could trust, one who had known him in his days of glory. The prince arranged to buy supplies and horses, but while Badr went off to collect the purchased goods a slave who had overheard the transaction slipped away and alerted a nearby patrol of Abbasid soldiers. Finding themselves surrounded, the two brothers dived into the Euphrates. The soldiers called to them, promising their safety if they turned themselves in. Abd-er Rahman was almost across when he saw his younger brother turn and head back to the soldiers. Abd-er Rahman yelled at him to swim on but the boy, apparently exhausted by the swift current and ready to be cajoled by the promise of safety, swam slowly back.

When Abd-er Rahman dragged himself out on the far shore

of the river he turned to see his brother's head sliced off.

Badr caught up with his prince weeks later in Palestine. Abd-er Rahman's sister had sent along a freedman named Salim and a quantity of money and jewels. The three crossed the Isthmus of Suez and entered Africa, where the Abbasid authority was tenuous. Salim felt impelled to seek his fortune where his family came from, in Syria. Abd-er Rahman and Badr were thus left to wander the North African coast as noble refugees down on their luck.

At twenty Abd-er Rahman was a strikingly handsome prince. He was tall, with light-colored hair that fell in curls to his shoulders. His one bad eye was almost sightless but it was not a very noticeable flaw. He rode well but his demeanor was less that of a military hero than of a poet. He wrote passable verse, they say, though we have only a fragment or two of it. And he spoke in resonant tones and phrases like a trained orator. Such a man at such a time attracted legends as a finely crafted lute draws musicians.

One story, which may possibly be true, tells of the time he came to a principality in what is now Morocco. By coincidence the governor was named Abd-er Rahman ibn Habib. Before the wanderers reached the capital, a Jewish soothsayer who was kept handy in the palace had made a curious prediction: A man of royal descent named Abd-er Rahman, identified by curls that dangled over each temple, would one day rule the whole African coast.

The governor of the province thought the matter quite simple: He himself had the proper name (a very common one in that time and place) and need only curl his hair to fulfill the prophecy. The Jew pointed out, however, that power cannot be conferred by hairdressers; the governor had no royal lineage and he was therefore the wrong Abd-er Rahman. When the royal Abd-er Rahman turned up, with curls, name and ancestry to match the prophecy, the governor sent for the Jew and congratulated him on the fulfillment of his prediction. He added, however, that an assassin would shortly snuff out the career of the new Abd-er Rahman. The Jew, worried that his prophecy would end in murder, led the governor down a Talmudic path of argument. There were two possibilities: Either the stranger was not the Abd-er Rahman of the prophecy, in which case it would be not only criminal but useless to kill him; or indeed he was the man chosen by destiny to rule, in which case nothing the governor could do would alter the heaven-decreed fate of the young man. The rabbinical logic was inescapable and the governor was left to wonder about the futility of knowing the future if one can do nothing to change it.

Unaware of such close shaves, Abd-er Rahman and Badr went up and down North Africa for four weary years. The fear, hate and envy that dog a politician out of power made him a discomforting guest. It was clear that he was unfit for anything other than a throne. Since thrones were scarce and empty thrones still scarcer, his hosts hurried him on his way. He followed a road well traveled by other Omayyad exiles—west to the shores of the Atlantic. When Abd-er Rahman joined the circle of refugees they persuaded him to see his last hope and theirs across the straits in Spain.

Badr was sent to sample the political waters, to talk to Omayyad followers and see how they might welcome a prince of the family. Badr crossed over in June 754 and began the subtle diplomacy that was to deliver Spain to the Omayyads.

Visigothic chaos in that peninsula had given way to Moslem chaos. Passions, rivalries, intrigues and doctrinal crusades had been carried from Syria like so many loathesome itches picked up at a tavern. Kalbites fought Kaisites as if they were still nomad clans quarreling over sand and oases; egalitarian, puritan and sanctimonious sects struck at the entrenched aristocrats in palace and mosque; Berbers, forced to farm the flinty Guadarrama mountains, assailed the Arabs who had taken the fertile valleys. Their rebellion, which had broken out in North Africa, spread to Spain with a raucous cry for blood and land.

When springtime weather brought thoughts of a holy war— for God and whatever loot might be vouchsafed to the truly pious—the mullahs would rally a semblance of Islamic unity. They would point to the infidel enemy holed up in Galicia or across the Pyrenees. The troops went through the eastern passes and spilled down on the Franks and the Jewish towns along the Mediterranean shore in the region called Septimania—in memory of the Seventh Legion that once held that smiling land for Rome.

After crossing the western end of the Pyrenees the Arab-Berber armies swept through Bordeaux and galloped toward Tours. All Europe lay open to the armies of Islam. It was a blessed lark—amply rewarded by loot if you survived and by God's grace and all his gorgeous houris if you died. It was on the old Roman road that skirts the River Clain between Châtellerault and Poitiers that Charles Martel, the Hammer, turned back the tide.

It was said then and has been repeated ever since that Charles Martel saved Europe from Islam, and Christianity from extinction. Actually there is some doubt that the Islamic leaders ever threatened—or hoped—to win Europe to the Koran. The conquerors of Spain scarcely paid lip service to proselytizing. True, they imposed tax penalties on infidels, but these were not onerous. Christians and Jews were accepted by the invaders as "People of the Book," to be protected, patronized and pitied. If a Roman could still be found offering a libation to his household god he might be persuaded by the sword to cease his heathen practice, but such scandals must have been rare, since paganism lingered largely in the mind and was never a fertile source of martyrs.

Some Christians and Jews chose to be converted to Islam, either because it was a likely road to political, commercial and social advancement or because the new religion held a more vivid celestial promise than did the older creeds. Most clung to the beliefs they were born with and paid the extra bit it cost. They settled in separate communities, mainly in Cordoba, Seville, Merida and Toledo. Churches were usually divided so that part could be used as a mosque. Theoretically Christians could build new churches if they had the proper permit but the Moslem bureaucracy was difficult when it came to issuing the necessary papers. Synagogues were usually left intact. Plainly the Moslems were not out to build a pure Islamic state. Most in those early days were not enthusiastic about a state at all.

There was a fantasy prevalent in Syria and North Africa, voiced in particular by the conqueror of Spain, Musa ibn Nusair, according to which the cavaliers of Islam would carry the banners of the Prophet in a gigantic sweep through Spain, Gaul, the forests of the Slavs, through great Rome and greater Byzantium and back home finally to Syria where there would be a grand fete, a sharing of the booty and the glory. Europe would be left exhausted to slumber in barbarism until Islam might choose to pluck again its ripened fruit. The dream was fanciful, however, and statecraft was ultimately forced upon the Arabs.

In any case the tide that washed over the Pyrenees began to ebb at Poitiers. To those who settled in Spain south of the Douro, Gaul was a far-off adventure, of lesser importance than the questions of whether the governor at Cordoba favored this or that faction, was mild or bloody, was obdurate or subject to manipulation by his harem or his councilors. Spain was still seething like molten metal and it was uncertain what shape it might take when it cooled.

When Badr crossed the straits in June 754, the government of Spain was in the hands of Yusuf al-Fihri, a weak but amiable man who looked like a king but was moved like a pawn in the hands of his chief adviser on military and civil matters, al-Sumail. Al-Sumail had lately been disappointed in Yusuf, who had been very slow in coming to his aid when he was besieged by troublesome rebels at Saragossa. The chief minister was therefore ready to look kindly on a replacement for the governor.

Badr did not approach the formidable al-Sumail directly. He scouted among the kinsmen of his Omayyad master and drew an elegant picture of the young Abd-er Rahman as the family's steppingstone to fortune. The Omayyad politicians then chose to approach al-Sumail at the moment when he was most at odds with Yusuf. Unfortunately, according to some accounts, the minister was also laboring under an oppressive hangover at the time. He is supposed to have used elaborate profanity concerning Yusuf and to have tearfully recalled that the Omayyad dynasty had always been good to his family. He finally sent the emissaries off with profuse promises of support.

When Badr and the Omayyad chiefs came again to al-Sumail to confirm that backing they found the minister sober and clear-eyed. In that condition he was unshakably convinced that he would rather work with the figurehead he knew than take his chances with a glamorous new pretender. If Abd-er Rahman should come to Spain, the prime minister told the emissaries, he would rise high but never as high as he would like. It could probably be arranged for him to marry one of Yusuf's daughters and thus join himself to the governor's fortunes. However, at the first sign of an ambition to rule Spain al-Sumail would crush him. That was the message that Badr was to take to his master.

The Omayyad courtiers assured al-Sumail that his kind offer would undoubtedly be accepted. They then hurried off to conspire against him with the Yemenites, who were clearly out of favor and out of patience. Money, promises and enthusiasm poured from the Yemenites at the first mention of a possible change in the political weather.

Badr hurried back to Morocco where his prince was in some uncertainty whether he was being entertained by his Berber hosts or being held for ransom. If Badr did not come back with good news and hard cash the prince's future was unpromising.

Badr arrived in spectacular style. When his ship was sighted the prince hurried down to the beach, and when Badr saw the prince he did not wait for the ship to lower a boat for him. Instead he leaped overboard and swam ashore to deliver his great news.

Badr paid off the tribesmen with money supplied by the Yemenites, thus assuring an affectionate farewell. Unfortunately, one of the Berber hosts who had missed the payoff swam after the boat and clutched at a rope alongside demanding his share. A Yemenite, impatient to make history and angered by such ill-mannered importunity, drew his scimitar and cut off the man's hands, which still clutched the rope. The gentle prince, it is said, turned away in horror.

The Yemenites rallied to Abd-er Rahman as soon as he established his headquarters at Torrox, just east of Malaga along the coast. Yusuf and al-Sumail were having their hands full at Pamplona, where the Christian Basques were fighting back against disorganized Moslems. At first al-Sumail counseled a diplomatic overture. He sent a three-man delegation including the royal secretary Khalid, a master of the delicate literary embroidery so esteemed in diplomatic correspondence. Khalid was the son of Christian slaves but he had embraced Islam and developed an eloquence in Arabic that endeared him to Yusuf, who lacked such skills. The three envoys brought along an array of gifts: two horses, two mules, two slaves, one thousand gold pieces and a variety of handsome robes, tunics, scarves and slippers.

They left the gifts at an outpost not far from Torrox and appeared before Abd-er Rahman with no more than soft words and the promise of Yusuf's daughter, that inevitable bargaining chip, if the prince would give up all claim to the emirate. The Yemenite politicians at this point concluded that they could get more out of Yusuf by selling out the prince's hopes than they could by fighting. As they dickered, the prince and Badr saw their future wane. Then, in one of those quirks of history, a literary tempest broke. Khalid, who had drafted the highly poetic proposals of his governor, called for an answer in a style that matched his own. The Yemenites were plainly at a loss and in the ensuing wrangle thought they detected a sneer in Khalid's high-flown rhetoric. The discussion was as barbed as any symposium of prideful literary critics. In the end the Yemenites ordered Khalid to prison. Negotiations broke off and the two other envoys departed hurriedly, stopping only to pick up the mules, slaves and gold that had been meant for Abd-er Rahman. When they reached Cordoba al-Sumail declared that he had never had much confidence in negotiations and that he would have to drive the prince back to Africa or kill him in Spain.

A bleak winter enshrouded Cordoba, so that hostilities had to wait until spring. Early in March the prince was parading through the towns of the south while advance teams of politicians fine-tuned the crowds to acclaim him as emir. He had no visible symbol, no battle standard. This was a serious omission in his effort to rally popular support, and it was rectified by one of the Yemenite chiefs who put his own turban on the point of a spear and tossed it up to Abd-er Rahman. That became his sign and the symbol of the Omayyad dynasty that was to come after him.

Abd-er Rahman marched along the southern bank of the Guadalquivir pushing north and east from Seville while Yusuf kept pace with him along the opposite shore. When both sides were almost at the point where the old Roman bridge leads to the gate of Cordoba, Abd-er Rahman began to parley.

He said his troops were on short rations (probably true) and that he felt no match for the forces against him (probably untrue). He was prepared, he said, to forgo all claim to the emirate if his army were allowed to cross the river for food and drink. Then the two leaders would work out a treaty of peace.

Yusuf sent a supply of oxen and sheep and permitted Abd-er Rahman's troops to cross the Guadalquivir. On the following morning when Abd-er Rahman saw his soldiers fed and positioned at the gates of Cordoba he mounted his high-spirited horse, waved his sword and acted the heroic warrior. This betrayal of Yusuf's hospitality was a tactic of war that did not trouble his subordinates. Heroes on prancing chargers tended to frighten politicians, however. Gallant leaders inevitably leave a trail of corpses. The Yemenites began to think it had been a mistake to replace the weak and manageable Yusuf with this overly grand descendant of Caliphs. It is perilous to live close to greatness, they remembered.

As the day wore on the grumbling grew louder. Abd-er Rahman, perhaps on the advice of Badr, let it be known that he preferred to go into battle astride a mild and humble white mule. The Yemenite chiefs appreciated the gesture as an indication of his prudence and malleability. At the very least it proclaimed an exquisite tact.

Reports of the battle agree that it was short and decisive. Yusuf and al-Sumail escaped with their lives, though each lost a son in the fighting. The Yemenites and their allies poured through the gates, bent on sacking Cordoba and leaving it a smoking ruin. Abd-er Rahman, however, with a handful of his guards, held off the looters, allowing them only the bare minimum of silks, a little gold, no women and no slaves. He saved the palace and the harem from invasion. In gratitude one of Yusuf's daughters offered the prince her favorite handmaiden, Holal, who shortly thereafter became the mother of a future Caliph.

In the mosque of Cordoba—then a rather modest affair that was a church on Sundays—Abd-er Rahman performed his first act as an imam in Spain. (Religious elements had to be mixed with the secular in the formula for Mohammedan power.) Though he had always taken religion lightly, in the Omayyad manner, Abd-er Rahman led the Friday prayers with impressive punctilio. He then delivered a sermon in which he pledged to govern justly. His audience understood that this was all part of the ceremony and very likely many of them were already engaged in one of the numerous plots then afoot to destroy him.

Thus began the Omayyad emirate in Spain. It was still theoretically a satrapy of the Syrian empire, still nominally subservient to the Caliph in Damascus, but the cord that linked the two capitals was frayed. It was to become merely ornamental and would finally be severed by another and later Abd-er Rahman.

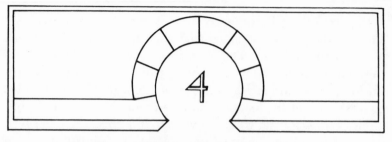

A Jewish Princedom

When Abd-er Rahman listened to the solemn oaths of fealty from the warlords of Moslem Spain it was understood that a man's word was only as reliable as the political weather—which was then notoriously unstable throughout the Iberian peninsula. Cordoba, the seat of Abd-er Rahman's power, was a capital without a country. Al-Andalus was an emirate with boundaries that varied from day to day depending on the market price of treason.

For forty-five years before the coming of Abd-er Rahman al-Andalus had been a colony of a Syrian empire, happily remote from the imperial center. The Caliph of Damascus was nominally the ruler. In the beginning, therefore, Abd-er Rahman, known to his newly found constituents as "The Immigrant," thought it politic, however nauseating, to lead Friday prayer services in the name of that same Abbasid dynasty that had cold-bloodedly murdered every Omayyad who could be sniffed out of hiding.

To have omitted this ceremonial bow to the murderers of his family would have carried fearsome implications. It would have been construed to mean that all links with Damascus had been severed, that Abd-er Rahman no longer thought of himself as an emir on a long leash held by the Caliph but as an independent prince. It would have upped the price on his head and sent assassins swarming over Cordoba. He was not ready for that.

It was all the emir could do to keep his grip on the capital. The defeated Yusuf had gone to Toledo and his vizier al-Sumail to Jaen to rally forces for another try at the throne. If one promised politicians power and their followers loot; if one clothed self-aggrandizement in a cloak of clan loyalty or revenge or religious dogma, one could easily put together the machinery of revolt. Indeed such adventures were vehicles for the upward mobility of Andalusians.

While Abd-er Rahman was away from his capital mobilizing the countryside in his defense, one of Yusuf's sons sneaked a raiding party inside Cordoba and defeated the garrison. When Abd-er Rahman raced back to rescue the city the young rebel quickly decamped, taking with him two of the handsomest ladies of the court. The young man was persuaded to give up the ladies when it was pointed out that Abd-er Rahman in his conquest of Cordoba had gallantly defended all residents of the harem and had left their honor intact.

Accordingly a tent, well stocked with food and wine, was pitched along the road. The ladies were left there to await in comfort the arrival of Abd-er Rahman. The emir rescued them in good time and then continued the chase. He pursued not only the sons of Yusuf but all the varied forces of the old regime, including those of al-Sumail. He caught up with the chiefs near Granada where they surrendered, abjectly swearing fealty forever.

The return to Cordoba was triumphant, with Abd-er Rahman riding joyfully between Yusuf and al-Sumail. Abd-er Rahman was later to comment on the vizier's exquisite manners. "All the way from Elvira to Cordoba," he noted in admiration, "Sumail was at my side, yet his knee never touched mine; the head of his mule was never in advance of mine; never did he ask me an indiscreet question; never did he commence a conversation before I addressed him."

It was a remarkable capitulation from a man who only a little while earlier had sent away the emissaries of this same Omayyad prince with a warning that he would break any man who aspired to supplant his puppet Yusuf.

Though Yusuf was not as mannerly as al-Sumail, both were treated with such courtesy as stirred resentment from the less gallant politicians of the court. The ex-enemies were given the run of Cordoba, except for Yusuf's two sons, who were restricted to the palace grounds. The young men were hostages but they enjoyed an elegant incarceration.

Al-Sumail had obviously thrown in his lot with the winner and Abd-er Rahman frequently called on him for advice. Yusuf, on the other hand, was a reed on which any conspirator might play a tune of royal restoration. One morning he was missed from his quarters. He had slipped out of the city and was on his way to Merida where his supporters had already recruited an army of twenty thousand Berbers and an array of ambitious Arab chiefs.

The forces of Abd-er Rahman met the rebels on a rainy morning near Seville. In an ancient preliminary rite of battle one of Yusuf's Berbers, a man of Goliathan proportions, stepped forward and challenged a champion of the other side to single-handed combat. A slightly built Abyssinian David, without a slingshot, charged bravely at the challenger, who slipped and went down on his rump in the mud. Thereupon the Abyssinian used his scimitar to chop off both legs of his huge enemy. The emir's loyal supporters, seeing divine intervention in the slimy terrain, sang out, "God is Great," and routed the rebels, lopping heads with divinely inspired vigor.

Yusuf might have escaped but he was recognized as he tried to slip through a village and was assassinated by a farmer who rightly read the political auguries. Yusuf's head was brought to Abd-er Rahman, who was then beginning to regret those generous Omayyad gestures that so often tended to miscarry.

He had Yusuf's older son put to death but spared the younger one because he was still in his teens. The emir found it impossible, however, to believe Yusuf would have undertaken a rebellion without at least the knowledge of the puppet-master al-Sumail.

When al-Sumail was found dead in his room one morning surrounded by wine, fruits and sweets, the official report had it that he had died of apoplexy following a party. It was later rumored that he had been strangled but, even if that were so, the delicate necessity to lie about murder seemed to betoken a new and gentler era in royal sensibilities. Henceforth Abd-er Rahman would continue to be merciful to his enemies, but a single betrayal of his kindness would be likely to prove fatal.

Revolts popped up like weeds in a garden newly wrested from a jungle. The most bitter outbreak was a war waged with frantic determination for nine years by a schoolteacher named Shakya, who claimed descent from the Prophet by way of his daughter Fatima. Calling for a return to the literal interpretation of the Koran and making much use of his mother, who by convenient happenstance was also named Fatima, Shakya shook the Berber masses. He was one of those messianic leaders who periodically have roused Islam with a mix of puritanism and theocratic politics. It is a very heady brew, appealing to those who are born powerless and to others who, for the moment, are out of power.

Shakya's guerillas would descend on the emir's forces like lightning bolts, then vanish. In the end Shakya was killed by one of his own men. It is not known whether the assassin was disenchanted with Shakya as a messiah or as a politician. In any case that most serious threat to the Omayyad emirate faded away with the leader's death.

As inner stability grew, Abd-er Rahman felt bold enough to drop the name of the Abbasid enemy from Friday prayers. However, he dared not yet proclaim de jure the independence that was evidently his, de facto. His position was all the more precarious because his domestic enemies had a foreign prince over the border with whom they hoped to conspire.

When the original invaders, Tarik and Musa, romped through Spain and sent the Visigoths flying they did not regard the Pyrenees as an effective barrier to empire. Moslem commanders had swooped over the eastern end of the mountain wall down on the land of Languedoc—so called because the inhabitants said "oc" for yes instead of something like "o-ile," which the Franks preferred.

It was a land of pleasant vineyards even then and very popular with Jews, who had come up with the Roman legions and settled there in great numbers, particularly around Narbonne. They owned and farmed extensive properties from Toulouse to Marseilles and, by and large, lived like Roman gentry. They held slaves as did other patricians though often they worked beside them in the fields.

The Jews took Roman names, Roman dress and Roman civilities. In evidence is a tombstone found near Narbonne. It bears a carved Menorah and is dated 688. It marks the simultaneous, and therefore somewhat mysterious, death of a man named Justus, aged thirty, a lady named Matrona, twenty, and Dulciorella, a girl of nine. All, according to the tombstone, were children of Paragorus and grandchildren of the late Sapaudus. The names of these long-vanished Jews are spelled out in Latin but at the end is a line of Hebrew, reading: "Peace upon Israel." It testifies to the easy cultural assimilation and religious separation of Jews in the latter days of the empire.

When the Franks drifted from the milder Arianism to Catholicism the political weather turned nasty for the Jews of Languedoc. Their persecution, however, was nothing like as bad as that suffered by their brethren south of the mountains, where Visigothic kings and bishops were offering Jews a choice of baptism, expulsion with spoliation, or death. Archbishop Julian of Toledo in the seventh century was outraged at the thought that the Jews of Narbonne not only were still living well but were converting Christians. (Julian was particularly vehement because he owed his fate and his high rank to the conversion of his parents, who had been born Jews.)

Another bishop, Agobard of Lyons, deplored the evident popularity of Jewish cooking. He wrote of the disappointing results of trying to win over the Jews: "While we, with all the humanity and goodness which we use toward them, have not succeeded in gaining a single one to our spiritual beliefs, many of our folk, sharing the carnal food of the Jews, let themselves be seduced also by their spiritual food."

Perhaps the sheer vigor of Jewish conviction in those years was attractive to Christians as Christianity had been attractive centuries earlier at a time when Judaism had grown stale and priest-ridden. One of the factors in the Jewish exuberance that prevailed was the talismanic quality of the number seven. Did not God make the universe in six days and rest on the seventh? Is not the earth to be tilled for six years and lie fallow for the seventh? Is there not a new empire sweeping al-Andalus and may it not be the instrument of the Lord to fulfill the prophecy and usher in the true Messiah in this, the seventh century since the fall of the second Temple in Jerusalem? Surely, the Jews thought, they were living at a great turning point for the world. They therefore welcomed the Moslems who came down over the mountains.

When Charles Martel stopped the Moslems at Poitiers they fell back to Narbonne. There Moslem and Jew had to withstand a siege without hope of relief from the divided and embattled emirate at Cordoba. The Frankish troops occasionally diverted themselves by converting the local farmers outside the walls to Christianity at swordpoint. And from time to time the Moslem chiefs sallied out of Narbonne to replenish supplies and counter the Christian missionary swords with Moslem scimitars. So went the battle for souls, with the peasantry flipping from the Koran to the Cross and back again.

The whole province was uncertain whether to bind itself to the emirate of Cordoba or to the Frankish kingdom. Charles Martel's son, Pepin the Short, had renewed the siege of Narbonne four years before Abd-er Rahman came to Cordoba. It was to last another three years but hostilities were not unremittingly grim. On the contrary, there seem to have been lengthy and not unfriendly negotiations between the besiegers and the besieged.

What actually went on inside the city is much disputed by chroniclers. The story varies with the religio-political views of the reporter. Some say that Pepin promised a quasi-independence to the Goths within Narbonne. Others find this curious because there were very few Goths in the city. And when the siege was lifted in 759 whatever Goths there were swiftly vanished from the region.

On the other hand there is no doubt that there were a great

many Jews of a very independent turn of mind in Narbonne. And when the seven-year siege was over they emerged not only as independent landowners, with extensive vineyards and slaves to tend them, but with all the appurtenances of political power. A good part of Narbonne had become an autonomous principality headed by a Nasi (Hebrew for prince) proclaimed as a scion of the House of David. The story of how this came about suffers not so much from a paucity of reporting as from excessive embroidery that hides the hard facts.

This much is known: The Moslems were under the governor-ship of a man named Matrand. He is called "king" in some accounts but these were written centuries later when kings were fashionable and Moslem titles of caliph and emir and wali had become outmoded. In any case, during Pepin's long siege Matrand ruled Narbonne under arrangements negotiated with the Jews of the city and perhaps with a handful of Goths. Apparently they all coexisted under a contract that could be abrogated unilaterally by any party to the agreement. After vainly trying to persuade Matrand to compromise, the Jews and Goths dissolved the compact and sued for a separate peace.

The head of the Jewish delegation to the peace talks, who has come down in history only as Isaac, made the arrangement clear to Pepin in these words:

"Sire, do not believe that we are committing treason, for Matrand has no power over us, nor do we hold anything from him except that, in return for the protection he extends to us, we are paying him a certain sum annually. Besides, we ask that there should always be in Narbonne a king of our nation, because there ought to be one in the future just as there is one today. It is on his order that we have come to you; he is of the family of David hailing from Baghdad."

The mention of Baghdad is significant because the Jews of Narbonne seem to have conceived a loyalty not to Matrand nor to whoever was in power in Cordoba but to the ultimate source of Moslem legitimacy, the Caliph of Baghdad, who happened to be one of the fierce Abbasids of the black banners, the sworn enemies of the emir of Cordoba. (In 762 the new dynasty had moved the capital from Damascus to Baghdad.)

The Franks, though sworn to eternal hostility against all infidels, preferred the infidel who was far away to the one who was just across the border. The Jews felt likewise. There was, therefore, a community of interests among Pepin the Short, the Jews of Narbonne and the Caliph of Baghdad. They were bound to one another by that pragmatic political equation: "The enemy of my enemy is my friend."

In time Narbonne fell with the aid of the Jews. The Moslem garrison did not surrender, however, until after some bloody fighting at the gate. There Pepin's horse was shot from under him. As he lay helpless on the ground, at the mercy of his enemies, a Jewish horseman galloped up and dismounted. He helped the king of the Franks into the saddle. Pepin then rode on to victory while the Jewish cavalier, fighting on foot, succumbed to a Moslem cavalry charge.

So the reports ran at the time and commentators (at least, the Jewish ones) were still referring to the incident three hundred years later. Some historians suggest that the story confuses the incident at Narbonne with a similar rescue of the tenth-century emperor Otto II, by a Jewish knight. Could there have been two such Jewish sacrifices on the battlefield for Christian royalty? Was it the beginning of a long series of such services that were to enhance both the prosperity and the danger of Jews in Europe?

Whether as part of a political balancing scheme, or out of personal gratitude, the Jews received a third of Narbonne along with extensive lands in the region, to be ruled by their own prince, who would owe no tribute to Church or lord but only to the king of the Franks.

Pepin the Short and his queen, Bertha of the Big Feet, as she was known, were disposed to be friendly to the Jews. The king did not see himself as a mere chief with a tribal inheritance and a parochial constituency. His domain ran from the shadowy eastern forests of what is now Bohemia, inhabited by wolves, bears and "irrational and unlettered people" (as his legates reported), to the western sea; from the land of the Bretons in the north, where, according to sophisticated travelers "brothers and sisters shared the same bed ... and lived by rapine, like savage beasts," south to the Moors beyond the mountains. He was the heir of two traditions. One was Roman, imperial, secular and civilized. The other was Christian but based not so much on the Christianity of the bishops as on the Christian roots in Judaism. Pepin fancied himself in David's line as well as in Caesar's.

When Pepin and Bertha were crowned, Pope Stephen was careful to anoint the king according to the ancient Hebrew royal ritual, describing him as another David. The emphasis on Hebrew lore was so strong that Pierre Riché, an authority on the society that gave birth to Charlemagne, wrote: "Nourished on the Old Testament, Carolingian culture felt very close to the Jewish tradition. Frankish liturgy, morality, religious laws, and even the politico-religious system resembled Jewish custom so closely that some historians have conceived of an 'occult influence of Judaism on the Christian conscience.' "

So fashionable were Jewish ways that many young Franks celebrated the Sabbath at synagogues because they fancied the rabbinical style of sermon. The Jews made little effort to attract outsiders but did nothing to discourage them either. Rabbis took a respectful stance toward Jesus, referring to him as a great teacher who, alas, was crucified as a magician. In their version he was not entombed in a cave but buried in a cabbage patch. (Mohammedans also insisted that Jesus had not been crucified but had simply ascended to heaven leaving his shadow behind.) Seduced by Jewish intellectualism, food, women and the Old Testament, some Christians were converted. This enraged the bishops but did not seem to irritate their titular superior, Pepin.

A Jewish prince did indeed arrive in Narbonne, but precisely who he was is still wrapped in learned controversy. There is a text that asserts "King Charles [presumably Charlemagne] the royal issue of Pepin the Short and Bertha of the Big Feet sent to the King of Babylon [i.e., the Caliph of Baghdad] requesting that he dispatch one of his Jews of the seed of royalty of the House of David."

This is not very far-fetched because the Caliph traditionally recognized as spokesman for the Jews of his realm an "exilarch" of distinguished genealogy who was treated with royal punctilio. Moreover, the notion of founding a friendly Jewish dynasty might well have appealed both to the Caliph and to Charlemagne as a counterweight to the Jews of al-Andalus.

The chronicle resumes: "He [the Caliph] harkened and sent him one from there, a magnate and sage, Rabbi Makhir by name. And [Charlemagne] settled him in Narbonne, the capital city and planted him there, and gave great possession there at the time he captured it from the Ishmaelites [the Arabs]. And he [Makhir] took to wife a woman from among the magnates of the town . . . and the King made him a nobleman and designed, out of love for [Makhir] good statutes for the benefit of all the Jews dwelling in the city, as is written and sealed in a Latin charter; and the seal of the King thereon [bears] his name Carolus . . . this Prince Makhir became chieftain there. He and his descendants were close to the King and all his descendants. Anyone who came to molest him because of his hereditary landholdings and his high office was himself molested by the power of the King of France . . ."

Some say that the first prince of the Jews in Narbonne was not Makhir but a pretender to the power and glory of the exilarchate in Baghdad. Defeated politically, he was forced to flee the country. This renowned scholar, Natronai, who had contended for the title by dazzling philosophical and theological rhetoric, supposedly arrived in the south of France by ship and was instantly hailed as lord of the Jews, recognized as such by Charlemagne.

Then what about Makhir? There are scholars who ingeniously reconcile all manner of data to arrive at a simple solution: Natronai and Makhir, they say, are alternate names for the same sage and hero.

And what should be made of that celebrated champion, William of the Curved Nose, count of Toulouse, memorialized by troubadours, both Jewish and Christian, in such works as the *Chanson de Guillaume* and *Le Moniage Guillaume?* True, the monks who chronicled William's life made a monk of him, al-

though a pretty rough-and-tumble one. Yet there are tantaliz-
ing questions: Why did William, who led the Frankish forces in
wresting Barcelona from the Moors, refuse to press the siege
until the Jewish festival of Succoth was over? Why did he wait
to enter the city until the Sunday after Rosh Hashonah? And
why did he forbid all military action on Saturdays? Was he a
monk or a rabbi in arms?

And what is to be made of noble escutcheons in the region,
inscribed in Hebrew as well as Latin, bearing lions and six-
pointed stars? There are not only vignettes of known Jewish
troubadours, such as the celebrated Bofilh, in doublet and hose,
strumming lyres amid chivalric trappings, but numerous *chansons de geste* celebrating the lineage of the families of Makhir
and others. These chansons helped to convince some historians
that it was the Jews who taught the Spanish grandees to swell
with pride over a proper family tree.

For almost four hundred years the Jews of southern France
would defy their enemies—mainly churchmen who saw them
as competitors—by invoking the hallowed pledges of Carolingian kings. Their property was safeguarded against the ambitions of feudal lords and bishops. The Jews remained royal vassals, subject only to the king. Even Charlemagne's son Louis
(variously called *le Debonaire* and *le Pieux*) enthusiastically renewed the royal contract with the Jews. Although the Church
venerated Louis as "the royal monk" he resisted the anti-
Semitism of the clergy and even of the pope. Technically Jewish affairs were left in the hands of a *Magister Judaeorum.* (Some
say that only Jews held that title; some say Jews never held it;
and others say Jews sometimes held it.) In any case the magister was a royal servant, a point of contact with the prince of the
Jews. The king had a good deal of business to transact with
Jews. He issued special charters to Jewish travelers and traders
who could bring the products of distant civilizations to the
court at Aix-la-Chapelle. In one such charter given to a certain
Abraham of Saragossa, Louis proclaimed to the world that this
Jew, by his handshake and his Hebrew oath, "had entrusted
himself into our hands and after an oath We have received him
and hold him under our protection."

A Jewish vassal could hold vassals in turn and represent their interests in court as any baron of the realm would do. More to the point, perhaps, King Louis decreed that even to threaten the life of a Jew would bring down on the offender a fine of ten gold pounds, a fortune in those years when gold, which had become scarce, commanded a very high price in all the markets of the world. Jews had the right to own non-Christian slaves, though not to export them, and any attempts to convert those slaves to Christianity as a means of depriving Jews of their property was discouraged by royal command.

To see how tenderly Jewish sensibilities were considered, observe the niceties of a Carolingian court of law. A Jewish defendant preparing to testify did not take a Christian oath, which would have offended his soul. He placed his hand on the five books of Moses—in either a Latin or a Hebrew edition— and declared: "So may God help me, the same God who gave the law to Moses on Mount Sinai, and may the leprosy of Naaman, the Syrian, not afflict me as it afflicted him, and may the earth not swallow me as it swallowed Dathan and Abiram; I swear that I have committed no wrong against thee in this matter."

The judge could not test the Jew's veracity in the same way he would have if a Christian were on trial—by the ordeal of fire, scalding water or the whip. He would first have to prove that such investigatory procedures were sanctioned by Jewish law.

And Jewish counterfeiters were merely fined some gold for their transgression while slaves caught in such crimes were whipped. (The fact that slaves were unlikely to have the gold with which to pay their fines may have something to do with that distinction.)

A judge was always aware that his decision might be appealed by the Jewish defendant directly to the king, and such a prospect imposed a certain moderation on his pronouncements. For all this, the Jewish community paid a modest tribute to the royal coffers.

If a Jew sought redress from another Jew he answered only to the Jewish courts. Jewish law, however, was slowly creeping into Frankish law and even into Church canons. For example, a synod went directly to the Talmud for a precept according to which the dowry of a woman who died in the first year of her marriage must be returned to the family that provided it.

Of greater use to the king than the tax the Jews paid were their connections abroad, their readiness to travel, their familiarity with foreign languages and foreign ways, in short their diplomatic resources. Charlemagne began the trend, it is said, by sending a man named Isaac (as many Jews seemed to be), accompanied by two Christian knights, to woo the worldly but devout Caliph of Baghdad, Haroun al-Rashid. Or perhaps, as other historians have it, Isaac was sent by Haroun al-Rashid to negotiate with Charlemagne, or, as still others contend, Isaac shuttled between the two. Furthermore, some suggest, Isaac may have been the father of the intrepid William of Toulouse, thus wrapping up in his person a number of history's loose ends. Again we deal not with facts but with highly suggestive shadows.

All these and still greater ambiguities of history were to hang over the Frankish Jews for centuries. The great good fortune of the Jews of Narbonne served only to underscore their difference from the general population and therefore to isolate them. After all, no Christian peasant could be spared the ordeal of fire and the boiling pot if the law so decreed; he could not carry his grievances to the king; nor could he usually hold his land against the claim of any noble of the Church or state.

Jewish leaders, even before the rule of Pepin the Short, involved themselves in court and Church affairs. Even in the sixth century Jews appeared in the funeral corteges of noted ecclesiastics, chanting Hebrew hymns as they marched along. Some high churchmen were touched but more were scandalized by the ubiquitous Jews. Before the Carolingians came along with their Old Testament bias, politicians played with the Jews. For example, King Chilperic I, a coarse and small-minded man, kept at court a Jewish jeweler named Priscus whose skill was much admired. The king tried to persuade Priscus to become a Christian. To do so he organized a grand debate on the relative merits of Christianity and Judaism. It would be Priscus versus Gregory, bishop of Tours, who would be assisted (like it or not) by Chilperic himself.

Gregory, one of the most subtle and learned theologians in the Church, had an abiding contempt for Chilperic and rather respected Priscus. Medieval debates were intellectual tournaments, held with pomp and a system of scoring that depended on pedantically perceived hits.

We do not have a record of the points made by each side but in the end Gregory ruled that it had been a draw, a most remarkable verdict by a bishop upholding the superiority of Christian doctrine against a Jewish jeweler. The story, recorded by Gregory himself, testifies not only to the jeweler's extraordinary skill and stubborn courage but to the bishop's astonishing fairness.

Chilperic, unrestrained by the bishop's scruples, flew into a tantrum and ordered Priscus, along with a number of other Jews, to accept immediate baptism. The king offered to act as godfather but, although some Jews gave in, Priscus declined the honor. He was thereupon tossed into prison, where one of the newly converted, a man named Phatir, strangled him.

Gregory later reported that some accomplices to the murder were executed although Phatir himself was pardoned by the king and fled to Burgundy. There some relatives of Priscus found him and exacted their family vengeance.

Of far greater importance to the Christian and Jewish worlds was the unexpected conversion to Judaism of Bodo, a German priest and noble, who had risen to be a deacon in the imperial court of Louis the Pious. There seems to have been an affinity between Christian theologians of a pedantic and disputatious turn of mind and Jews who pondered the Talmud when they were not negotiating at court or dodging pirates on the high seas. Christian prelates and Talmudic scholars alike relished the minutiae of faith and the letter-by-letter dissection of Holy Scripture.

In 837 Bodo asked the emperor Louis for permission to go to Rome. Was it, as some suggest, to seek solace for a spirit troubled by doubt? When he got to Rome was he disenchanted by a high-living and dissolute papal court that made the rabbis seem chaste? Or did he use the trip to Rome as a pretext to escape the eyes of his superiors while he maneuvered a long-plotted transformation?

In any case the bishop turned up in Saragossa where he had himself circumcised, grew a beard, took the name of Eliezer, married a Jewish lady of that city and began to devote his days to pondering the Talmud. His Christian critics described his new way of life this way: ". . . sitting each day in Satan's houses of worship, bearded and married and profaning the name of the Nazarene and his Church, even as do all Jews."

Bodo seems to have been a testy sort. On fire with his new-found faith, he preached to his retinue urging them to follow him even unto circumcision. Only his nephew was persuaded, however. This so infuriated Bodo that in a self-righteous passion he sold all of his stubborn servants to a passing Arab slave dealer.

The Bodo/Eliezer affair stirred the Church on both sides of the Pyrenees and provoked a fierce polemical duel between the apostate and a Cordoban Christian theologian named Paulus Alvaro Cordobes. The momentous debate, which was at first couched in the sweet sad tones a man may use to a misguided brother, soon gave way to fierce invective. Always, however, they underscored their diatribes with quotations from Scripture, seeking to confuse and confound each other. Even the papacy took note of the raging controversy. We are left, however, with only one side of the debate, because the monks who were keeping the record thought it indecent to preserve the words of the renegade Bodo. Nevertheless, this has not prevented Jewish scholars from imagining what his arguments must have been.

Many in Spain were amused by a certain underlying irony in the situation. It was well-known that Alvaro was Christian only because his Jewish grandparents—or great-grandparents—had been obliged to accept baptism at the hands of the Visigoths. Thus Jews could entertain a characteristic pride of ancestry in the logic of Alvaro and at the same time marvel that the circumcised gentile Bodo could argue so like a Jew.

The Moslems of Spain were so sure of their power that they could enjoy the antics of Christians and Jews. The diversion was well-timed. The foreign threat had not faded away beyond the Pyrenees. Charlemagne had been persuaded by a group of pro-Abbasid dissidents to come over the mountains and crush the Omayyad Abd-er Rahman. The strategy, hatched in the Saxon capital of Paderborn, miscarried badly, however. A Berber army landed prematurely by sea before Charlemagne had crossed the Pyrenees. What with ineptitude and possibly treachery the advance force was wiped out.

Saragossa was supposed to surrender as soon as Charlemagne appeared but the would-be traitors were outmaneuvered and Charlemagne settled down to besiege the Moslem stronghold. Then he received word that the Saxons were up in arms again and back he had to go to Paderborn.

It was in 778 at the pass of Roncesvalles that Christians, Basques and Moslems, in a temporary alliance based on xenophobia, ambushed and annihilated Charlemagne's rear guard. An anonymous troubadour, seeking to cover the bare bones of history with a shred of panache, wrote into his *chanson* a trumpet part for Roland, warden of the Breton March, who fell in that minor mountain engagement and so won a literary immortality his life would not have earned him. His fictitious trumpet call closes a Frankish prelude to the glories then being prepared for Moslem, Christian and Jew in Cordoba.

Ziryab Sets the Fashion

Those who were crucified or beheaded during the rehearsals for the climactic scene of Cordoba's civilization may be pardoned for lacking the long view of history. Actually, however, there were visible, palpable intimations of future glory during the reign of Abd-er Rahman I. In his thirty years of rule the "Immigrant Emir" succeeded in reconciling most of his Moslem subjects to one another; he converted most Christians within his realm to the curled slipper, the white tunic, the style, language, tastes and, in some cases, the religion of Islam; and he managed to put to good use the Jews as technicians, artisans and sophisticated agents for the transnational osmosis of diverse civilizations of the Mediterranean world.

There had been wars and revolts under this first Omayyad prince of al-Andalus, but at the end of his reign there was a peace such as the country had not known since the heyday of Roman rule. The Christian kings of the north were kept securely behind the frontier marked roughly by the Douro River. The Abbasid army in Syria was apparently unable to seriously trouble the Andalusian satrapy by assassination, direct assault, subtle subversion or conspiratorial alliance with Frankish barbarians.

In addition to conferring political health on his state Abd-er Rahman exhibited a characteristic Omayyad style. He was a reluctant, if competent, general but an ardent aesthete, lavishing his favor and his money on poets and artists. The Great

Mosque had begun to rise on the ruins of a Visigothic church across the road from the Alcazar. And along a stream northeast of Cordoba the emir built himself a gracious palace, which, in tender nostalgia, he called al-Rusafa, after a similar royal retreat on the banks of the Euphrates where he had played as a much-loved princeling before the annihilation of his family.

When he was not quite sixty but clearly on his way to death from an illness difficult to diagnose at this distance, Abd-er Rahman set about the last great task of a ruler—the naming of a successor. (Moslems might have saved themselves a good deal of bloody warfare if they had established primogeniture as the rule of succession. True, it might have seated some incompetents, perhaps some criminals or idiots, on the throne but that is an inevitable risk and at least it would have prevented some of the ferocious civil wars that plagued their history.)

Abd-er Rahman passed over his oldest son, Suleiman, and his youngest, Abd-Allah, to choose the middle prince, Hisham. It was a rare choice, for Hisham was the gentlest of the sons of Abd-er Rahman. Even more astonishing than his selection was the agreement won from his brothers to live abroad and let him rule without making themselves available as the usual fraternal foci of conspiracy.

The brothers were no doubt encouraged to accept an African exile by the forecast of the palace astrologers that Hisham would not live very long. Perhaps it was that same horoscope that prompted Hisham to a career of saintliness, so alien to Omayyad gusto.

Here was an Omayyad emir, clad only in a simple white robe, walking the streets of Cordoba in sun and rain, carrying food from the palace to homes of the poor, consoling the sick and praying not with the high priests, the imams, but with the people. Even the mullahs were shocked. Piety was all very well for a priest and it is good embroidery for a royal legend but it is a quality not usually associated with a working ruler.

Hisham went further. He welcomed a holy man, Malik ibn Anas, who had founded still another variation of Islam in Medina. Malik appealed to Hisham not only because of the merits

of his philosophy and his apparent aura of sanctity but also because he had somehow earned the enmity of the Abbasids,
whose torturers had twisted one of his arms out of its socket and
subjected him to the bastinado. Hisham not only took in the
refugee but blessed the new Malikite brand of Islam with his
favor. The Malikite theologians thus became a new and arrogant political faction.

Like most self-righteous leaders—even the most saintly of
them—the emir was not moved to compassion for those who
did not accept his ideology or his theology. The non-Malikites
suffered political eclipse. Christians and Jews who had thrived
under Abd-er Rahman now found themselves ignored by everyone in official circles except the tax collector.

Hisham also embarked on what seemed to be a noncontro-
versial architectural innovation, but later events were to prove
this innocent diversion a source of horrors. He rebuilt the
Roman bridge over the Guadalquivir at Cordoba. It seemed a
sensible thing to do—like adding a minaret to the Great
Mosque—but his successor and the next generation of Cordobans were to suffer dearly for it.

Saint or no, the emir could not ignore the military aspects of
his job. When the weather was favorable he dispatched the
army on its routine holy missions to combat infidels in the Asturias or over the mountains in Narbonne. For the most part,
however, all was quiet in the emirate and the people of al-Andalus credited their serene and saintly ruler with divine favor.

In 796, after a reign of only seven years and a life of barely
forty, Hisham suddenly died, thereby validating the astrologers' predictions. However short and holy was his life Hisham
had obviously enjoyed women from a very early age. Or perhaps he merely regarded concupiscence as a royal duty. He became a father while he was still in his early teens. On his deathbed he chose as his heir Hakam, who was then twenty-six years
old, barely fourteen years younger than his father—and
Hakam was not the oldest of his children.

The choice of Hakam could be regarded as the fond whim of
a father who sees in his son the very opposite of himself and

finds the image both startling and fascinating. Where Hisham was a pious man burdened with the prophecy of early death and with his eye fixed on the world to come, Hakam was more on the wild side—a characteristic Omayyad.

The Malikite sages, whom his father had imported and cultivated into a political force, depressed the young prince, though he painstakingly followed their arguments as intellectual exercises. To the imams, Hakam seemed as threatening as sin. Not only had he been bored with their theology but he was also given to hunting, which they thought a scandal. And, though he called himself a devout Moslem and had made the pilgrimage to Mecca, he could not be weaned from wine, dissolute friends and casual lovers.

When he took over the emirate the mullahs prayed for him in ways that bordered on sedition. They asked for divine assistance to lead their emir to repent his sinful ways. Such prayers have a deadly ring. They lead crowds to throw stones at the sinner while they pray for his soul. An emir is not immune to such holy dangers. They awoke in the hitherto sociable young prince an uneasiness that gave rise to a deadly fear of conspiracy—that paranoia that is the disease of power.

Hakam was showing symptoms of that malaise a year after his subjects knelt before him swearing their fealty. The rhymed criticism of a satiric poet named Ghirbib ibn Abd Allah seemed to the emir to be a deadly dagger. He made his displeasure known and the poet left for Toledo where there were always rebels looking for a cause. Ghirbib's verses took on a more acid tone and young men and women delightedly recited them in the salons of disgruntled intellectuals. Many of these were new Moslems freshly converted from Christianity.

To control them Hakam sent one of his tame but wily new Moslems—a man named Amrus, a native of Huesca. It is possible that the emir gave Amrus no specific instructions but only wished aloud that he might be rid of the plotters in Toledo, a common device of rulers confronting a messy job. Amrus set about doing the bidding, spoken or unspoken, of his master. He built a tower along the winding Tagus River, a little north and east of Toledo. In the courtyard, his men dug a huge ditch of ambiguous purpose. The dissidents of Toledo welcomed the new tower because, Amrus explained, when it was finished the garrison would have plenty of room and need no longer be quartered on the townsfolk. It is hard to tell whether careful planning or supreme good luck brought to Toledo at that particular time the crown prince of Cordoba, a tall, graceful, four-teen-year-old Arab with the blue eyes and long blond hair that betokened the Omayyad partiality for Gothic concubines. His name, like that of his great-grandfather, was Abd-er Rahman.

Ostensibly Hakam had sent Abd-er Rahman on a ceremonial expedition to the frontier and, seemingly as an afterthought, Amrus courteously invited the prince to break his journey in Toledo. He called on the notables of the city to join in welcoming the heir to the throne. A formal reception was to be held in the new tower on the Tagus even though it was still incomplete.

The Toledo dignitaries gathered outside the walls of the castle and were met by a smiling Amrus and his lieutenants. When they were presented to the boy prince they were charmed by his innocence and amiability. Amrus led the way into the fortress through winding corridors with walls of raw masonry until they reached a passageway barely wide enough for one to pass. Each of the guests went alone down that long tunnel, the men in handsome tunics, the women in their silkiest veils. The end of the passage was a rectangle of blazing sun. Into that rectangle, one by one, they disappeared.

Did they vanish so quietly that the courtly elite of Toledo went pressing on unthinkingly toward the hot sunlight? Or at some moment was there a sense of unease, perhaps the sudden balking by those near the front, a moment of panic before Amrus' guards pushed on the backs of those at the end of the line, moving them like cattle down a chute, bellowing at the smell of blood?

Some historians say that five thousand Toledans were decapitated that afternoon, their bodies flung into the dry ditch in the courtyard. Others suggest that there could have been no more than seven hundred victims. All agree that the young crown prince, Abd-er Rahman, astonished and horrified, turned his head away from the tower and wept. It was certainly true that from that day forward for the rest of his life Abd-er Rahman exhibited a nervous tic in one eye.

The day was thereafter referred to as "The Day of the Ditch." To the converted Christians, prominent among those slain, it was a reminder of the fragility of their safety under Islam. To born and bred Moslems it was an example of an unfortunate "excess" of power. On the rebellious spirit of Toledo it imposed a shocked hush and a fourteen-year interval of civil peace. For the emir Hakam the Day of the Ditch was a point of no return. Terror bred revolt and revolt bred terror, so that all political communication was reduced to an antiphony of screams.

Throughout al-Andalus some of the dissidents were crucified alive and others only after they were dead. Their bodies hung on crosses along the Rasif, the road that runs between the Guadalquivir and the walls of the Alcazar. The emir Hakam, writing anguished poetry in the night, may have found some comfort in those grisly markers.

His uncles, the ambitious brothers of his saintly father, had been thrown into prison very early in Hakam's reign. It was a futile security measure where no security was possible. The only safe uncle was a dead one, and so the two were killed by an assassin who was smuggled into the jail.

The walls of the Alcazar were reinforced, the moat was deepened. New arms were stored in the palace. New slaves were groomed to replace old guards whose very survival was suspect. A new chief of internal security was appointed—an erstwhile Christian called Rabi. But the fountainhead of treason lay in the new part of Cordoba that was linked to the old by the Roman bridge that Hisham, in his innocence, had rebuilt. To Hakam that bridge was a link to a pest house. The wind that blew up from the south seemed to carry a deadly infection.

In saintly Hisham's time the leaders of the new sect of Malikites had built their homes and schools there because it was a short walk across the bridge to the palace, mosques and courts of Cordoba. The converted Christians set up shops in the new quarter to do business with the rising middle class. Craftsmen, apprentices and workmen of all sorts settled there to do the jobs required by a thriving new community. The place became known to Cordobans as "the Suburb"—cleaner and greener than the alleys of the old city, and still convenient.

When the crosses with their grisly burdens disturbed the view across the river, the Suburb began to grumble. In short order the mood became as threatening as it had been in Toledo. There were angry public meetings in the suburban mosques although it was well known that spies and informers were everywhere.

When crowds demonstrated angrily over a grossly lopsided decision by the chief of market police, Hakam ordered a commission of inquiry. This led to the arrest and crucifixion of the leaders of the demonstration. That did not stop the grumbling. So far had disloyalty spread that no Moslem could be trusted to collect taxes in the Suburb; the job was left to Christians.

On March 25, 818, a soldier, involved in a shouting argument with a blacksmith in the Suburb, drew his sword and killed him. Crowds gathered in the suburban center, and by mid-afternoon the emir, returning from a hunt, could feel the sullenness hanging like dark clouds. From the back of the crowd came jeers and boos. His guards cleared the way to the bridge and picked up ten troublemakers. They were crucified on the spot. The emir galloped across the river into the palace, barely making it in time. The riots spread from the Suburb to the city, where markets shut down. Merchants joined with workmen, artisans and slaves. They carried pickaxes and hacked away at the gates of the Alcazar.

The emir's lieutenants, prepared for such an emergency, rallied their forces south of the river and proceeded to press in on the rioters, burning their houses and their markets as they marched to the bridge. The rebels were trapped between the flames of the Suburb and the army of the emir. Troops hedged them in, killing as they came.

The frightened emir was all for massacring every man, woman and child and had made a good start at it when some of his legal secretaries reminded him of the advisability of appearing to follow proper form. A commission of judges was established to recommend sound legal procedures while troops continued to block every alleyway that might offer an escape for the rebels. After three days of deliberation the judges decided to crucify three hundred of the leaders and to expel every other living being from the Suburb. Every building was to be razed and the ground sown with grain. It was to be declared forever uninhabitable, so as to leave the emir with one less nightmare.

Some twenty thousand exiles fled to Toledo, where for years they were called, with the awe due to spectacularly failed revolutionaries, "the Suburbanites." Many more, however, left for North Africa, where settlements soon sprouted under names such as "Andalusian town." A few of the more venerable Malikites were allowed to find new quarters and safer politics in old Cordoba. Only after the healing time of more than a century did any Cordoban dare to build a home again on the left bank of the Guadalquivir.

Hakam went into seclusion, consumed with either fear or repentance—depending on the political coloration of the chronicler who was telling the story. After the frenzy of the massacre he pardoned at least some of the surviving lawyers and mullahs, even though they confessed their involvement in the rebellion. He even forgave a Jew who for a year had sheltered one of the rebellious mullahs. The contrite emir said that he admired the Jew for risking his life in a gallant gesture.

To some this behavior argued a sincerely repentant heart. Others saw in the emir's behavior a consuming fear of retribution, either worldly or divine. In those comparatively innocent times massacres tended to haunt their perpetrators and were not exorcised by geopolitical excuses or historical imperatives. History was then highly personal and none of those who played great parts were unconscious of the tragedy.

Hakam was not altogether mad nor altogether hateful nor altogether anything but pitiful. After the massacre he shut himself into his palace with his wives and his eunuchs. He imported two hundred guards—mainly from Narbonne—who knew no Arabic and would therefore find it difficult to conspire with the people against him. These tall, grim men, isolated in their barracks, became known as "the deaf and dumb" because no one could communicate with them. The emir saw some safety in that gulf of silence.

In the middle of May 822, Hakam emerged from his harem long enough to confirm what everyone had already taken for granted—that Abd-er Rahman, the second Omayyad of that name and the second son of the emir, would be next in line. Hakam then went back to the harem, to the love of his wives and concubines. There he wrote a testament in verse to his son and heir. The poem is an apologia pro sua vita; it is a plea to history to find him guilty but with an explanation:

"Just as a tailor uses a needle to sew together pieces of cloth, so I have used my sword to reunite my divided province. . . . Ask my frontiers if any place is in the power of the enemy; they will answer 'nay!' But if they answered 'Yes!' thither would I fly clad in my cuirass, and sword in hand. . . .

"Ask also the skulls of my rebellious subjects which, like split gourds, lie upon the plain, gleaming in the sunshine. They will tell you that I smote them again and again. . . . If I spared not their wives and children, it was because they threatened my family and myself; he who cannot avenge insults offered to his family is devoid of honor and despised of all men. What if, after the exchange of sword thrusts, I made them drink deadly poison? I did but repay the debt they had compelled me to contract. Of a truth, if death overtook them, it was because destiny willed it.

"Peaceful then are the provinces which I hand down to thee, O my son! They are a couch on which thou mayst repose undisturbed; I have taken care that no rebellion shall break in upon thy sleep."

The emir, having made the strongest case he could in his own defense, died shortly afterward in the collective bosom of his grieving wives and concubines. Having known the emir's fears, lusts, sentiments and literary aspirations, they seemed to have loved him for his most vulnerable moments, his many failings and his few virtues.

Abd-er Rahman II thus inherited, along with a nervous twitching of the eye contracted on the Day of the Ditch, a vast and lovely country as quiet as a tomb. It was also one of the richest countries in all the Mediterranean littoral. Poets were beginning to speak of al-Andalus in the breathless hyperbole previously reserved for the wonders of Byzantium or Cathay.

The bloody peace that Hakam won was now yielding a rich revenue. Every city in the peninsula paid its taxes promptly, uncertain whether the new emir was like his pious grandfather or his bloody father and taking no chances. Farmers sent in either bags of money or great supplies of malt and wheat to stuff the emir's granaries. Patricians who wanted exemptions from the military draft paid well for the privilege, and the vast bureaucracy extracted money from the issuance of permits. For example, there was a permit, with fee attached, for the use of falcons in hunting. There were fees collected from manufacturers who applied for the advertising advantage of appending the seal of the emir to their product, and there were the handsome proceeds derived from the emirate's own looms and ceramic factories.

All this princely business was facilitated early in Abd-er Rahman's reign by the establishment of mints in al-Andalus. Under previous administrations the bronze oboles and the silver dirhems were coined in North Africa but, in the expanding economy, people were running out of coins and being reduced to barter. This was awkward for the captains and merchants in the river and ocean ports.

Abd-er Rahman II was by nature neither a businessman nor a lawyer, though he did passably well in both fields when he had to. Architecture was closer to his heart. He built a new palace near the Alcazar, not out of extravagance but out of respect for custom, for no king was expected to live in the house of his predecessor. From the terrace of his new home he could view all of Cordoba. He had his engineers lay conduits and build viaducts to bring water down from the mountains, not only to splash in the marble basins of the palace but to play in some 850 public fountains that sprouted in the markets and wherever the streets were wide enough throughout Cordoba.

The place was alive with the sound of splashing water. A millennium later anthropologists would design a theory according to which the Arabs, whose ancestors were forever seeking water in the desert, flung it about like beggars with a windfall when they saw streams cascading down the Andalusian hills in spring.

Near the front of his palace Abd-er Rahman set up an elegant sunlit room, known as the *madjlis*, where he would sprawl on cushions each morning while his secretaries and viziers rendered their accounts and while commoners presented their petitions in the ancient desert manner. He would dictate his correspondence, allowing his secretaries to put their own poetic gloss on routine business. Proud of his talents as a poet, he would formulate the delicate imagery and learned allusions that he thought fitting for diplomatic exchanges or higher literary criticism. Whatever the content, every letter was sealed with the ornate expression of proud humility: "Abd-er Rahman is content with the will of Allah."

Actually the emir was not a pious man, though he was the nominal mullah of mullahs, the supreme religious leader as well as the supreme military power in al-Andalus. Like most absolute monarchs he was not altogether his own master. In religious affairs he dared not flout the mullahs as a class for he knew they could damn a sinning monarch to an earthly assassination while praying for his soul in the hereafter.

He could not ride roughshod over his military chiefs, for who would then protect his absolute majesty? He could not even be too high-handed in administering the law because he had entrusted the complicated and delicate procedures, policies and appointments of the courts and police to a man whom he dared not lose, because he was far too efficient. This was Yahya ibn Yahya, who had impeccable credentials, because his grandfather had come over to al-Andalus with Tarik.

As a young man Yahya had burned with a theological and

revolutionary zeal. It was said that when he studied at the feet of the venerable Malik, in the days when saintliness was in vogue in Cordoba, he would not move from his master even when an elephant thundered past the door. While other students raced out in high excitement he remarked that he had come to Cordoba to seek wisdom, not to gaze at strange beasts.

Later, when the emir Hakam barred the Malikite theologians from political influence, Yahya rose along with the other students of the Suburb to denounce tyranny and godless government. He had to flee for his life to Toledo but Abd-er Rahman II cheerfully rehabilitated all erstwhile revolutionaries. The emir was always saddened by necessary brutalities and outraged by unnecessary ones.

Yahya, grown older, felt the sweet temptations of power and glimpsed a social rationale for tyranny. He found the new emir a touch too soft. Yahya kept judges, lawyers, litigants, market squabblers and chiefs more or less in line by stern decrees and draconian punishments. The emir had to admit that Yahya did the job efficiently, albeit more harshly than he would have wished. A tough sergeant is invaluable to a mild commander.

Yahya even dared to reproach the emir for his mildness and occasionally to instruct him in morals. Abd-er Rahman merely smiled. He was happy to have a minister who practiced the stern and pious virtues in his name, leaving him to be concerned with diplomacy, art and the intellectual and sexual gratifications of his harem.

Abd-er Rahman hungered for the delights of women—not only their sexual excitement, of which he was a celebrated connoisseur, but their music, poetry and conversation, all of which enhanced the love affairs on which he thrived. His prowess in the harem became legendary. He was known to have fathered forty-five sons and forty-two daughters. The number of his wives and concubines is not known, but the emir enjoyed a rapid turnover. Those who provided sons achieved the honored status of "princess-mothers." They were given their freedom and retired from active duty except in cases of a lasting and mutual ardor.

Scouts canvassed the peninsula for attractive virgins. To

qualify they had to be not only sexually stimulating but also exceptionally bright or talented in the arts. Many were imported, for the emir admired blond and blue-eyed girls from the north as well as the black-eyed, dark-skinned graduates of music academies of Arabia and North Africa. The schools of Medina turned out the most celebrated singers, with elegant manners in bed and out of it.

The scouts had to inquire into the genealogy of all candidates, for the emir was interested in the families of his wives and lovers. There were some who had to take special training after being chosen. For example, a delicate Basque princess named Kalam figured in a treaty concluded with her kinfolk after their minor rebellion was put down. She was only thirteen but very promising. The agreement with the Basques stipulated that she was to be sent to Medina or Baghdad, where she was to be educated in the arts of enlivening the court as well as the bed of a cultivated, energetic and pleasure-loving prince. Neither the girl nor her family appear to have had the slightest objection, since the opportunities thus unfolding were likely to be far greater, safer and more entrancing than any she would have had among her people.

Not all of the wives of Abd-er Rahman II were mere amusements or the pleasant vehicles of a noble posterity. Some tended not only to influence but also to rule the ruler of al-Andalus. Tarub was one such wife. No reliable description of her has come down through the centuries but it is clear that she overwhelmed the susceptible emir of Cordoba. There is no suggestion that her charms were literary, musical or conversational. Her commercial sense, however, was highly developed. Tarub would keep her door closed to the pleading Abd-er Rahman until he deposited bags of gold or gems at her doorstep. She commanded a very high price indeed from a man who had an extensive array of women to gratify his extraordinary appetite. Abd-er Rahman was not the man to batter down a door and take a wife against her will. He regarded such conduct as fit only for Goths, Germans or the strange men of the British Isles who had just left off painting themselves with interesting vegetable dyes. He preferred to win a woman's favors with poetry, but if she preferred gold he was ready to meet her price—at least in Tarub's case.

Tarub may have influenced the politics of her ardent lover, but only in petty ways: the appointment or dismissal of a bureaucrat, perhaps, or the naming of a mosque in her honor. Unlike some harem women Tarub did not think in large terms. In the end her grasp for power was as crude as the price in gold she put on herself. She hatched a plot that almost killed the emir and would have plunged an infant civilization into chaos.

Her partner in that fateful enterprise was a eunuch who was highly trusted by Abd-er Rahman. Abu al-Fath al-Nasr was the son of Christian parents in Cremona. Just how he came to be among the castrated elite is not known. He was one of a group of bright and handsome young men who found themselves in Lucena, that center of Jewish science and medical practice where surgeons would biologically prepare candidates for their confidential service to the prince.

Al-Nasr grew up speaking only the Romance tongue of his parents. He picked up his Arabic in the harem. Abd-er Rahman came to trust al-Nasr's advice on a variety of matters far afield from the domestic problems of the palace.

Was al-Nasr beguiled by Tarub or was it the other way around? In any case their partnership in politics was to end in disaster, but that came near the end of the reign of Abd-er Rahman II and should be told in its proper place. There were other figures in this glittering court who were beginning to give it that distinction that in time would become the hallmark of Cordoba's civilization.

For example, there was that master of illusion, Abbas ibn Firnas, who makes Merlin seem an awkward amateur. He amused the lesser intellects of Cordoba with sleight-of-hand tricks but delighted the emir and the ladies of the harem with subtler arts. He developed a formula for making crystal in which a sky of dazzling stars would appear in a goblet. Then, by a slight motion of the hand, he would change the light and make the glass appear to cloud over into a storm.

He taught Abd-er Rahman bits and pieces of philosophy gleaned from Indian, Chinese, Hebrew and Persian mystics. For the literati, Firnas developed a system of scanning Arabic meter that enlightened those courtiers who fancied themselves as poets.

He was not only a poet and prestidigitator but also something of an athlete. His physique was almost as celebrated as his intellect. His mind, however, tended to overreach his physical powers. Reveling perhaps in the myths that teemed in his brain, he fancied himself at least the physical equal of a bird and much wiser than Icarus. He fashioned a tight-fitting suit out of an animal skin to which he had craftsmen sew "feathers" of silk. He attached wings (made of who knows what material) that he could activate with his arms. Accompanied by a vast throng of Cordobans, always delighted with the eccentricities of the court, Firnas climbed one of the hills that rise above the road along the Guadaliquivir. He stood at the edge of the cliff—that was mercifully not very sheer—and leaped. For an instant he hung poised on his wings like a hawk at the summit of its soaring. Then he tumbled down. His constitution, his pride and his sense of humor seem to have survived the roll in the gravel on the hillside.

Also sharing the emir's delight and the acclaim of the Cordoban crowd was al-Ghazal—the Gazelle. He was an Arab named Yahya ibn Hakam al-Bikri, who even at the age of fifty was celebrated for his good looks, his slim waist, his movements graceful as those of the gazelle that was honored in his nickname.

His verse was not the customary wash of languorous sighs. He satirized most of what he saw in as crisp a style as the soft sound of Arab poetry would allow. It is an indication of Abd-er Rahman's permissive attitude to the arts that the Gazelle could choose his targets very close to the throne. For example, he caricatured that forbidding theologian and arch-policeman Yahya ibn Yahya in verse that asked why only theologians grew rich in service to the state.

Yahya stormed in the emir's presence against the insolence,

even the blasphemy of such poets. The emir's smile cooled Yahya's temper. Abd-er Rahman would not agree to discipline his erratic Gazelle but he conciliated the fierce Yahya by promising that, at least during the important fasts of the Islamic calendar, his court would abstain from satire and conspicuously sensuous pleasures. Copulating on holy days or even in holy months was a sin so heinous in Yahya's eyes that he forced the emir to do penance for his pleasure.

Shining above all other luminaries in the Cordoban court was one man who influenced far more than the style of poetry. He set the fashions for men and women, established a style of cooking, developed a new music and devised new instruments to play it. He introduced toothpaste and taught women how to form their eyebrows.

Abu al-Hasan'ali ibn Nafi came out of the court of Haroun al-Rashid in Baghdad. His dark skin and flashing black eyes gave him the stage name Ziryab—meaning blackbird in Arabic. (If, on the other hand, one chooses a Persian derivation, it is translatable as Goldwater.) As a young man, though already married and the father of four children, he was a pupil of Baghdad's most celebrated entertainer, Ishak al-Mawsili. At a command performance before the Caliph, Ziryab won such royal acclaim that Ishak found him unbearable. Fearing that his master's jealousy could be murderous, Ziryab fled to Kairouan, where he wangled employment at the provincial court to maintain his family while he put out feelers for other posts. At the time—shortly before the accession of Abd-er Rahmin II to the emirate—one of Cordoba's most distinguished musicians was a Jew named Abu l-Nasr Mansur who, like many of his people, had access to foreign news and gossip from kinsmen scattered around the world. Mansur heard of Ziryab's talents, of the scandal at Baghdad and of his present availability. He put in a good word for Ziryab with the emir Hakam, who, even though he was then winding up a brutal reign, still considered himself a poet and patron of the arts.

Hakam agreed to try out Ziryab at Cordoba, and Mansur sent for him. When the singer arrived at Algeciras with his several wives and four young sons, Mansur was waiting at the pier with news both good and bad. The emir who had invited him was dead. Ziryab instantly prepared to take the next boat back to North Africa, for he knew that newly crowned rulers rarely fancy the favorites of the old regime. But Abd-er Rahman had been persuaded by Mansur that Ziryab was a living wonder and that this was a chance to steal a gem from the crown of Haroun al-Rashid.

Abd-er Rahman sent down to Algeciras one of his most distinguished eunuchs with a convoy of mules, carrying glittering trinkets for the musician and his family. The eunuch, a man of impressive bulk, was elegantly fitted out and ornamented as befitted one designed to serve so close to the emir. He came bearing gifts and smiles and glittering promises. Ziryab, Mansur and the eunuch traveled up the highway to Cordoba in a gala procession. The emir, after one conversation with Ziryab—which must have been scintillating—went considerably beyond the eunuch's promises. Ziryab was to be given a salary of two hundred gold pieces a month, very handsome by any standard, plus a midsummer bonus of five hundred, a new year's bonus of five hundred, and one thousand gold pieces on each of the two high Islamic holidays. In addition his household was to be provided annually with two hundred bushels of barley and one hundred bushels of wheat. He was given a small palace in town and several villas in the countryside, each with a farm that produced a pleasant harvest. Overnight, Ziryab became a wealthy man.

One wonders why Abd-er Rahman thought it proper to lavish all this on a musician. Was it merely to assure a flow of pretty concerts? Not likely. The emir was rich and generous to a fault, but this was more than an extravagant caprice; it was beyond what even he would pay for amusement.

In view of what Ziryab later accomplished one must assume that Abd-er Rahman chose to make this a deliberate investment in civilizing his peninsula. His bloody father had left him a relatively peaceful land, and a rich one, but it did not yet shine in the world like Baghdad or Byzantium. It was still an outpost on the edge of a backward continent. Ziryab was to teach al-Andalus at least the superficial graces that would save it from the grossness of mere wealth.

Of course, he was to bring the refinements of life primarily to those who could afford it. He would not sing his wailing ballads to farmers in the fields or to slaves aboard the galleys. The poor, however, were never far from the extravagantly wealthy. Those who served at parties in the palace quickly picked up the new songs and new styles. Those who watched the parade of the gentry in their latest hairdos mimed them in the back streets.

Ziryab's earliest enterprise, undertaken shortly after his arrival in Cordoba in 822, was more that of a minister of culture than of a court entertainer. He set up a school of music open not only to harem novices and court entertainers but also to aspiring boys and girls of Cordoba. The new school was not patterned after the old conservatories of Baghdad, which permitted only minor variations and very subtle refinements of venerable models.

Ziryab introduced a fresh style of playing, new themes and even a variation in instruments. For example, he modified the old four-string lyre by adding a fifth string and devising a new plectrum fashioned from an eagle's claw instead of wood. He found it more sensitive and soon no fashionable Cordoban would touch wood to a lyre or to any of the other mandolinlike instruments then in vogue.

He himself composed for the double-flute, the drums and voice as well as for strings. His method of recording his compositions was simple and effective, if inconvenient for his household. His most inspired melodies would often occur to him in the middle of the night, in a twilight of the mind between waking and sleeping. At such times he would call for the two most talented musicians of his harem, Hindah and Ghazzalan—unless he was fortunate enough to be sleeping with one of them. They would rush to his room clutching their lutes and he would then teach them the song that had run through his brain. After it was imprinted on their fertile minds, Ziryab could then resume his sleep or whatever might be his pleasure.

Ziryab was a cautious revolutionary who did not abruptly overturn all that had been taught or practiced. When he came to Cordoba the court was much enamored of three singing maidens from Medina. (At least they were maidens when they came to Cordoba, though in time each of them presented the emir with a son.) These talented women had organized an orchestra and chorus for the emir along traditional Baghdad lines. Ziryab joined in the general approval of the Medina trio but worked with them to modernize their repertoire. He was careful also to cause no upheaval in the music school headed by Mansur, the Jewish musician who had championed him. Mansur slowly faded into relative obscurity but never regretted having brought Ziryab to Cordoba. He was content to glow by reflection.

Ziryab was an adept in all the manifold forms of art, trivial or profound. He had plucked his sense of style and taste out of the perfumed air of the Middle East. Much of what he worked with were cultural relics left by the Greeks and Romans, fertilized and transmitted by the Jews, seasoned and preserved by the Arabs. Food fascinated him as much as music. He found the Andalusian middle-class cuisine interesting but a trifle uncouth.

In the mornings the Cordoban lady of the house, or perhaps her Sudanese cook, would prepare the batter for the day's bread and take it to the community oven to be baked. Then the ingredients of the main meal of the day would be bought and the menu prepared. It might be lamb's head or lamb meatballs or spiced lamb sausage or lamb heart or lamb livers—to be cooked in butter, or baked or grilled over a wood fire in the courtyard outside the tiny kitchen. Ziryab codified these ingredients in imaginative recipes, stylishly setting the ubiquitous lamb in an array of side dishes.

There would be white cheeses, and cakes of honey or almond. There would be vegetable soups and chicken breasts molded into balls mixed with grain. There would be fish, marinated like *escabeche* (pickled fish), fried or baked or rolled into balls. Puddings would be made of chicken breasts, flour and milk.

The menu of the poor was limited in quantity but there was a wide choice and an adventurous appetite, for the middling-rich had not yet had the centuries it takes to create wholly separate class worlds. And al-Andalus was then a horn of plenty. The fields, fish and fowl were not fenced off from the poor.

Before Ziryab there had been no style in the presentation of food. It was all lumped in platters on a bare wooden table or, if the household had some pretensions, there might have been a cloth of coarse linen.

Ziryab laid down an order of service that was quickly followed in the palace, then in the villas of up-and-coming courtiers and businessmen, then by Christians and Jews and finally by the poor. The regimen spread to Seville and Jaen and even to the northern borders of al-Andalus. It was to be taken up in Gaul and even in Britain. It would be followed for generations, indeed for a millennium.

The meal, Ziryab decreed, must begin with soup and proceed to the meat course if there be no fish. Then should come the fowl, followed by sweets—usually cakes of almond and honey, fruit dishes flavored with vanilla, bowls of pistachios or other nuts.

And the table should not be bare, he insisted. He introduced coverlets of exceedingly fine leather. To meet the needs of such style he went into the market stalls and taught a generation of leather workers how to cut, skive and tool an elegant table covering.

He also found fault with the gold and silver goblets the wealthy used to hold their rose-perfumed water or, in scandalous cases, wine. They seemed to him to be clumsy, pretentious and fit only for Teutonic chieftains. Ziryab organized glass factories to produce a delicate crystal. Soon the tables of al-Andalus dazzled with the lights of tapers reflected in glass.

Forks and table knives were still undreamed of, even by Ziryab, but he redesigned the wooden spoons universally used for soup. For the rest, there were only fingers, which seemed quite serviceable, washable and as capable of elegance as were the diners themselves.

The women of al-Andalus were much in the eye of this ardent aesthete. He admired their beauty but could not leave them in their uncultivated state. In Cordoba near the Alcazar he established a school where he taught women the use of depilatories to leave their limbs, face and underarms unmarred by hair.

He disapproved of the conventional hairdo—a part precisely down the middle, temples and forehead covered, braids running down the back. Instead he cut the ladies' hair short, shaped the hair to the head, lifted the veil of hair from eyebrows and ears and made visible the lines of the neck, which he thought quite fetching. The ladies listened, the barbers cut and the men of Cordoba found new fascinations.

He prescribed a fashion calendar for the tunics, shirts, blouses and burnooses, which were usually made of cotton or linen. From April to June, he decreed, bright colors should be worn by both men and women. Silks in blues, greens and yellow should flutter over their tunics. From June to September white should predominate everywhere. For winter Ziryab recommended long cloaks trimmed with fur. Every attorney, every rich farmer hurrying to the capital swirled his cloak, and furriers multiplied in the market.

Ziryab was not content with remodeling the look of his adopted country. He worried about its intellect. Accordingly he cultivated Jewish doctors and even brought astrologers from India who mingled with their wizardry some of the fundamentals of astronomy. He had them teach chess to the emir's court and from there the game spread to the tavern.

He called on philosophers to help interpret his dreams and those of the emir. Above all he sought out the riches of art from wherever his reports gave clues of their existence. He wanted Cordoba to sample carvings, mosaics and, above all, the ideas recorded in the parchment scrolls of the world's great libraries. He stirred the appetites of the emir and the court of Cordoba to receive these works, but how was he to find and bring it all to this outpost on a barbarous continent?

For that purpose he had one resource. It was the same resource his Christian neighbor Charlemagne had found and put to use—the Jews. They were the adventurers, the people who knew strange languages, who could find kinsmen everywhere from Gaul to China, who could navigate, who could travel in Moslem lands, where Christians were not welcome, and in Christian lands, where Moslems were anathema. The Jews opened the windows of Andalusia.

By Goat to China

The director of posts for the Caliph of Baghdad was a master spy and the head of counterintelligence as well as postmaster general. In his headquarters were maps of the Caliphate and the fringes of the world that dangled beyond it. Radiating across the known world were lines representing caravan routes of Medes and Persians, military roads of Greeks and Romans, camel paths, mountain trails and barely navigable waterways.

These were the routes over which crawled or sailed processions of merchants, messengers, diplomats, pirates, soldiers, smugglers, beggars, tempters of youth, enemies of order and purveyors of salvation. They went on camel, mule, horse, barge, dhow, galley and foot.

Their routes reached from al-Andalus into India, China, Egypt, Carolingian Gaul, Rome, Byzantium, Muscovy and the Jewish kingdom of Khazaria.

To watch over these pathways of infection and defection and to keep the business of empire in motion took a network of postmaster-spies. They had to provide relays for imperial couriers, ceremonially accommodate visiting dignitaries, collect tolls and tribute from passing caravans. One such busy provincial bureaucrat of the ninth century was Abdul Kassim Obaid Allah ibn Khordadbeh, the son of a governor, who cultivated a personal fancy for maps, travel and travelers' yarns.

His job was therefore most congenial to his taste. He ran the post office—although this scarcely does justice to the office—in

Djibal, once a province of the Medes before Cyrus' brought them under Persian rule. Now it was a part of Baghdad's empire. Through Rayy, the main city of Djibal, ran one of the most ancient caravan routes of the world, the Khorosan Road, linking the Middle East to the Far East, those lands of impassable mountains, teeming jungles, fierce and preposterous beasts, wise men and uncountable riches.

Khordadbeh closely questioned the travelers who passed through Rayy. Possibly over sweet wine and pastries, he drew from them their stories and, with the discrimination of an experienced reporter, pieced them together into an authoritative geography text entitled *The Book of the Roads and the Kingdoms.*

In it he devoted a chapter to what he called, "The Routes of the Jewish Merchants called Radanites." Learned scholars have long pondered that word and heatedly argued over its derivation. Is "Radanite" a reference to the name of Khordadbeh's own city of Rayy? Not likely, the experts think, because the Jews began their voyages in the west, most frequently in al-Andalus, not in eastern Persia. And Rayy was not a terminus. Travelers passed through it as they passed through far greater cities.

Some suggest the Rhone as a source for the odd term. Rhone merchants, sailors and shipowners—many, if not most, of whom were Jewish—were called in Latin *Nautae Rodanici* (sailors of the Rhone). Scholars are more likely to credit the Rhone than Rayy as the source of the term but they are not enthusiastic about that either.

Some discount place names entirely and theorize that Radanite is merely a corruption of Rabbinite. Ingenious but unconvincing. The likeliest bet, scholars suggest, is the theory that traces the word to the Persian phrase *rah dan,* meaning "he who knows the way." That Persian phrase has interesting cognate descendants including the English "road."

These, then, were the people of the open road—the Jews. But why Jews?

Actually, if there had been no Jews to cross-fertilize Cordoba and the world beyond with goods, arts and ideas, the people of the ninth century might have sunk into exclusive watertight enclaves. Jews were the only ones who were free to travel the world without being suspect as carriers of either the Moslem or Christian creed. They were multilingual, they were not tied to the land by oaths of fealty, they had kinfolk everywhere, and they were, in general, literate in at least one language.

There were also Arabs and Berbers sailing the southern shores of the Mediterranean, trading in the bazaars of North Africa, and loading slaves and other merchandise in ports all along the East African coast. In general, however, Moslems were averse to travel among the infidel.

Increasingly in the ninth century most Moslems—even the worldly Syrians—were excluded from Christian markets and Christians were virtually barred from Moslem waters. The once-thriving port of Marseilles, where Syrian vessels used to unload wine, spices, papyrus and oil for Charlemagne's court, was now idle. Conversely, "the Christians could not float a plank on the sea," as the Arab commentator ibn Khaldun noted in later years.

Though Arab sailors still ran some of the traffic from Andalusian ports to North Africa, the long voyages to the east on which Abd-er Rahman and Charlemagne relied for the creature comforts and intellectual stimulus of their realms depended on Jews. These were no peddlers on muleback trading out of their saddlebags but navigator-adventurers, crossing oceans and scaling mountains to fetch from emperors and businessmen a remarkable miscellany of diamonds, lions, rare books, Greek vases, German slaves and anything or anyone else that was marketable, interesting and, by any manner of means, portable.

It was these traveling Jews and their Arab competitors who gave Europeans their first taste of sugar, rice, cinnamon, mace and apricots. They introduced Europeans to the aroma of sandalwood and musk, and taught them the medical uses of asafetida, camphor and the aloe plant. They brought to Gaul the Arab comforts of the mattress and sofa. And, though some rabbis protested, Jews brought in the incense for use in Christian churches.

Some of the spices and papyrus were cut off when the Syrians left the business but Jewish travelers supplied most other exotic commodities to Cordoba.

Some historians contend that Europe entered the Dark Ages when trade and communications were severed between the Islamic and Christian worlds. Perhaps, but the Radanites kept the door sufficiently ajar to allow a nourishing interchange in the twilight before events in China, Venice, Russia and elsewhere combined to ruin them. While Abd-er Rahman II ruled Cordoba and the Carolingians held their empire together the Radanites distributed to the kingdoms of semibarbarous Europe the necessary luxuries of the pre-Renaissance.

It would be a mistake to imagine that what the Radanites brought back did much to civilize the savage heart or ameliorate the rough life style of the Central and Northern Europeans. The ninth century may have looked pleasant in Cordoba and Byzantium, but chroniclers took note of the frequent famines in the interior of the continent when "men ate men; brothers ate brothers, and mothers their children . . . when a third of the human race died in Gaul and Germania." Nevertheless, the burgeoning metropolis of Cordoba survived splendidly, thanks in large part to the Radanites.

The postmaster of Rayy, Khordadbeh, described in some detail the voyages of those Jewish travelers. And his account has been seconded by those of others, including that of a chronicler who worked not far from Rayy. His name was Ibn al-Fakih Abu Bekr Ahmad ben Muhammed ben Ishak al Hamadani. In the year 903 he completed a work called *The Book of Lands*.

The two texts differ in only minor ways, chiefly in the spelling of place names, which were largely a matter of personal preference, anyway. Khordadbeh's account is considerably fuller and some scholars suspect that it was the original from which al Hamadani cribbed the essentials of his story. Khordadbeh describes the linguistic abilities of the Radanites this way: "These merchants speak Arabic, Persian, Roman, the language of the Franks, Andalusians and Slavs." Presumably they also spoke Hebrew although in al-Andalus, at least, that language was reserved for holy matters. Arabic was the language for love, poetry, business dealings, medicine and science.

"They take ship in the land of the Franks on the Western Sea, and steer for Farama," Khordadbeh wrote.

That suggests that many of the Jewish commercial travelers brought their cargoes of furs and slaves down from the north, perhaps from Charlemagne's capital of Aix-la-Chapelle (now the German city of Aachen) or perhaps from Troyes along the Rhone valley, to Marseilles. Some Jews had followed the Roman legions north as others had gone west with them to the Iberian peninsula. When the Romans fell back or melted into the countryside the Jews stayed to pioneer along the frontier.

Now, as merchants, they traveled the Roman roads to the sea. The trip of four or five weeks on muleback or on foot was broken by stops along the way, for in most major towns there were Jews who extended a generous hospitality to commercial travelers, particularly those who shared their lineage. Jewish voyagers came out of the gloom of primordial forests to spend a Sabbath eve in a hut lit by ritual candles; to pray; perhaps to sip a glass of wine; to talk of politics, of business, of how this one was lost at sea and that one was still missing on a tropical island or a snowbound Alpine pass. Perhaps they lit a candle to memorialize those who were presumed dead on the road.

Roads and trails often petered out into what a contemporary described as "wooded haunts of savage beasts and swampy wastes." Northern and Central Europe were covered by vast, dense forests of birch, beech, maple and oak. Through them roamed bears, fierce tusked boars, stags, wild goats and aurochs (a kind of buffalo that has long since vanished). Wolves padded at the heels of travelers and howled at village gates during the night. Charlemagne had commissioned wolf hunters with trained dogs to curb the packs but still in winter wolves besieged Slav villages.

Spring floods often washed out any signs of a trail, and savage winters decimated villages, sharpening the appetite of the clamoring wolves. The people of the forests offered both danger and salvation. Some were anchorites who had fled from the world to the forest for ascetic delights of the soul. Others were bandits hoping for easy pickings from merchants or holy people on the move.

Through it all the Jewish merchants led their mules, sampling the world's beauties and horrors, gathering wonders to retail them in the bright islands of civilization to the south. The world's astonishing variety colored the minds and spirits of these people and served to make them seem odd to those who stayed home, tilled the fields and built the cathedrals.

A few of the Jewish merchants must have set off from their own principality of Narbonne. Although that city was then a port of some consequence it presented a problem, for the ships that left its quays had to navigate the chronically tempestuous waters of the Gulf of Lions, which must have tossed around the frail tenth-century dhows as if they were corks.

Those who originated in Cordoba had the benefit of comparatively straight roads running under sunny skies to Algeciras or to Malaga. There were inns along the route, fellow Jews, and the family comforts of Andalusia until they came to the sea.

In fair weather the Mediterranean leg of the voyage might have been more comfortable than muleback but the ever-present threat of pirates must have made the Radanites edgy. Roving corsairs, seeking rich cargoes and slaves, or distinguished rabbis to hold for ransom, swarmed in the seas around the Spanish coast. The only protection against them was the three-hundred-vessel fleet of Abd-er Rahman II. Some of these were swift sailing ships that could outrun a pirate raider. Others were huge galleys rowed by slaves and armed with flame-throwing arbalests and catapults. The navy tried to keep the islands of Majorca and Minorca free of marauders. Watch-towers dotted the Andalusian shore to give the alarm by means of bonfires if any enemy approached. In some places fortress-monasteries had sprung up. These were mannned by volunteers who, for a limited time, would practice an austere religious withdrawal from the world while exercising their military virtues in guarding the coast. The warlike monk embodied an

Islamic tradition of shining spirituality in mortal combat with evil.

The forts and galleys of Cordoba were in place to protect the peninsula not only against piracy but also against invasion. It had been only a short while since the Norsemen, in 844, had harried the Atlantic coasts, burning, looting and raping. They had sailed up the Guadalquivir to seize and sack Seville. When they were routed from that city, which they left a shambles, a group of them, in love with the sun and the allurements of southern civilization, settled down with Andalusian wives in the countryside. Adopting Islam and Islamic ways, they contributed their blue eyes and blond hair to future generations.

Once beyond the reach of the Cordoban navy the Jewish merchants sailed at their peril. It is likely that they skirted the shore and put into port wherever there was a congenial Jewish congregation. In any case it usually took four or five months to reach Farama at the mouth of the Nile—now Port Said. There they had to load their furs, swords, cloth, ceramics and jewels onto camels. Slaves were walking cargo. The distance across the Isthmus of Suez is given by Khordadbeh as "25 parasangs"— roughly eighty-eight miles. It took a caravan some five days to cross that strip of sand joining Asia and Africa.

The merchants unloaded their camels at Kolzum—Suez—a hot and busy port where ships, with Indian, Chinese and Malaysian captains, lined the harbor, waiting to be commissioned for trips to the Far East. From Kolzum they sailed some seven hundred miles down the Red Sea, past the Sinai Peninsula on the port side, past the Hejaz, to Jidda, teeming with pilgrims bound for Mecca. From that steamy port they rounded the Arabian peninsula at Bab el Mandeb, sailed through the Gulf of Aden and into the Indian Ocean.

Once there they employed a navigational technique discovered some eight hundred years previously by an Egyptian sea captain named Hippalos. Before the time of that ingenious navigator it had taken the better part of a year to pass Yemen, cross the Gulf of Oman to the Persian side and then coast down to the mouth of the Indus at what is now Karachi. Hippalos saved many months by mastering the timetables of the monsoons. He found that if he caught the monsoon that blows from the southwest in July, he could sail from the Gulf of Aden across the open sea to the Indus in only forty days. The Radanites always planned their overland treks and sea voyages to bring them to Aden in time to catch the monsoon at their backs.

Some would stop to trade in Sind while others would go aboard Chinese junks bound for Java, Sumatra, Cynkalon (Ceylon) and finally to the promised land of commerce, Cathay (China).

Not all of the Jewish merchants made the voyage clean through from the forests of Gaul to the islands of the South Seas. For the most part they concentrated on one or another leg of that prodigious trail, meeting and trading with their fellow Radanites at juncture points along the way.

For example, there is the highly adventurous and profitable career of Ishaq, "the Son of the Jew of Oman," as he is known in medieval chronicles. He came from a thriving Jewish settlement in Oman, traveled to the courts of India and China, and died in Sumatra as the consequence of a lifelong antipathy to excessively greedy bureaucrats. Although he never reached the Western world the goods he carried undoubtedly found their way to Cordoba.

Ishaq would disappear from his native Oman for a decade or so at a time. On his return, he would astonish the townspeople with his wealth and his stories. Many of these were retold by historians of the time, notably Buzorq ibn Shahriyar of Ramhormoz, who in the early part of the tenth century put together a travel book called *The Wonders of India.*

Ishaq told his admiring audiences in Oman—in both synagogue and palace—of how on his way to China he would put his merchandise on the backs of goats because "the road over those precipitous heights is like a series of steps which only those animals could climb."

He told how he swapped stories and gems with a king "seated on a golden throne encrusted with rubies, he himself being covered with jewels like a woman." Ishaq brought back such souvenirs as "golden fish with eyes of rubies lying on a bed of musk—and that of first quality," according to observers.

One is entitled to be skeptical of tall tales allegedly told by a Jewish merchant to whet the interests of his customers and then retold in a book by an Arab chronicler dealing in exotica. Still, there are other details of Ishaq's life that have the ring of plausibility.

He is said to have landed one day in Oman after a voyage of some years. His ship was loaded with valuable cargo from India, China and the South Sea Islands. He was met by a eunuch with the odd name of Foulfoul who came down to the dock with thirty slaves and demanded an altogether excessive tax in the name of the local sultan. Ishaq angrily refused. A little tax, a little bribe were to be expected, but Foulfoul's demand was confiscatory, he felt.

He proceeded to organize the Port of Oman. While ostentatiously preparing to sail and vowing never to return, he apparently persuaded other Jewish merchants to gather their families and show every sign of impending emigration. They issued a joint statement, which was recorded in these words:

"We are going to be deprived of every means of existence when ships no longer call here, for Oman is a city the inhabitants of which get everything from the sea. If the small amongst us are thus treated, it will be worse still for the great. Sultans are a fire that devours everything they touch. We cannot resist and it is better for us to go away from before them."

There is no record of precisely how the strike ended but since the Jewish community continued to be an important part of the life of Oman, one is tempted to guess that their demands were met. Ishaq did hoist his anchor and sail off in the direction of Sind. He turned up at a place that was then known as Serboza on the island of Sumatra where, once again, the local governor demanded an exorbitant tax, estimated at twenty thousand dinars in tenth-century Omani currency. This outraged Ishaq once more but before he could sail off, the governor resorted to the most expeditious means of collecting: He killed that stubborn Jewish merchant and took his entire cargo.

Not all of the Radanites went by way of Farama and the Red Sea to Yemen and Oman. Some sailed from the western ports to Antioch, then came overland to the Tigris, which they sailed to Baghdad, then down to the new port of Basra on the Persian Gulf. Basra had been built because the older port city of Obolla had become so infested with flying and crawling insects as to irritate business relations. After Basra the route led down the Persian Gulf past Qatar to Oman, "the forecourt of China," as the medieval geographers termed that stretch of coast.

Khordadbeh traces another route, which was far more dangerous but more attractive to the Jewish adventurers. It led them through the great metropolitan centers of North Africa, which was pleasant, but then over a most rugged and perilous mountain route to the legendary Chinese sources of musk. That word, derived from the Sanskrit for testicle, was then applied only to the aromatic oil produced by the sex glands of a species of diminutive deer found in the valley of northeastern Asia. It was much valued by the ladies of Cordoba, Seville, Byzantium and even Aix-la-Chapelle. Such treasures were more marketable than rubies.

The musk route led from Spain across the straits to Tangier, the bustling capital of North Africa, where the Sabbath could be celebrated in style among great throngs of Jews, not as in the lonely huts of Bohemia. The travelers would then head for Kairouan, only a few centuries old but already the major station where caravans could be assembled for the trek eastward.

The caravans crossed the desert to Cairo, headed north up the blazing Sinai Peninsula, through Palestine (then controlled by the Egyptians) and on to the splendors of Damascus. They usually stopped at Kifa, some ninety miles south of Baghdad. It was a pleasant watering station on a tributary of the Euphrates, occasionally used as a capital by the Abbasid Caliphs. There Omayyads and Christians were scarcely welcome, but Jews were as neutral as the landscape and more nourishing.

In Babylon the Jewish merchants who could spare the time

stayed a while to pay reverence to the scholars of the great Talmudic schools of Sura and Pumbedita. Both of these academies
were somewhat past their prime but their chief scholars were
still issuing authoritative guidelines for Jews everywhere. Every
passing caravan brought letters from distant parts of the world
asking the sages for the most delicate exegesis of dogma.

The letters would be kept, along with copies of the answers,
filed by some ingenious, long-forgotten system so that when
similar questions were asked the scholarly authority need only
pluck out answers sanctified by earlier sages. In Spain, Gaul,
Rome, Byzantium, Kairouan and all the regions in between,
Jews were thus given the same or similar prescriptions and pro-
scriptions, the same solutions to the same conundrums—all
supported by textual references and ingenious, if involuted,
logic. Of all the correspondents, it was said, the Spanish Jews
were the most demanding.

Rabbi El'azar of the Jewish city of Lucena, for example,
wrote repeatedly to explore the ramifications of levirate marriage—that is, the obligation of a bachelor to marry his
brother's widow. The rabbi might ask: Suppose a man has a
son by his handmaid; on top of the duties thus incurred does he
also have to marry his sister-in-law?

It might be a year and a half before the answer would come.
The messenger from the academy at Sura would pass through
the Moslem suburbs and arrive at the gates of Lucena where
Jewish sentries would admit him.

He would solemnly carry a bundle of manuscripts wrapped
in linen through the broad sunlit avenues to the synagogue,
where the requisite ten men would sit cross-legged on mats
murmuring pious pleasantries. Opposite them young men
would wait in awe for the truth to be expounded.

When the dignitaries of the city and the deans of the college
arrived at the synagogue, the cord tying the packet was cere-
moniously cut with a knife. The answers of the sages of Sura or
Pumbedita were then given a first reading in the drowsy,
prayerful drone of semisanctity. Accommodations were then
arranged for the messenger, and the *responsa* put away for more
leisurely examination.

Some of the letters sent to Lucena gave the academicians' views on whether schoolmasters should whip their students (the learned answers seemed a trifle ambiguous); whether one is permitted to speculate in the market, cornering commodities to raise prices (the venerable Natronai of Sura said no); whether a modest interest could be taken in return for extending credit (certainly not, said Natronai); whether a pregnant cow should be slaughtered (the answer cannot be summarized in a parenthesis).

In time the wise men of Lucena, who themselves were issuing *responsa* to their troubled brethren up in Gaul or Septimania, would gather to parse every sentence of the Babylonian answers. Each phrase was painstakingly scrutinized, dissected, weighed, interpreted in a variety of lights and shadows, experimentally fitted to this situation and that. In the end it might be accepted, criticized, modified or sent back for further clarification, which might come in a couple of years. So it went, and men grew pleasantly old pondering the wondrous logic of far-off sages.

Rabbi El'azar, perplexed by questions revolving about the duty to marry a brother's widow, went to Sura, himself, to debate the matter. He spent twenty to thirty years there pondering that problem, among others, and informing the Babylonian wise men of what was happening in Lucena, Cordoba and Granada so that they might incorporate the Spanish experience in their replies to puzzled Jews around the world.

Other rabbinical Radanites came on similar missions. Rabbi Petachia, who was born in Ratisbon (now Regensburg) on the Danube, came to Babylon a little after the prime of the Radanites, but his notes probably apply to the ninth or tenth as much as to the eleventh century.

"Baghdad is very large," the rabbi reported. "To go round it is more than three days' journey. In the city of Baghdad there are a thousand Jews. . . . They all walk about, wrapped in their praying scarves of wool with fringes."

The rabbi met there the "head of the academy . . . Rabbi Samuel, the Levite, son of Eli . . . full of wisdom both in the written and oral law and in all the wisdom of Egypt." He met fellow rabbis, including one who prophesied on the basis of astrological computation. The cautious Petachia, however, explained that he was careful to take no written notes of such interviews, because he did not want to be thought a believer in unapproved teaching.

He noted the fact that nobody in Baghdad, whether Jew or Moslem, "looks upon a woman, nor does anybody go into the house of his friend lest he should see the wife of that neighbor who would immediately say unto him: 'Insolent man, wherefore art thou come?' "

If a rabbi from the Danube could be astonished at such a preoccupation with female chastity, a Jew from Cordoba must have found it ludicrously archaic. In Spain women were not the prisoners of their husbands in practice, whatever may have been the theories of mullahs and rabbis. It is hard, however, to doubt any of the reporting by Rabbi Petachia after reading his remarkably accurate description of an elephant he encountered in Nineveh:

"Its head is not at all protruding. It is big and eats about two wagonloads of straw at one time; its mouth is in its breast, and when it wants to eat it protrudes its lip about two cubits, takes up with it the straw, and puts it into its mouth. When the Sultan condemns anybody to death they say to the elephant: This person is guilty. It then seizes him with its lip, casts him aloft and kills him. Whatever a human being does with his hand it does with its lip; this is exceedingly strange and marvelous. Upon the elephant's back is set a structure like a citadel within which there are twelve armed warriors; when the beast stretches forth its lip they climb up using it as a bridge."

After the pleasant valley of Babylon many of the Radanites would strike out on the most celebrated caravan trail, the Khorosan Road. It wound through Persia, skirting the desert and climbing toward Afghanistan. Some of the travelers would transfer their loads from camels to goats when they scaled the fierce and windy heights of the Hindu Kush, where peaks rise about twenty-five thousand feet. Then they would descend the precipitous slopes to Bokhara and Samarkand, where the sun would warm them again. After what must have been a rest so sweet as to tempt them to stay forever they pushed east across the Pamirs and down to Khoten in Sinkiang, China.

The fourth great route of the Radanites was followed in pursuit of the slave trade. The trail ran overland, south and east from the great northern slave mart of Verdun on the Meuse in eastern Gaul. The Romans had built some roads through the Rhineland and into Thuringia. Sections of these were still usable in the ninth and tenth centuries, and Charlemagne had built others. Once the merchants reached the land of the Slavs, the landscape grew wilder and the going more difficult. Both people and beasts constituted terrible dangers, but the commodity sought was worth the risk.

The world's civilization thrived on slaves. They were used on farms, in households, workshops, armies and navies. War yielded a steady supply of prisoner-slaves. However, the business was constantly threatened by religious considerations. It was thought impermissible for Jews to corral Christian or Moslem slaves and the rabbis did not approve of their buying or selling other Jews. Missionary zeal was beginning to limit the number of pagans. Only in the German and Slavic forests or in black Africa was there a supply of "primitives" who could be enslaved without making the righteous blush.

Prague was the great slave market of Central Europe, where soldiers brought their prisoners, where creditors endeavored to turn their debtors into cash, where bankrupts ended. The Radanites bartered spices, swords, tin or wheat for slaves. These might be picked up on the way east for the Byzantine trade or west for the markets of Verdun or Cordoba.

The eastward trail wound through the Balkans to the Jewish kingdom of Khazaria tucked away between the lower reaches of the Volga and the northern Caucasus. This kingdom had come to dominate the Crimea, barring the advance of Islam from the south and of the Vikings from the north. It was a power with which the Byzantine emperors had to dicker.

No one seems to have heard of the Khazars before the sixth century. It is suggested that they were nomads who swept in from Central Asia. They evinced an apparent kinship with the Turks. Some scholars trace linguistic connections to the Magyars. The Khazars seem to have practiced a religion in which the fate of mankind was determined by a perpetual contest between benevolent and malicious demons who could only be propitiated by shamans holding intimate relations with the spirits.

The Khazars, presiding over a military and commercial crossroads, encountered both the Christians of Byzantium and the Moslems of Persia and Arabia. They were duly impressed with the magnificence of the ambassadors from both sides, who came to pay their respects at the court of the two kings of the Khazars. (Actually the nation was ruled by a pair of monarchs, one of whom reigned as a symbol while the other held the power—until, according to a predetermined schedule, the time came for the ruler to yield the throne. At that point he was garroted. The symbolic king had nothing to do with politics, lived a ceremonial life and died a natural death.)

In time the Khazar rulers became aware of a certain primitive quality in their beliefs, a lack of philosophical depth and ritual grandeur. Accounts differ as to details of the end of paganism in Khazaria, but all agree that at some time, probably in the seventh century, the royal authorities decided that the time had come for the Khazars to adopt one of the great religions of the world. Accordingly a grand debate was held.

A bishop represented Christianity and a mullah spoke for Islam. There were many Jews in Khazaria and the community sent up a rabbi to join the competition. The rabbi won, but whether it was because his philosophical jousting was more adroit, his religion more venerable or his ethics more appealing, it is impossible to know. Geopolitical scholars suggest that the rulers of Khazaria might have concluded that for a country caught between two fiercely competing cultures it would be tactically wise to choose a neutral ideology. (To choose Judaism for protection suggests a beguiling innocence and a certain irony.)

Perhaps all of these factors weighed in the minds of the royal arbitrators. In any case the ruling king and the reigning king and all the courtiers were properly circumcised and became observing Jews. Many of the people went along with the new religious fashion although the kingdom was famous for its wide toleration. This happy trait may have been a holdover of the pagan spirit, blended with the urbane and tactical wisdom of the rabbis, who knew that all victories are transitory and that even the likeliest of bets are to be hedged.

Although the Radanites rejoiced in finding so curious an anomaly as a Jewish kingdom in the Caucasus, and though they eagerly spread the word of the enlightenment, the trip was perhaps more trouble than profit.

Rabbi Petachia described the strange customs of the Khazars and of the people who lived to the north of them in the land of Kedar. (Actually, though, it may well be that, by the time the rabbi reached that part of the world, the Moslems had conquered and converted the Khazars from their Judaism. However, regardless of doctrinal allegiances the popular customs were still as they had been in the centuries when Khazaria was Jewish.) The cavalrymen of the plains, whether Jew, Christian or pagan, still "put pieces of flesh under the saddle of a horse, which they ride and, urging on the animal cause it to sweat," the rabbi wrote. "The flesh getting warm, they eat it."

In the countryside he observed that "the inhabitants live in tents; they are far-sighted and have beautiful eyes because they eat no salt and live among fragrant plants. They are good archers, bringing down birds whilst on the wing. They perceive and recognize each other at more than a day's distance."

In Khazaria the rabbi was struck by the seemingly perpetual mourning that preoccupied the women, obliging them to keen over the memories of long-vanished parents, children, cousins and even more distant relatives. It does not seem to have been a merry place.

Those Jews not enchanted with the spectacle rode along the southern shores of the Caspian Sea to Samarkand and then across the plains, over the Pamirs and into China.

Few of the Radanites could have made the entire journey

from Cordoba to China and back again. It took a year just to go from Cordoba to Babylon. And when Charlemagne sent the courtier Isaac on his mission to Haroun al-Rashid, the round trip took more than four years, although it must be pointed out that the voyage home of that Jewish ambassador was slowed somewhat because he was bringing back an elephant as a gift to the emperor.

Most commercial travelers went only part of the way, dickering with their colleagues for merchandise picked up along other legs of the trail. A man might go as far as Farama or Kolzum and there shop among the wares brought by other Jewish travelers from Sind or China. The business was operated by a network of Jewish merchants.

That highly profitable and adventurous Jewish monopoly in trade and ideas declined at the end of the ninth century and ended in the middle of the tenth. There were a number of circumstances that drove Jews from the seas and from the caravan routes.

The T'ang dynasty, which had unified China and opened it to foreign interchange, was overthrown. The new emperor, Wu, proved xenophobic and dramatized this tendency by a fearful massacre of Moslems, Christians, Jews and Parsees who had settled in some of the larger Chinese cities. Many of the foreigners survived but were then cut off from the outside world because the Tartars, taking advantage of the old dynasty's collapse, had ringed the borders of China, blocking all traffic in or out. The Jews inside China gradually adapted to Chinese ways, intermarried and wedded their Judaism, complete with Hebrew calligraphy, to a Confucian dialectic.

At about the same time Venice rose as a commercial capital and resolved to drive all but Venetians from the Mediterranean. By the time the First Crusade put the gloss of sanctity upon commercial rivalry, only a relative handful of Jews were left to gather the crumbs of trade in the forests of Eastern Europe or the Islands of the Pacific.

Some old Radanites retired to Majorca or Minorca where they taught the mysteries of navigation along with those of the

Talmud and the Cabala. Many more settled down in the cities of Andalusia with the profits of an exuberant century of trade available for investment in the welfare of Jewish cities and Jewish schools, and in the Islamic emirate itself that spread its mantle over them.

Could the Jews have contributed substantially to Cordoba and finally to Europe if they had not had the financial profits and the rich experience of such purposeful wandering over the world? And would they have achieved that polished cosmopolitan perspective which enabled them to survive the frenzies of their time if they had not found the world so richly various and national boundaries so absurd?

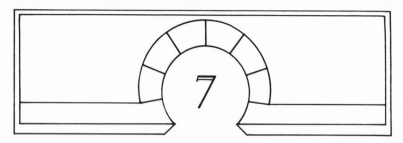

Martyrs to a Tyranny of Smiles

While the Jews went about their worldwide business, tilled their farms around Lucena, Seville or Granada, wrote love ballads or religious hymns, prayed, sang and chopped each other's logic, a fever beset some of their Christian neighbors in Andalusia. It was feared that the fever might become epidemic and disrupt the well-being of Jews, Christians and Moslems in the emirate of Abd-er Rahman II.

Some of the more ardent Christians found it too difficult to maintain their faith in a land that offered no overt persecution. Christian businessmen, courtiers, professionals and farmers thrived as did Jews or Moslems. Some were given a hand in managing the bureaucracy of the emirate. Some had military posts and some were among the emir's advisers. Christians paid an infidel's tax, but it was not oppressive. Their churches were open, and bells tolled, merrily or sadly, depending on the occasion.

All this beguiling peace, however, was working a subtle erosion of Christian integrity, it was felt. Christians dressed like Moslems, talked like Moslems, read and wrote Arabic, and verged on thinking in Arabic. One fierce Christian, the lay theologian Alvaro, complained of the scandal: "My fellow Christians delight in the poems and romances of the Arabs; they study the work of Mohammedan theologians and philosophers not in order to refute them but to acquire a correct and elegant Arabic style."

He complained that young Christians could not even write a letter to a friend in "their own language"—Latin. Arabic was their tongue and they reveled in its beauties, though it outraged priests and monks. The emir would toss coins to Christians as well as to Mohammedans when they turned a pretty phrase or conjured up a striking image or made music of their words. Unlike the Jews the Christians did not have their own cities and centers of learning in Andalusia. There were monasteries and convents throughout the country but in general these were communes for a relative few, not facilities for the laity.

It is true that beneath the surface there was an endemic hostility among the believers in Islam toward all rival faiths, including Christianity. Occasionally boys would toss pebbles at a priest, upset a tombstone or spit at a Christian funeral, but this sort of mischief was scarcely enough to rally the comfortable Arabized Christians. It would not weld them into a force capable of resisting the soft blandishments of Moslem toleration.

The Christian clergy, fearing the ultimate assimilation of their followers, preached unrelenting hatred of Mohammed and Moslem teachings, which they frequently distorted for their purpose. Some of the more audacious priests were in regular communication with the Christian kings of the north and others sought sanctuary there, but even those refugees took with them their Arabized names, clothes and customs. The emirate took little notice of such things. A few unarmed priests would be of little help in a Christian invasion, which, in any case, seemed well beyond the capability of the disunited kingdoms of the north.

The process of smothering the Christians with smiles continued, with only an occasional conviction of some zealot for conspiracy or blasphemy. Those who saw a demonic temptation in this Arab embrace grew more desperate as the years went on. Eulogius of Cordoba was a case in point. He was a third-generation Christian whose grandfather crossed himself and called for divine vengeance every time he heard the muezzin chant from the minarets.

It is typical of the irony of those times that the family of Eulogius had prospered exceedingly under Moslem rule. One brother of Eulogius was rising rapidly in the civil service and two others were doing very well in business. Eulogius and his sister Anulo were expected to redeem the family from the perils of assimilation by a life of piety and good works. Anulo was to enter a nunnery and Eulogius a monastery.

Eulogius, however, always exceeded the requirements of any assignment. He not only studied with the priests of St. Zoilus but also, without the blessings of Church or family, sneaked off to attend the fire-breathing sermons of a militant abbot named Spera-in-Deo (Hope in God). There he met Alvaro, who, like Eulogius, was seeking to balance his family's material prosperity with a passionate Christianity. The two became friends and together steeped themselves in the recorded lives of Christian martyrs, concentrating on tales of excruciatingly painful heroism.

Eulogius fasted, stood lonely vigils and was duly ordained. He soon became a model of self-tormenting piety, with but one ambition—to die gloriously for his Church. The emirate of Abd-er Rahman II, however, stubbornly refused to oblige the young man, although there were some at the court who thought that so earnest a wish of the infidel should be granted. One of these was Abu al-Fath al-Nasr, the eunuch who had the emir's ear on many of the subjects on which his active mind continuously played. It was al-Nasr and another eunuch named Masrur who were entrusted with supervising the expansion of the great mosque of Cordoba. Al-Nasr's taste for architectural aesthetics was as developed as his skill at harem intrigue. He also had the passionate hatred for Christianity that is characteristic of an apostate. Al-Nasr had been born and raised a Christian. His acquired Mohammedanism was emphatic and defensive. He was therefore not as amused as was the emir at the preoccupation of a few young Cordobans with the splendors of martyrdom. After all, the Romans had encouraged a similar taste for sanctified dying and ended up with their rulers hopelessly seduced by their glorious victims, although, of course, there were other geopolitical, economic and historical reasons for the conversion of emperors.

While the sons and daughters of solid middle-class Christians seemed to be intoxicating themselves with visions of crucifixion, burning and torture, the emir thought it a passing fad of the young, however macabre. Al-Nasr, on the other hand, considered it an affront to the established values of the state. A very pretty young lady named Flora was an example of the most wasteful madness in the eyes of Nasr and others like him. Flora's father was a devoted Moslem but her mother was a Christian who, despite all the necessary pretenses at conversion, had retained her faith and secretly nourished her two daughters on the *Lives of the Saints.*

Flora and her sister Baldegotho would sneak off to church to hear mass whenever their brother, a pious Moslem, was not watching. In Islamic families brothers were duty-bound to guard not only the physical but also the spiritual chastity of their sisters. This constraint not only was bothersome to the two young women but also forced them to keep secret the very beliefs that they felt it their duty to proclaim as loudly as possible. Accordingly they ran away to a Christian family. Their brother, shocked by what he regarded as a gross violation of his sisters' minds, searched all the convents in the area and then stirred the police to raid the homes of several priests and toss them into jail.

On hearing of the dangers faced by the priests in their behalf, Flora came out of hiding and bravely told her brother that she was a Christian, fully prepared to defy the worst torments he could invent. The much-troubled brother alternately beat his sister and pleaded with her to come back to Islam. He added the warning that apostasy from the Prophet's creed was punishable by death.

Flora took the beating, resisted the plea and defied the warning. Her brother then took her to the local judge, to whom he explained that his sister, who had always been a faithful daughter of Islam, had been "perverted" by the Christians.

When questioned by the judge Flora denounced and disowned her brother, proclaiming herself a Christian ready for martyrdom. The judge, who could have passed the death sentence then and there, looked kindly upon the ardent young woman, and merely ordered two guards to hold her while a third whipped her neck and shoulders. He then turned her over to her brother for proper religious instruction. Flora was locked up in the harem of her brother's house but somehow climbed walls and leaped to the street. She found her way into the Christian underground, where, in a secret shelter, she was joined by her sister and, in time, encountered Eulogius.

Whether it was Flora's daring escape, her beauty, her passionate religiosity or an overwhelming combination of all three allurements, Eulogius fell in love with Flora in his own highly spiritual way. Reinhart Dozy, a scholar with a penchant for the lyrical, puts it this way: "He conceived for Flora an exalted affection, a love purely intellectual, a love such as may be conceived in the habitations of angels, where incorporeal souls are swayed by sacred desires."

In a letter to Flora written six years after their first meeting, Eulogius recalled: "Holy sister, time was when thou didst vouchsafe to show me thy neck all torn with the lash, bereft of the lovely and abundant tresses which once veiled it. It was because thou didst look upon me as thy spiritual father, and deemed me pure and chaste as thyself. Tenderly I laid my hand upon thy wounds; fain would I have sought their healing with a kiss, but I dared not ... when I departed from thee I was as one that walketh in a dream and my sighs ceased not."

Flora disappeared into the underground, surfacing only occasionally to offend Moslems, who bridled but refused to grant her the martyrdom she sought. Eulogius wrote voluminously and passionately not only for Christian virtues against Moslem vices but for Latin poetry—even secular Latin poetry, as long as it was not overly licentious—against Arabic verse with its seductive music. Flora wrote letters too, proclaiming her Christianity to all who would listen. The two were to meet again, but only in prison after the radical movement had thrown into panic the middle class of Cordoba and was beginning to shake the emir's complacency.

The movement was unwittingly given a major impetus by a zealous but somewhat garrulous priest who, though he venerated the saintly martyrs, had no such ambitions for himself. His name was Perfectus and, according to Christian historians, he was marketing one day when a pair of Moslems led him into a discussion of comparative religion. It was a topic that a more knowing Christian would have avoided.

At first Perfectus tried to dodge the challenge, reminding the would-be debaters that his opinions, even if expressed in a personal conversation, could send him to his death. The friendly Moslems assured him that they would not turn him in, no matter how horrendous his opinions might be. They merely wanted the views of an intelligent Christian concerning the Prophet.

Perfectus began by calling Mohammed a "false Prophet," and then expatiated on that theme until he ran away with himself, finally referring to him as "a servant of Satan." That was too much for the Moslems, who walked off in fury. Days later they spotted Perfectus in the market again and shouted to the crowd, "He has blasphemed against Allah."

The crowd did not lynch Perfectus, because Moslems had a profound respect for the law as long as it was in the hands of their coreligionists. Instead they took the priest to a judge, to whom the priest denied that he had ever said anything against the Prophet. It was a performance that Eulogius and Flora would have found shockingly close to blasphemy.

In any case his evasion was of no use, since there were unimpeachable Moslem witnesses ready to testify against him. That he had uttered his blasphemy in private was a poor defense, from either the Christian or the Moslem point of view. The judge handed down the death sentence but left the actual date of execution to be decided by the man whom Abd-er Rahman II had made his general factotum—the eunuch Abu al-Fath al-Nasr.

Al-Nasr let Perfectus languish in jail for months until the merriest of Islamic holidays, the one that closes the fast of Ramadan. It was a marvelous summer day in the year 850. Crowds poured in and out of the great mosque and milled about the market as at a carnival. Boats of all sorts, their pennants streaming in the wind, circled the columns of the old Roman bridge and sailed up and down the Guadalquivir.

Everyone, from slave to lordly relative of the emir, dressed in white as ordained by that fashion-setter, Ziryab. Al-Nasr had planned the execution of Perfectus to be the wittiest of amusements on that festive day. Although executions have always been exciting popular spectacles—particularly when the principal actor is unquestionably guilty of some hideous crime such as blasphemy—al-Nasr's entertainment probably did not delight the emir. Such displays, however necessary for the security of the state, had never amused him and now, as he grew older, they troubled him. He did not attend.

The imminence of death and the ignominy of having it treated as a public show worked wonders for the spirit of Perfectus, however. He no longer tried to evade the inevitable. All the way to the execution block he shouted imprecations against Mohammed as, among other things, "a child of hell." It is probable that even al-Nasr's holiday mood was shattered by the prophecy that the doomed man uttered from the scaffold. As if speaking with divine foresight Perfectus told the crowd that before another Ramadan al-Nasr would be dead.

It is difficult to calculate the effect of so melodramatic a prophecy. Al-Nasr's behavior in the months that followed suggests a frenzy characteristic of people who feel they have little time left. Al-Nasr was probably brooding about his survival prospects if his sponsor and protector Abd-er Rahman, now nearing sixty, should die. The likeliest heir was the melancholy prince Mohammed, who had always disapproved of al-Nasr, a feeling reciprocated by the eunuch with redoubled venom.

Al-Nasr much preferred the cynical, pleasure-seeking, high-living Abdallah, the son of the emir's favorite wife, Tarub. It was she who had been clever enough to sell to the emir what he could have commanded. Tarub, too, feared that Abd-er Rahman would choose Mohammed, denying her boy the throne and herself the power behind it.

The two of them pooled their fears and hopes. Tarub suggested a limited but swift massacre of the emir, Prince Mohammed and whichever others of the emir's forty-five sons might stand between Abdallah and the throne. Al-Nasr agreed, first because the plan seemed to assure his future as the man to whom the next emir would be much in debt; and second because it was too risky to turn down Tarub, who could still manipulate the emir on such matters as the control of eunuchs.

Al-Nasr prevailed upon a physician, who had newly come to court, to brew a potent poison. The doctor did as he was told, but at the same time sent word to the emir to be careful when taking any medication offered by al-Nasr. That same evening Abd-er Rahman loudly complained of intestinal troubles and al-Nasr promptly appeared with a phial of medicine, which he highly recommended. The emir suggested that al-Nasr taste it first just to make sure that it had no unpleasant after-effects.

The eunuch had to comply or confess that he had knowingly offered poison to the emir. He gulped it down, excused himself and ran to the doctor, pleading for an antidote. The dispassionate physician, feeling his obligation to save any life on any side of any political controversy, dosed al-Nasr with goat's milk, highly recommended in such cases. It was too late, however, and al-Nasr expired in excruciating agony. Tarub survived the failed plot. Either the emir never suspected her or she was capable of charming him even in her most murderous moments.

Although the court tried to hush the matter, word of al-Nasr's death spread quickly through Cordoba, provoking enthusiastic celebrations in the Christian underground. The prophecy of Perfectus had been fulfilled and the militants were prepared to forget their prophet's earlier aversion to martyrdom. They were ready to make a saint of Perfectus. Actually they had given him a funeral worthy of a saint even before they knew the truth of his prediction. They were using Perfectus as a rallying point and the funeral procession looked very like a political demonstration. The death of al-Nasr, seeming to be an act of divine retribution, spurred the radicals to new efforts at self-martyrdom.

Typical of these radicals was Isaac, a highly paid secretary in Cordoba's bureaucracy who, seized with the spirit of the Christian revival, decided to enroll himself in the monastery of Tabanos, which his uncle had built in the hills near Cordoba. Not only his uncle and aunt but also a number of other relatives had all come to live in that forbidding fortress. There they mortified the flesh and memorized *The Lives of the Saints* until Isaac felt emboldened to seek the road to glory.

He went to a judge and asked him with beguiling humility to expound the law of Mohammed. The judge had barely begun to outline the first principles of the doctrine when Isaac shouted that it was all a lie, that Mohammed would drag the judge and all other believers in Islam to hell. The astonished judge lost his head and slapped Isaac. Then he apologized, declaring that the monk must be drunk. When Isaac insisted that he had never tasted wine, that he had deliberately insulted Mohammed and earnestly desired to be put to death for his faith, the judge sent him to prison.

Such incidents were occurring more and more frequently. At a solemn moment when worshipers in the great mosque were rising and prostrating themselves, two eunuchs who had become monks shouted that hell was yawning for Moslems. A judge who had been leading the services rushed down to protect the eunuchs from the crowd and hustled them off to jail.

Some judges tried to fight the glamor of martyrdom with ridicule. A merchant who had taken the Prophet's name in vain was paraded through the city mounted on an ass, with his face to the tail. The militants were outraged and demanded the dignity of a painful death. Would-be martyrs sprouted all over Cordoba, screaming insults against the Prophet and demanding dire punishment. The judges yielded only when popular anger demanded what, to the Moslems, seemed no more than simple justice. An indication of the remarkable judicial restraint is the statistic that only eleven Christian militants were executed at the height of the martyrs' frenzy in two months of that dreadful year of 850. It is true that some of the executions were accompanied by the dismemberment prescribed for such offenses, but by and large, there was no reign of terror.

Martyrdom was more troublesome than the usual sort of rebellion. Its practitioners could easily turn every defeat into victory. The state itself seemed threatened. The bureaucracy and the courtiers were not the only ones to worry. The ordinary law-abiding, church-going Sunday Christians saw their security endangered by their overly zealous coreligionists.

Where Christians had mingled freely with their Moslem and Jewish colleagues at markets or salons or in offices, they were now suspect, forced to disclaim any connection with these mad people bent on suicide. Jews, too, felt menaced. Though they might seem secure in their own schools and synagogues, and in the cities that they controlled, they still needed a peaceful interchange with their neighbors and their rulers. They had known enough fanatically religious movements to mistrust them profoundly. It was axiomatic that a Jew was safest in the urbane society that took its religion seriously but not so passionately as to inhibit conversation or learning or business. Any movement that carelessly sacrificed lives for ideology tended in the long run, it was felt, to sacrifice Jewish lives. The multigenerational national memory of Jews recalled the dreadful days of the Visigothic kings who found it convenient to demonstrate their recently acquired Christian piety on the bodies of Jews.

Jews therefore joined Christians of the middle class in upholding the genial status quo of the emirate. They were part of the alliance of the middle class and middle-aged against the wild youths who had devised the seemingly foolproof tactic of suicide, the one crime that cannot be deterred by death. It frustrated the establishment.

In desperation the emir summoned a council of bishops and designated as his representative a Christian layman called Gomez, the son of Antonio, the son of Julian. Gomez does not seem to have been a very devout Christian, but at least he was politically reliable, and the emir could not be choosy in the crisis. Gomez was certainly opposed to martyrdom, whether of himself or of others. Like many Christians who kept their religion for special holidays or very private devotions, he had done well under the emirate. He was a skillful writer and enjoyed wide acclaim for his elegant style. The emir trusted him and

Gomez fancied that he had achieved a position in which he could exert a benign influence in behalf of his fellow Christians and all people of common sense. Now a handful of boys and girls were upsetting this serene prosperity and might end by making even Gomez suspect in the eyes of his Moslem colleagues.

Gomez tried to make that point at the council meeting. He pointed out that the martyrs were not only accomplishing their own deaths—which should not occasion prolonged mourning—but also threatening to bring on a wave of persecution against all Christians, many of whom had no taste or ambition for saintliness. Gomez suggested that the assembled bishops issue a decree condemning the martyrs and warning others not to follow them. He also favored episcopal action to place ringleaders such as Eulogius in preventive detention.

The presiding ecclesiastic, Reccafred, metropolitan of Seville, thought such measures practical but theologically troublesome because the Church could not condemn martyrdom in principle without drastically revising *The Lives of the Saints*. The martyrs had a defender in Saul, bishop of Cordoba, but the reputation of that cleric was a bit tainted. The Cordoban clergy had elected him to his post but he failed to obtain the emir's approval, which was legally required. Thereupon, according to correspondents of the time, Saul promised the royal eunuchs some four hundred pieces of gold if they would put in a good word for him with the emir. To give the eunuchs the necessary financial guarantee, Saul offered them a lien on the Church's revenues in Cordoba. The ploy worked but it created a scandal, shocking idealistic Christians and offending those who did not like to see the Church's money used to buy the favors of a Moslem emir.

The radicals were fond of throwing the bishop's bargain at the heads of any conservatives who criticized them. At the council, Saul tried to create a record that would redeem him in the eyes of the zealots, or at least take the sting out of their incessant attacks. In the end the council refrained from criticizing martyrdom in general but forbade all members of the Church from presumptuously aspiring to such a crown.

Reccafred of Seville set about tracking down the militants and their supporters in the months that followed the council session. Even Saul, the bishop of Cordoba, landed in jail. Eulogius, apparently not yet ready for martyrdom, was routed out of hiding and thrown in a Cordoban prison. There the romance of Eulogius and Flora was played out in medieval colors. Flora had left her convent and, accompanied by another young lady whose brother had succeeded in having himself martyred, set out to find a judge who would have no mercy.

They made a bad choice. They went into court sweetly declaring Mohammed to be an adulterer and Islam to be a device of Satan. The judge did not fly into the expected rage. He tried to play the uncle. They were young and beautiful, with life ahead of them, he said. Reluctantly, when the young women adamantly refused to reconsider their blasphemy, he had them thrown into jail.

There Eulogius found them somewhat disheartened. The judge was stubbornly refusing to have them executed. If they persisted in their blasphemy, he threatened, he would send them not to a glorious death but to a rather undignified martyrdom in a brothel.

Eulogius then found his faith cruelly tried. He felt duty-bound to persuade Flora, whom he loved with a fine spiritual ardor, to go to any length to have herself killed. Never had any lover, spiritual or carnal, carried out so difficult a mission with such fortitude. The prospect of success tormented him only somewhat less than the prospect of defeat. "I send from me the light of day," he wrote in desperation to his friend Alvaro.

When he was not encouraging Flora to bring about her own death, Eulogius spent his time in prison writing essays on the vast superiority of Latin literature over Arabic. If only Cordoban Christians had been properly schooled in Latin grammar, he argued, they would be in a better position to maintain the high Roman virtues against the looseness of Arab morals. He also wrote a stream of letters encouraging resistance among bishops and priests.

When Flora and her friend returned from their final interview with the judge, reporting that they had at last goaded him into sentencing them to death, Eulogius wrote Alvaro that he was positively enraptured. The flesh, the devil and the angels must have fought a terrible battle in his heart or liver or wherever such medieval conflicts were resolved. In any case this is the way he reported the results of that turmoil in a letter to Alvaro: "As I heard the words fall from those lips sweeter than honey, I strove to confirm her in her resolve by pointing to the crown which was laid up for her. In adoration I prostrated myself before that seraph form; I commended myself to her prayers and, reanimated by her discourse, I returned with a lighter heart to my gloomy cell."

On November 24, 851, Flora and her friend were decapitated. If one is to take Eulogius' letters at face value, he celebrated the occasion. He wrote Alvaro: "Our virgins, instructed by us, amidst bitter tears, in the living word, have won the palm of martyrdom ... the whole Church rejoiceth in their victory; but I, above all, have the right to glory therein for I strengthened them in their intent when their hearts began to fail them."

Five days after Flora's execution most of the priests were freed from jail. Included in the amnesty were Eulogius and Saul, bishop of Cordoba, who could now boast an honorable prison record whenever radicals reminded him of how he had bought his see.

Abd-er Rahman II had ruled Cordoba as it grew to wealth and acquired all the trappings of a powerful and cultured state in the Mediterranean world. He had seen his countrymen learn to relish the amenities—the ideas, fashions, arts, frivolities and manners of civilization. He had imported into Andalusia scholars, musicians and poets—whether Moslem, Christian or Jew—who sang tastefully of life and love and occasionally of God.

Because the emir had enjoyed his self-image as an enlightened ruler, he bitterly resented those who drove him to dark deeds that betrayed his sunny nature. He had savored his palaces, his music, his women, his ninety children, but on a September day in 852 Abd-er Rahman felt utterly defeated. He was horrified as he had been just before his coronation when he bore witness to the nature of power in a ditch near Toledo where the dissidents of that day went to their ignominious death. Now, more than three decades later, his eyelids still blinked uncontrollably when those broken bodies rose to the surface of his mind.

In the thirtieth year of his reign, in the fifty-fifth year of his life, Abd-er Rahman II stood on the terrace of his palace overlooking the Guadalquivir and the teeming highway that ran alongside it. His eye wandered from the multicolored traffic to the gibbets that brooded over the road. Each gallows bore the mangled corpse of a Christian zealot who had spat at Islam, at reason and at toleration. He called to his guard to have the bodies burned. Then he fell to the ground in an apoplectic fit from which he never recovered. So died the second Abd-er Rahman, up to then the greatest ruler of that name, but only a prelude to the last.

The Luck of the Mountain Boy

History seemed to have lost her way for sixty years or so after the death of Abd-er Rahman II. Al-Andalus languished among misfortunes that, for all their extravagance, were without grandeur. It was a time of casual rapine and anarchic murder.

For months before the old emir died, his wives, sisters and daughters had discussed the succession with the most influential men in the palace—the eunuchs. These slaves had come to count for far more than princes, who, after all, held their positions by accident of birth, while the eunuchs had been selected and fitted, at considerable pains and expense, for their station in life.

Most of them had been bought or kidnaped from Eastern Europe when they were boys. They came in at the port of Pechina on the southern coast, where traders, generally Jewish, inspected them for physical health and whatever signs of extraordinary intelligence might be evident across the language barrier.

Those chosen were bought and sent up to Lucena, where deft surgeons adapted them to carry out responsibilities anywhere in the emir's household, including the harem. The casualty rate on the operating table was fairly high—a fact that was reckoned into the price of eunuchs. Jews handled the business not because of any particular predilection but only because they had organized and staffed the best medical schools and facilities. Actually the Christian courts of Europe had their own busy emasculation center in the slave market of Verdun. The custom had been followed for centuries at the cultivated courts of Baghdad, Damascus and Byzantium. Christians from the wilds of Northern Europe took much of the bad along with the good from the cultivated Arabs, Persians, Greeks and Jews who were patiently instructing them in the ways of civilization.

The palace at Cordoba was traditionally managed by eunuchs. In the harem their charges included hundreds of women and their servants. These were not only the emir's wives but also those of his predecessor. Though retired from the bed these women, whom royalty had once loved, were accorded elaborate dignities. There were also numerous female kin of the emir—unmarried or widowed daughters, sisters, aunts, cousins, friends and guests. And there were the numerous progeny of all these women. All had to be fed, served, housed, clothed, schooled and entertained in royal style. Their various tastes had to be indulged within and often beyond reason.

The eunuchs had to manage not only the harem but also all of the domestic arrangements of the emir, including the household guard, stables, and quartermaster corps. They had to engage doctors, run diplomatic errands, entertain—with an exquisite attention to politesse and protocol—all foreign visitors. They supervised architects, engineers and workmen who repaired, maintained, improved and expanded the palace and the public buildings. They were expected to know which poets and musicians were best to cultivate and which to ignore.

Some eunuchs became generals and led princes into battle. Most who survived the fierce politics of the harem became freemen. Often they were rich, powerful and celebrated. Yet, even in their glory, they bore the names that were given them when they entered royal service. The odd relationship between them and their masters was underscored by their names. These had an affectionate, familiar sound, like those given to beloved pets, and often they signified no gender. A fat young eunuch (they quickly put on weight) from the wild Adriatic coast

might be called Yakut (Hyacinth) or perhaps Bishr (Gaiety) or
Badr (Full Moon). Well-loved wives and concubines might be
given such names. On emancipation eunuchs and other top-
ranking slaves would be allowed the honor of appending the
family name of the emir to their own, as if they were in fact
their master's faithful children.

The death of Abd-er Rahman II did not catch the harem
unprepared. Tarub, the favorite, had been scheming relentlessly in behalf of her son Abdallah. She had actually won over
the college of eunuchs but when the moment of decision came,
her alliances fell apart. The emir's death left her completely
vulnerable. While he lived she had been a mighty power in the
palace. If her son was chosen to succeed she would again be the
maker and shaker. In that moment of the emir's death, however, she was not the queen but the dependent of the eunuchs.

Those who had been with the emir when he died could testify that he named no heir. As soon as he breathed his last the
eunuchs locked the palace gates and went into executive session. Although most were heavily in debt to Tarub for past
favors and many had pinned their hopes on her promises, she
was powerless at the moment to either reward or punish them.
Neither she nor her son nor anyone else knew that the emir was
dead and the throne vacant. It was a rare occasion in a courtier's life. Each of the eunuchs was free to think without intimi-
dation. For a brief moment they could give themselves to such
abstractions as the national good, the popular will, the verdict
of history.

At such times it needs only one man to unlock the larger
feelings of politicians. In this case it was a eunuch who had
made the pilgrimage to Mecca—a particularly onerous obligation for the faithful in al-Andalus, since the trip was likely to
take more than a year. This hadji pointed out that Abdallah
was flagrantly irreligious, a libertine and a blasphemer. Those
who supported him would have to answer to their consciences
but, more awesome than that, they might have to answer to the
people, who sooner or later would curse the names of the eunuchs who had given them Abdallah. Such curses could be
fatal.

The devout eunuch swung his confreres from Abdallah to the only other candidate—a prince who was known to be a favorite of his late father. Having decided to make Mohammed the next emir the eunuchs had to act quickly. Fortunately for them Abdallah was indulging in one of his wild parties so they could slip quietly through the palace to the quarters of Prince Mohammed. He was a dour man who expected at any moment that brother Abdallah would take the throne and promptly commit fratricide as his first official act. When the eunuchs arrived, that panicky prince, expecting only a signal of doom, began to plead for mercy. Once assured that he was the emir-elect he let himself be smuggled—in women's clothes—into his father's apartments. There the eunuchs could protect him while they proclaimed him the emir.

Mohammed was a well-organized but unimaginative ruler. He had good reason to be grateful to the harem, for it had brought him to power, but he was also painfully aware that the eunuchs who had made him could unmake him. Moreover, the conniving Tarub might be more dangerous in defeat than she had been in her years of triumph. The new emir, therefore, put a wall between himself and his family circle. Whatever politics was discussed in the harem remained no more than ineffectual gossip. The eunuchs were relegated to strictly managerial functions and the ladies to the ornamental or the amorous.

Mohammed began by economizing on the arts. There would be no more royal largesse tossed to a poet for a pretty verse or to a wit for a spontaneous bit of word-play. Women and artists were now less welcome at the palace than generals, admirals and the recruiters of mercenaries from the outposts of Europe.

There was some point to the emir's concern for the defense of his realm. True, he had succeeded in establishing friendly relations across the Pyrenees with Charles the Bald, but on all the other fringes of the emirate and even at its heart there was trouble. Mohammed had to confront another series of incursions by Norsemen, who sailed down the Atlantic coast in sixty-two high-prowed ships. Two of them were captured by the Cordoban navy off the Algarve. And when other Vikings tried to sail up the Guadalquivir to sack Seville a highly disciplined army sped down the highways that lined the river to prevent any landing.

At Algeciras the Vikings—called, in Arabic, "Madjus," meaning idolators or fire-worshippers—succeeded in burning the biggest mosque in the city. This would later be replaced by a new structure built from the wood of captured Norse ships.

Mohammed also had to put down the customary outbursts at Toledo, whose fractious citizens always welcomed a new emir with a fresh rebellion. As ever, the city was a refuge and rallying point for young Christian radicals ambitious to be martyred. The Toledans had chosen Eulogius to be their metropolitan and he was busily rousing the young people to pursue a glorious death. At one point a Toledan army threatened Cordoba itself and was defeated only by a bloody ambush, which netted Mohammed's bounty hunters some eight thousand heads.

The revolt was crushed when the royal engineers cut the underpinnings of a bridge out of Toledo. The Cordoban army, pretending to retreat, had galloped over just as the last supports were delicately whittled to a perilous point. When the Toledans whooped in pursuit of the emir's men, the bridge supports gave way and the rebels plunged to their deaths in the Tagus River.

Eulogius was in Cordoba at the time, relying on his title of metropolitan to stave off for a little while the martyrdom toward which his life was pointed. He was picked up in a raid by police looking for a young girl of a respectable Moslem family who allegedly had been spiritually seduced by Christian proselytizers. The authorities were not overjoyed at his arrest. If he had been slain in battle or fallen off a bridge his death would have been seen by everyone as a fortuitous event. But to execute him would inflame the martyrs' movement all over again.

The trial judge held that propagandizing Christianity, though certainly a crime, was not a capital offense. A beating would do. But Eulogius outfoxed them by shouting hair-raising insults at the Prophet and his works. Eulogius was sentenced to die but high officials took turns pleading with him to retract the more outrageous of his blasphemies.

Sure that his time had come and determined to make a grand exit, Eulogius did not waver. On his way to the block a eunuch slapped him. Eulogius mildly turned the other cheek. The eunuch obligingly played his part and slapped that as well. Minutes later the headsman struck. Eulogius was ultimately canonized, as was the young lady he had sheltered. The Christians now rose up shouting pious war cries. Some were Mozarabes, who had retained their faith while rising in the Moslem world. Others were Muwalladun, renegades whose fathers or grandfathers, possibly for the sake of a better job or a promising marriage, had spoken the fateful words: "Allah is Allah and Mohammed is his Prophet." A person was considered a Moslem if he was born of Moslem parents, and for all believers and the children of believers the penalty for apostasy was death.

Many joined the uprising because throughout Andalusia, from the Asturias and the Basque country to Elvira, Merida and Seville, petty chiefs were thumbing their noses at Cordoba, all eager to exchange the status of vassal for that of monarch, even if the "kingdom" were as independent as a hair is of the head. Where no lord's banner waved, bandits took their toll of the traffic across the crumbling emirate.

The most successful of these was a man who flavored his banditry with a rough and appealing populism. For almost half a century he was to ride the capricious political winds of the peninsula. Omar Hafsun proudly included in his ancestry a Visigothic count named Alphonse. Although his family had dropped their Visigothic Christianity for Islam they kept their Christian leanings warm, if well hidden, while living in the style of rustic Moslem nobility in the mountains north of Malaga.

In those disordered times, when the law of Cordoba did not run very far into the hills, a young man, prickly about his honor, was likely to vindicate it with his own sword. In a minor quarrel over an insult, fancied or real, young Omar killed a neighbor. His father, remembering when the killing of a man was inevitably followed by the killing of the killer, promptly disowned his son to clear his own skirts but then packed him off to the hills with ample provisions.

Hafsun gathered around him a small group of other young men, footloose products of those uneasy times when people rolled away from their families as if the sandy soil could no longer hold their roots. The little band of friends took up the trade of highway robbery, but they were such clumsy amateurs that they made easy game for the local constabulary. A judge had Omar Hafsun whipped for petty theft and then set him free. The young man, grateful that the judge knew nothing about the earlier killing in his village, decided not to press his luck. He headed for North Africa, where he found work with an exiled Andalusian tailor. A customer who spotted Hafsun's origin babbled about the fortune awaiting a young man with courage to reap the rich harvest of anarchy. Hafsun panicked. If a stranger could identify him so could the police, he reasoned. He fled to his kinfolk in the hills of Malaga who, he knew, would shelter him. An uncle not only granted him a secure refuge but also saw in his nephew's mixture of banditry and populism a possible political resource. His uncle taught him to rally followers by decrying such obvious evils as taxes and the snobbishness of Arab aristocrats. Hafsun quickly learned how to combine the allurements of loot with the ennobling rhetoric of class warfare.

He took over a ruined Roman fortress on top of Mount Bobastro above what is now the railroad junction of Bobadilla. He had some forty followers to start with but others found their way to his castle because the times were bad, policing ineffective and government service underpaid.

Omar Hafsun thrived on early successes. He basked in the applause of his followers and became brave, even gallant, in order to satisfy the image they had of him. He spared those victims who fought back bravely. He treated his men squarely, sharing the booty justly and lavishing honors on those who put up a good fight. Pleased with what he saw in the mirror, Omar

Hafsun began to think that he indeed had political importance.

Local authorities sent expeditions to dislodge Hafsun from his castle, but these were so resoundingly repulsed that the commander-in-chief of the emir's army traveled to Bobastro to see this young warlord for himself. He proposed that Hafsun and his band join the emir's forces in a campaign against other rebellious clans. The emir would pay and provision Hafsun's troops and establish a garrison at Bobastro to expand and strengthen its fortifications.

Hafsun took the offer and led his men with some distinction through a series of bloody battles. Then he was ordered to Cordoba, where he and his men were treated as country bumpkins by the dandies and courtiers of the capital. Offended, he led his men back to the mountains of Malaga. There he drove out the emir's garrison, keeping for himself the commander's mistress. Some say he wooed her; others say he raped her.

Now he could inveigh against the citified Arabs with a personal vengeance. When other rebel chiefs called for help he dashed off to rescue them from the emir's attacks. And when the crown prince al-Mundhir again attempted to hire him, Hafsun played with him, seeming to come to terms, only to betray him into a humiliating defeat. This set all of Andalusia to laughing at the prince who had been gulled by the mountain boy. By lightning raids and threats and shifting alliances, by footwork and by virtue of the vacuum of public authority, Omar Hafsun came to dominate much of the countryside.

The crown prince al-Mundhir, thirsty for revenge, was on the point of starving Hafsun in a viselike siege of Bobastro when word came of his father's death. Al-Mundhir hurried to Cordoba to be proclaimed emir. Although early in his emirate he succeeded in cleaning rebel chieftains out of strongholds they had held for years, his big test was still Hafsun. Once again he laid siege to Bobastro, vowing never to lift it without Hafsun's abject surrender. Once again, however, the mountain boy had the rarest of luck.

At the crucial moment al-Mundhir fell ill and sent for his

brother Abdallah to take command. Abdallah, now in his for-
ties, was a man of long-frustrated ambitions. He was the same
age as al-Mundhir almost to the day. (They were born of different mothers, who shared the lively old emir's affections alternately.) Since their father had publicly designated al-Mundhir
to succeed him, Abdallah's only hope was that his brother
would die before siring any princelings. Al-Mundhir had been
in power for twenty-three months and was still without a son.
Here he was, helplessly ill and dependent upon his brother.
Doctors were busy bleeding the emir and utilizing whatever
other therapies had been mentioned by Galen. The illness had
not seemed grave and yet suddenly, one morning shortly after
the Abdallah's arrival, the emir was dead.

Historians now feel certain that one of the doctors had been
prevailed upon to put a drop of poison on the lancet with
which he bled the emir. There was never a confession of conspiracy and Omayyad historians tried to cover up the affair but
circumstantial evidence has since accumulated against Abdallah. Certainly his later career was to make the suspected murder eminently believable.

In any case Abdallah lifted the siege of Bobastro and took
the remains of his brother home to Cordoba. Hafsun was merrily harrying the rear guard and picking up whatever loot
could be had when he learned that he was attacking a funeral
cortege. Gallantly he withdrew his forces and allowed Abdallah
to carry home the body of his brother in due solemnity.

Under Abdallah the fortunes of the house of Omayyad foun-
dered. He plundered what was left in the treasury to squander
it on interminable military campaigns. Poets, singers, dancers
and artists deserted Cordoba for Seville, where Ibrahim ibn
Hajjaj presided over a court that made the emir's look shabby.
Ibrahim had once been an ally of Hafsun's but now he was a
nominal vassal of the emir. The only reason for his show of loyalty was the presence in Cordoba of his son, whom Abdallah
kept as a hostage for his father's good behavior.

Ibrahim attracted to Seville the flower of Andalusian culture. For example, there was the nation's leading linguistic au-

thority, Bedawy abu Mohammed Odhri. He was much respected by scholars, whether Moslem, Jew or Christian, for Arabic was universally regarded as the language of civilization and its custodian as something of a high priest. Bedawy regularly scolded courtiers for sloppy syntax and vulgar impurities. He also answered questions on grammar from puzzled correspondents in the way the rabbis of Sura and Pumbedita offered *responsa* to the morally or legally perplexed.

Also among the charms of Ibrahim's court was a lady named Kamar whom the prince had purchased in Baghdad at considerable expense. She was a poet who could be savagely scathing or sweetly lyrical. She had a fiercely independent mind, which she expressed with pungent wit. And she genuinely loved Ibrahim, prince of Seville. She was merciless in her treatment of court gossips and snobs who declared that brains were an impediment in a pretty woman. Answering those who charged that she came out of nowhere and was good only for writing clever verses and "conquering hearts by languishing looks," she wrote:

"By Allah, what men are these who despise the only true nobility—that which talent confers? Who will deliver me from the unlettered and doltish? The most shameful thing in the world is ignorance, and if ignorance were a woman's passport to Paradise, I would far rather that the creator sent me to hell!"

The cultivated Ibrahim tried to play the mountaineer Hafsun against Abdallah, although he was forced to do so with great subtlety, so as not to endanger his son in Cordoba. He continued to scheme with Hafsun even when that wily politician declared that he was returning to the Christian faith of his Visigothic ancestors. To many observers this suggested that, in Hafsun's eyes at least, the days of the Moslem emirate were numbered. A few Moslem allies of Hafsun fell away in horror but others like Ibrahim saw no reason to let religious differences interfere with either business or politics. And indeed Hafsun the Christian was very like Hafsun the Moslem.

The prospect of a return to power of Christianity seemed absolutely disastrous to at least one group. The Jews could ride out the ordinary conflicts among Moslem princes but the brutal days of the Visigoths had not faded from their collective memory. Much of the torment, they recalled, had been inspired by Church councils in which the terrible choice of forced baptism, exile or slaughter had been offered by bishops.

Moreover, Jewish historians suggest, the populist appeal of men like Hafsun threatened the economic interests of Jews. It was not reassuring to hear Hafsun's call to the mountaineers and tenant farmers to overthrow their Arab landlords, withhold the rent and terrorize the owners out of their property. After all, the Arabs had not only offered the Jews a congenial intellectual life, personal safety and religious tolerance but had also created the great market of Cordoba. There Jewish manufacturers, traders, artists and artisans sold their wares, bought their books and tasted the delights of a wider world.

To the Jews Omar Hafsun was a noisy, unpleasant, provincial warlord. They therefore remained stubbornly loyal to the emir, although Abdallah could be far more brutal than Hafsun to those who stood in his way.

In 891 one of Hafsun's Christian allies had taken the fortress of Poley (on the site of what is now Aguilar de la Frontera) barely twelve miles from Lucena. One morning in the spring of that year some three hundred of Hafsun's men marched to within a hundred feet or so of the wide moat and thick walls that ringed the Jewish city. It was a raggle-taggle army, some soldiers wrapped in farmers' cloaks, others looking vaguely military with helmets perched on their heads and improvised mail armor over their torsos. Some straddled mules and others plodded along on foot. They came dragging a string of covered carts. For a night they quartered themselves in the suburbs inhabited mainly by Moslems, although a number of Jewish families also had chosen to live there amid the cool vineyards and along the canals that watered the valley. Inside the walls the city, with its huge markets displaying the farm produce of the region, its shops, colleges, synagogues—all with a cool, white Arab look—was almost exclusively Jewish. A few Arab families lived with the Jews but these were either dignitaries or service people.

After a couple of days during which the rebels did no more than camp and cook, the battle began. In the middle of the night the attackers ran forward and heaved sandbags into the moat. They then planted ladders on the sandbags and attempted to scale the wall. Since for at least forty-eight hours the Jewish guards had been watching the preparations for attack they were ready with a supply of rocks to toss down on the invaders' heads. During the day the attackers fetched from their carts a variety of equipment, which they assembled into siege artillery. They pieced together a series of armored plates beneath which they hoped to crawl to the walls without suffering from the bombardment.

Bowmen came out of camp shooting javelins and arrows from under the protection of armor. Their volleys went on for hours without noticeable effect. The Jewish defenders answered with a steady avalanche of rocks and a storm of flaming arrows that occasionally set fire to the wooden framework of the armored shields. Then, under cover of a huge mantelet of woven armor and wood, the rebels brought out their battering rams—tree trunks lashed to fixed beams. The besiegers worked with difficulty under the flaming arrows, which threatened to set ablaze the ram and its supporting beams.

The battle of Lucena lasted for only a few days before the dispirited invaders packed up and went after easier pickings. All up and down the country loyalist cities were being besieged by rebels and rebel strongholds by loyalists. No matter who was the victor, each engagement ended in the customary looting, arson and rape, following which the tax collector would enter on muleback with retinue to pick up what was left, always keeping a share of the carrion for himself.

In the midst of this seeming disintegration of a once-promising culture sat the emir Abdallah. He was obsessed with the insecurity that afflicts most absolute rulers. Although his rule was indeed absolute where he could enforce it, the area of his power was growing ever more restricted. From time to time audacious rebel chiefs would ride up to the gates of Cordoba and fling their lances at the royal portal. Arab military ability, gallantry and heroism had been squandered to the point of near bankruptcy. Berber chieftains were setting up their own principalities with designated spheres for taxing and exploitation. Christian politicians played one petty ruler against another. Only the Jews fought and prayed that a strong central Omayyad government might somehow emerge from the chaos before new Visigoths and Vandals came.

Inside Cordoba there was no food in the great markets because even if farmers succeeded in harvesting a crop they would not trust it to the roads. Prices had risen to such absurd heights that even bread was a luxury for the rich. Soldiers who still fought under the white banners of the Omayyads grumbled more than ever at missed paydays and the lack of anything to buy even if one had the money to pay.

It was a time for jeremiads and these were being voiced in mosque and market. In the high and thunderous fashion of Old Testament prophets, the mullahs called once-glorious Cordoba "a vile courtesan . . . a sink of corruption . . . an abode of calamity." Abdallah's palace was "a house of iniquity." Hafsun's men were "a scourge of Allah," the mullahs proclaimed. These angry prophets were excited and poetic but they offered no advice to frightened people except to "think no longer of earthly things."

Abdallah, physically comfortable in his "house of iniquity," was inevitably suspicious of those who still stood by him, particularly those who stood too closely by him. He had ordered that a covered bridge be built from his palace over the roadway and into the great mosque to make him a less tempting target for assassins when he had to lead the prayers.

Now in his late sixties, he was still a striking figure—tall and straight, with the long reddish-blond hair of his Frankish mother. He had once had a flair for poetry but he had seen his talents shrivel as his appetite for power grew.

His corroding suspicions had led him to connive at the assassination of three of his brothers, al-Mundhir, Hisham and al-Kasim. Abdallah was equally wary of his eleven sons. He had taken the precaution of naming as his heir the oldest, Mohammed. This, he thought, would reassure the boy's mother, one of his most cherished wives. Also he hoped that it would end the usual sibling rivalries among princes, but actually it exacerbated them.

Al-Mutarif, five years younger than Mohammed, had his father's ambitions and his lack of scruple. It is generally assumed that the young man planted a suspicion in the fertile brain of his father concerning the crown prince's impatience to take the throne. Mohammed was therefore tossed into prison. He was about to be freed for lack of evidence of any treason when al-Mutarif was smuggled into his cell. There he dispatched his elder brother with a dagger. Most historians agree that Abdallah probably put the young man up to it.

If it was al-Mutarif's idea he paid for it. Five years later charges of treason were brought against him. For three days he fought off the party of soldiers who had come to his palace to arrest him. When he surrendered he was brought before his father, who ordered his prompt decapitation. The young man's remains were buried in the garden.

Understandably the other sons of Abdallah kept at a distance from their father and so survived in obscurity. Now an old man, sitting in the shambles of the empire he had stolen from his brother, Abdallah fastened on one small boy all of his remaining hopes for salvation at the hands of history.

Commentators, however critical of Abdallah's murderous insecurity, agree that his tender affections for the boy were owed, at least in part, to remorse. The boy was his grandchild, the son of his own firstborn, Mohammed, who was stabbed in his jail cell. Actually the boy had been born just three weeks before the murder of his father.

It must have been a strange life for the boy, to grow up in the tender affection of his grandfather who so terrified his uncles and all the world, it seemed. It was like living in the eye of a hurricane, gazing up at blue skies while all around, winds howled and wreaked utter devastation.

The child saw his uncles only rarely, for they lived away from the court in discreetly unassuming houses along the winding, white-walled streets of Cordoba. They came to the palace only when summoned and left hurriedly the moment they were dismissed. The emir had named his grandson as his heir and his sons did not begrudge the boy the honor or the danger of the royal smile. After all, the boy's father had once been summoned to that same destiny and had paid for it with death at the point of a dagger.

Grandfather Abdallah, beset by catastrophe, ruin and disgrace, cherished his grandson as if he were a sign of redemption. He presided over his education and applauded his every childish achievement. He prophesied great wonders for the child. The boy was the darling of the little world circumscribed by Cordoba's Alcazar and harem.

He grew into a short, stocky young man with the blond hair and blue eyes that distinguished this royal Arab line. As an adolescent he would touch up his hair with dye to get rid of the reddish tints he thought might give him a common, Nordic look. When, as a full-grown man of twenty, he sat astride his horse one could scarcely see his head above the mane. His stirrups barely cleared the saddle's edge. Nevertheless he managed a royal look.

On October 15, 912, when his grandfather died, this sheltered prince, glowing with youth and confidence at the age of twenty-two, was proclaimed emir of al-Andalus—Abd-er Rahman III. In a world of horrors he had been raised gently in a garden and was thus well prepared to preside over an age in which poets, traders and soldiers—Moslem, Christians and Jews—would sing hosannahs.

The Palace of the Caliph's Lady

The road that meanders northwest from Cordoba toward the dark crests of the Sierra Morena runs past a landscape of tilled earth laced by the blue ribbon of the Guadalquivir. Some five miles out of the city there is, on the right, a hillside covered by sentinels of cypress, feathery almond and writhing olive trees. It is hard to distinguish this hill from so many others. Still, it has a name given it more than a thousand years ago—the Mountain of the Bride.

Halfway up this slope there seems to be a village of solid low buildings, rising in tiers toward an edifice at the top where archways flare beneath a flat roof. The sun touches the little town to gold.

A narrow, rutted byway breaks off from the main road and climbs toward the town. Above the purple flowering weeds that bend on either side of the lane, scattered, slender columns rise. Many of them are broken off near their tops, suggesting ballet dancers frozen in mid-leap.

The road arches above the hamlet, then swings abruptly on to a gravel plaza where dusty trees cast a spotty, ineffectual shade. It is forlorn, like the parking lot of a summer resort in late fall. From beyond a narrow doorway set in a chipped and yellowing wall there rises a barking, yipping, whining clamor. A woman answers our knock. Broom in hand, kerchief about her head, she is framed by the gateway and set against the tilled landscape as in a medieval painting. She seems unaware of the uproar around her.

"The ruins are closed," she says. Then, because we have come from far away, she relents. As we step through the doorway the valley opens before us in a wide embrace. The lady sets down her broom beside the shaded kiosk where in season she sells souvenirs to tourists. She is the currently reigning mistress of what was once the beating heart of al-Andalus—the Madinat al-Zahra as Abd-er Rahman named it, the City of Zahra, or Sarah, as the Jews would say, or the Medina Azahara as the Spaniards call it now in syllables garbled by time and transliteration.

We scramble down muddy paths, the troop of yapping mongrels looping around, behind and ahead of us, pausing from time to time to lift their legs at the venerable rubble. Here and there the terraced mud walls are relieved by a chipped arabesque or what seems to be the fossil of a fern in a fragment of tile.

"There's the mosque," says the lady flatly, as if in fact it stood there, minarets, alabaster beehives and all. We walk past the remains, around corners and across weed-grown plazas to a promenade that commands the valley. At our feet are two large excavations that once were pools filled by splashing fountains. Spread out on the cracked paving stones at the pools' bottoms are shattered pieces of tile and stone, some bearing tendril-like Arabic letters. Not all are the deathlike chalk white one misguidedly associates with ancient art. Blues, greens and reds still glow on the tiles.

They have been meticulously arranged in groups, as one might sort out the pieces of a jigsaw puzzle before fitting them together. The lady of the Madinat al-Zahra sighs. The archeologists, who work here when the government has the money to pay them, have a formidable *rompe-cabeza,* she says—a headache of gigantic proportions.

We turn away from the empty pools toward the cool interior of the building whose arches flashed into gold when we saw them from the road. In this royal audience chamber, pillars of blue-and-pink marble—brought perhaps from Carthage or Tunis—still offer platforms for arches that leap above their Greco-Roman-Persian capitals. Beyond the arches is an intricate frieze, in which the sculpted stone is not as dramatic as the blank stretches where, ages ago, puritanical mobs stripped beauty from this place.

Horseshoe archways, like great keyholes, open into dark and silent corridors, where one may not go, the lady warns. The floor of white marble is cracked and overlaid by dust. It is said that marble was chosen for the floor of this room of royal meetings because of a legendary joke concerning the visit of the Queen of Sheba to King Solomon. It was quite acceptable to the Biblical courtiers that a queen should be beautiful, but it was unsettling to find her also clever, rich and powerful. The gossips therefore whispered that Sheba's queen might be supernatural. Perhaps she wore so long a gown to hide feet that in fact were hooves. The king, mindful of the rumors, granted her an audience on a floor of marble so highly polished that it seemed wet. The queen therefore walked daintily, lifting her skirts to her ankles and displaying a foot that was reassuringly human and feminine, pleasing the king and confounding the courtiers.

Above this chamber where Abd-er Rahman III received other queens as well as poets, jesters and rabbis, restorers have been working on the rafters that hold the high flat ceiling. They have been painting bright colors and abstract flowers on new beams that are faithful replicas of the old. This is "the rich room," as the Arab chroniclers described it, where Abd-er Rahman frequently held court, gazing beyond the heads of his nobles, eunuchs and wives to the cool valley, which was then covered with winding lanes and avenues almost to the shores of the river.

In this city, which was not only a working political capital but also a symbol of majesty, pleasure palace and art center, there lived perhaps as many as thirty thousand people, all fed, clothed and housed by the government. These included the royal accountants, clerks, historians, lawyers, calligraphers, administrators and supervisors who kept the wheels of government turning.

Some historians put the number of servants in the royal household at more than 13,750. Abd-er Rahman III was known to be very fond of women, not only in his bed but at conversation or in concerts in the family rooms of the home. In Madinat al-Zahra there were six thousand women, counting resident poets, hairdressers, musicians and dancers as well as wives, concubines, daughters, aunts and other assorted female kinfolk.

Each day, the bookkeepers noted, the population of the city consumed thirteen thousand pounds of meat along with innumerable birds and fish. Small game was to be had for a day's hunting. Pools were well-stocked with fish, which were regularly fed with dried vegetables and breadcrumbs. These made it unnecessary to spread nets in the mountain streams or add to the burden of the mule train that daily brought provisions from Cordoba. The people of this capital were housed and schooled in some four hundred buildings, most of them along the upper terraces, amid patios and gardens both formal and woodsy. Water was brought down from the *sierra* in two main aqueducts, which branched into a network of pipes serving homes, fountains and bathing pools throughout the city. Another network of ceramic pipes drained sewage from the terraces of the city across the flatlands to empty into the Guadalquivir. Some sources say there were as many as three hundred bathing places in the city. At least two of these were very large—one for the servants of the royal household; the other for workmen, farmers, tradesmen and porters who lived in the lower sectors of town.

Though numerous fountains splashed in all parts of the city—as they still do throughout Andalusia—none equalled the one in the chamber set aside for Abd-er Rahman's afternoon rest. Its gigantic central stem of carved stone had been brought from Syria. From it waters leaped and splashed into a basin of green marble adorned with twelve sculpted pieces in four trios: a lion with a gazelle and a crocodile; an eagle, elephant and dragon; a dove, hawk and peacock; a cock, hen and vulture. The stone of these animals sparkled with gold, pearls and other gems.

The city was the dream of a monarch in middle age. Abd-er Rahman III was forty-one when he conceived of this western Byzantium and forty-six when the first workmen were sent to dig up the fields in the shadow of the Mountain of the Bride.

It is hard to know what is true and what is ornamental in the history of this astonishing city. The chroniclers of the tenth century say that a concubine who had profited from the generosity of Abd-er Rahman—and perhaps from others as well—died leaving a tidy fortune for the purpose of ransoming Moslem captives held in the jails of Christian kings.

Abd-er Rahman sent emissaries throughout the Christian kingdoms but could find no one to be ransomed. Zahra, the love of Abd-er Rahman's sunny middle years, suggested that the money be used to build a shining city worthy of the emperor of the Western world. Abd-er Rahman, not unnaturally, found the idea attractive and decided to name the new city after Zahra. In this he seemed to have been somewhat neglectful of the lady whose bequest furnished at least the initial funding for the enterprise. On the other hand, Zahra was still alive and the other was not. The Koranic injunction against representational sculpture did not prevent the ardent ruler from adorning the main gate with a bust of his lady, to the fury of the mullahs.

The female head that topped the gate and the name of the Madinat al-Zahra are solid evidence for the story, but there is also a great deal of embroidery, which one may take for fact or fancy. For example, it is said that Zahra woke up one morning in her city and, gazing out of the window, with her loving monarch at her side, imagined that the white buildings nestling into the dark hills resembled a fair-skinned maiden in the arms of an Ethiopian. Finding that this racial mixture troubled his lady love, the monarch ordered the planting of almond and fig trees to lighten the complexion of the Bride's Mountain.

Other historians suggest that a prosaic political alibi under-

lay the fantasies. Abd-er Rahman had to explain to his constituency the lavish expenditures he was making for his new city at
a time when some people were suggesting better uses for the
money. Every Friday the mullahs preached their criticism, apparently undeterred by the fact that Abd-er Rahman had become, by his own decree, their superior, spiritually as well as
temporally.

Seven years before the first workman went up to Madinat
al-Zahra Abd-er Rahman had taken a step of enormous political importance. He had himself proclaimed Caliph, a far loftier
title than emir, which denotes a derived authority, a mere lieu-
tenancy. A Caliph is supreme under Allah. No longer need the
Moslems of Andalusia look to the rulers of Mecca, Medina,
Baghdad or Damascus for infallible spiritual guidance. The
emirate had been a cultural dependency of Syria. The Caliphate asserted Cordoba's position as the Islamic center of the
world.

The new title designated Abd-er Rahman and his successors
on the throne of Cordoba as "Prince of Believers and Defender
of the Faith." He added to his name the designation *al-Nasir li-
dini Allah*—"He who fights victoriously for Allah." All this he
topped with the standard Arab formula for proud humility:
"The Slave of Allah."

Abd-er Rahman did not take the Caliph's title as still another luxury, like the green marble fountain that played during
his siesta or the pleasant toy that spun mercury into dazzling
colors to astonish guests in his anteroom. The title of Caliph
was not a plaything but a political necessity.

In the early years of his reign Abd-er Rahman III had three
fronts on which to fight: rebellions at home; the perennial
menace of the Christian kings in the north; and the Fatimids
across the straits in North Africa. That sect, tracing their claim
to the mantle of the Prophet by a line descending from his
daughter Fatima, had grown powerful on a mixture of messianic faith and a very worldly political opportunism. Mes-
siahs, imams and Caliphs were multiplying in North Africa as
the old centers of power in Damascus and Baghdad fell apart.

Abd-er Rahman sought to checkmate these new rivals by announcing his celestial authority. To cap that victory he also stymied his opponents militarily by taking the strategically important North African port of Ceuta.

The Caliph's naval campaign along the African coast was aimed not only against the Fatimid threat but also at the flow of supplies and reinforcements to that aging but still troublesome rebel in the mountains of Malaga, Omar Hafsun. Early in his reign, Abd-er Rahman's fleet of regular and privateer warships took to burning whatever vessels they could catch bringing supplies from Africa to Hafsun. On land the armies of Cordoba did not wait for balmy summer weather, usually considered essential for proper military adventures. They struck even in winter at those chieftains who were more or less sympathetic to Hafsun, so that the old lion was left alone holed up in the church and castle he had carved out of rock at Bobastro.

In 914 Abd-er Rahman was fully prepared to storm the citadel or starve it to surrender but once again, as on so many previous occasions, Hafsun was reprieved by a seeming miracle. A year of poor harvests and searing drought had left Andalusia hungry and prone to disease that came in the wake of famine. Chroniclers described the epidemic but it is hard now to pinpoint the disease that wracked the usually healthy Andalusians.

In any case Abd-er Rahman had to hurry back to his capital to see that the royal granaries were opened in an orderly way to feed the hungry, to see that irrigation works were speeded to bring mountain water to more of the parched plains, and to keep in check the medical and social malaise that gripped the country.

The national disaster made a military campaign impossible and for the moment left Bobastro in the keeping of Omar Hafsun, his two sons and his daughter Argentea. That young lady had become seized with the martyrdom fever that still intoxicated young Christians, although it no longer provoked the mass hysteria that had troubled the days of Abd-er Rahman II.

In 917 old Omar, who had been launched on his career by the hot-blooded slaying of a neighbor, died peacefully in his bed at Bobastro. It took ten more years to rout the warrior sons of Omar from their almost impregnable lair. During that time Argentea loudly proclaimed her Christianity until Moslem judges, obliged to recall that she had been born a true believer, convicted her of the capital crime of apostasy. She was beheaded, a fate she welcomed as a victory.

When Abd-er Rahman finally led his forces into the castle of Bobastro he exhibited a profound respect for the valor and military skills of the old troublemaker. It offended him deeply to learn later that his more vengeful—and more militantly Moslem—lieutenants dug up the bodies of Hafsun and his sons (buried with crossed arms in the Christian manner), carried whatever remained of them to Cordoba and nailed them up on crosses. Moslems always had a horror of backsliders.

It is said that Abd-er Rahman was deeply offended by such unchivalric treatment of the enemy. It is true that he himself resorted to brutality now and then, but only when political or military exigencies—not personal spleen or religious dogma—seemed to require it. For example, he once had three hundred of his officers crucified after a disastrous campaign against the Christian north. They had led their troops in a disorderly, disgraceful rout. Abd-er Rahman, like most military commanders, always hoped that his troops would be less afraid of the enemy than of their own superiors. The necessary corollary to that proposition was the dread the Caliph had to inspire. He even felt it necessary to have one of his sons executed for conspiring to murder him and seize the Caliphate. Similarly, an unpleasantly ambitious uncle had to be sentenced to death.

Disillusionment in the loyalty and the political sagacity of his kinsmen and his class led Abd-er Rahman to distrust and then to loathe the power-hungry nobility. After he took the Caliph's title in 929—a date that formed a sharp dividing line in his reign and in his life—Abd-er Rahman found a political use for majesty. He elevated himself above the political scramble and shut himself away from nobles and plebeians alike. He cultivated the remoteness of semidivinity, except in the company of his intimate friends and the ladies of the harem, with whom he joked, laughed, drank, played and read poetry.

He no longer walked the streets of his city like a mortal. He did not use the bridge that the emir Abdallah had built to hide from his people, but instead he raised a wall of solemn ceremonial that was more durable and that the people valued more highly. For when they were allowed a glimpse over that high barrier they watched and relished a pageant of royalty, priesthood and power in which they shared the Caliph's pride.

His sons, as princelings of the dynasty, had to keep their distance from the people and the Caliph. They lived in villas where they might revel in luxury and safety so long as they did not seek to break their golden bars, or try to curry popular favor, or raise a faction or in any way exhibit an unseemly ambition.

Noble kinfolk were pensioned off and assigned to their deluxe cages with the unwritten, perhaps unspoken, but plainly understood instructions that they were to come to the palace only when summoned, go promptly when dismissed and never express a political idea. For advisers, administrators and executives the Caliph preferred men who were bought and paid for. They came from the class that all along had provided continuity in the civil service: the household servants, free or slave, castrated or intact.

Most of these new favorites were Eastern Europeans, though some were African. Once they might have played politics with a conniving prince or noble or with a lady known to have the Caliph's attention in and out of bed.

Now those temptations were removed. At the same time the lid was lifted from their ambitions. There was only one possible loyalty: to the Caliph from whom all blessings flowed. And no man stood between the Caliph and his servants. Another source of talent lay among the Jews and Christians. Against such forces the mullahs grumbled but did not dare to roar. It was, then, to magnify the majesty of the Caliphate—even more than to please his lady love—that Abd-er Rahman built his glorious suburb. Being an Arab and not a Goth, although genetically he was both, he built his city as an airy palace of delights rather than as a grim fortress. Some ten thousand workers, free and slave, were put to work on the project. They used fifteen hundred mules and four hundred camels from the royal stables plus another thousand mules that had to be rented by the day from private breeders and agents. These helped to spread the royal treasure throughout the booming economy that came with the pax Cordoba.

The Caliph employed the most distinguished architects of the kingdom and lured others from his fading rivals in the East. He assigned his son and heir al-Hakam to supervise the works and to refine the details of the architectural design, although each major step had the benefit of Abd-er Rahman's considerable taste.

Specialists were hired to select the best marble from the quarries of Carthage and Sfax. The Christian emperor of Constantinople thought it only tactful to send the Caliph a gift of 140 sculpted Greek columns with a suitably Corinthian elaboration that he thought might appeal to the Oriental strain in Abd-er Rahman. The Franks sent 19 columns, mainly from the Jewish area around Narbonne. These were interspersed with the sunny blue marble of Cordoba and the pink of Cabra, some forty miles to the south.

The buildings materialized with astonishing speed, considering the travel time needed for the imported materials and the grandeur of the scheme. For example, the mosque went up in just forty-eight days. To do the job the architects were assigned three hundred masons, three hundred carpenters and five hundred workers skilled in a variety of other building crafts. Though many of these were Christian or African slaves, most were free men who were paid an attractive daily wage.

In 945, just nine years after the ground was cleared, enough of the city was finished for the Caliph to move in with all of his family, his wives and concubines, his retinue of servants and slaves, his guard, his officers and his counselors. To populate the city with the lesser sort that would keep the wheels turning, the water flowing, the streets swept, the garbage collected and the market well stocked, the Caliph offered a handsome' cash bonus for settlers. The offer lured thousands.

The last roof of the city would not be in place until 970, and by then Abd-er Rahman would be dead and Cordoba in its last days. Still, Abd-er Rahman lived long enough to enjoy the splendors of the Madinat al-Zahra. Royal fetes were decreed ever more frequently and in ever grander style. Cordobans came out in great numbers to enjoy the carnival when the glittering celebrities of the time rode on carpets laid over the streets all the way from the old city to the new one. Every time a prince was circumcised or a general welcomed home from a skirmish on a distant frontier there was a royal reception that delighted the crowd and underscored the majesty of the Caliph. He sat on his throne in the audience chamber—the *madjlis*—amid its blue-and-pink columns and deigned to receive or to give sumptuous gifts with quiet grace.

Some of the more affluent officials who had thrived on favors from the Caliph occasionally returned some of their wealth in presents, designed partly to encourage further royal generosity and partly to display their rank and power. There are records, for example, of the gifts a grand vizier brought to his king and benefactor at what must have been an extraordinary spectacle. The presents included thirty bolts of silk, five luxurious tents, six Iraqi silk robes, forty-eight outfits for the Caliph's daytime wear and one hundred for evening use, one hundred Arabian horses (five of them with brocaded saddles), five prize mules, large quantities of gold and silver in bricks or in minted coins, seven white fox furs from Khorosan, one hundred marten skins from Siberia, four hundred pounds of silk thread for the royal weavers, one thousand shields and one hundred thousand arrows for the royal guard.

If this lavish display measured the grand vizier's gratitude for past favors, those favors must have been spectacular. They might well have constituted fortunes in land and tax-farming concessions. Actually, this particular official, Ahmad Abu Shuhaid, was one of a diminishing number of aristocratic executives. The Caliph's favorites among the slaves—whether generals, poets or jesters—required royal generosity but probably on a far lesser scale.

The Caliphate of Cordoba was not a society in which the overly fed battened on the misery of a beaten peasantry or on whipped and tortured slaves. True, the lords and favorites of the palace enjoyed luxuries that the puritanical Moslems thought scandalous. And certainly the small farmers, road menders and even the craftsmen in potteries and textile factories enjoyed few of those comforts. But the expectation of equality had not yet taken root and poverty was not of the desperate sort. No one went hungry or sold his children to feed himself, or lived in filth or fear. Such a claim could not have been made for any state in Europe, Africa or Asia in the tenth century and not for so very many in the twentieth.

Consider, for example, the pay of a building worker at Madinat al-Zahra. The scale ranged from one-and-a-half to three dirhems a day. A man getting the middling pay of two dirhems might hope that with a little bit of luck he could put by enough to buy a modest house in Cordoba, costing about two thousand dirhems, or one thousand days of work. This is very roughly comparable to the situation of an American in the late twentieth century who earns forty dollars a day and hopes one day to buy a forty-thousand-dollar house, if he can find one. His Cordoban counterpart could buy a horse for twelve days' pay—far less than what an American would have to spend for the prevailing mode of private transport. Admittedly such comparisons are rough, almost but not quite to the point of absurdity, since a thousand other factors would have to be included in the reckoning if one would draw the picture of an Andalusian workman's life on an American scale.

The ingredients of Andalusian prosperity did not lie in the natural riches of its soil, for other parts of the Mediterranean shores were more fertile, nor in any original technology the Cordobans brought to the production of life's necessities. The talents of Arabs, Berbers, Arabized Christians and Jews were directed toward the ornaments of life or toward its philosophical, religious, scientific or artistic substance more than to mere subsistence.

Still, Andalusian society in that gleaming century did seem to work. It fed its fishermen, miners, farmers, tradesmen and slaves. It supported sizeable armies and navies. It permitted an aristocracy to pay for the services of teachers, scholars, artists, shoemakers, clothes designers, jewelers, musicians, diplomats, dancers, doctors and priests. It paid the salaries of judges, lawyers, policemen and bookkeepers. And as a population of parasites demonstrates the vitality of the host, so did the relative prosperity of thieves, confidence men, whores, pimps and beggars.

There were bad years when drought or grasshoppers destroyed the wheat crops. Then even the Caliph had to do without the choicest bread from Toledo or Lorca grain, and made do with North African wheat or barley. Even in good years the farmers could scarcely keep up with the domestic demand for grain.

On the high mesa the steady winds powered mills of the sort used since Roman times and possibly even from the days when Celts peopled the place. Everywhere that water ran, mill wheels were set to catch the current. Some mills were mounted on rafts that could be moved to wherever water worked the hardest. Abd-er Rahman III was as preoccupied with water as were his desert ancestors. Aqueducts of the Romans and intricate Syrian contraptions, using horsepower to draw up well water, were combined into systems of irrigation. These spread the nourishment of the Ebro and the Douro through canals that crisscrossed the plain. Where nothing else grew, olive trees took over, covering the hillsides as they do even now. Olives, prime export items, were packed in baskets and shipped downstream or loaded on mules and headed for the ports of the south. There they would be put aboard vessels that could carry them throughout the Mediterranean world. Or perhaps they would be sent northward, where Jewish traders would pick them up for the trek over the mountains to Gaul or beyond.

The south was adorned with vineyards. Grapes and raisins

were sold in all the markets—for they figured prominently in Andalusian recipes—but much of the crop went into wine. The mullahs bewailed the apparent tendency of Moslems to follow the bibulous example of Christians and Jews. Whatever models they used, the ordinary subjects of the Caliph indulged themselves in local wines, as did the lords and ladies in the palace and in the princely villas. City dwellers drank in inns that flourished under the management of Christians, because they were the only candidates for the job. Though Jews joined with Arabs in singing the praises of a gentle alcoholic glow, most thought the trade of publican to be not quite respectable. And Moslems could not abide the double sin of drinking while tempting a brother in Islam to profit from the forbidden pleasure.

Actually alcoholism never became a serious concern for the state. Few drunks were seen in public and the sins of the powerful transpired behind harem walls. Hakam I had nationalized a part of the wine market, allowing his subjects to share their pleasure with the revenue department. For the sake of Moslem propriety the manager of the state wine market was always a Christian.

Almanacs of the time reminded gardeners of the proper season for the grafting of fig trees and the planting of sugar cane, cotton, cucumbers, eggplant, saffron, mint and marjoram. The highly lyrical calendars timed the appearance of peacocks, turtle doves, storks, quail and the swarming schedule of bees in the numerous apiaries. Rivers ran with mullet and shad. Around the shores the sea poured sardines into the fishermen's nets, which were slung on cork floats.

Seekers of quick riches panned for gold along the swift running Segre (particularly at Lérida) or along the banks of the Darro, the Genil or south of the Tagus. Miners worked a hundred feet below the surface digging for iron in the valley of the Guadalquivir, for mercury at Almadén, for silver at Murcia or Hornachuelos. Copper mines, originally worked by the Romans, employed as many as one thousand men each. Other Andalusians dried salt from the sea or dug it out of quarries, such as the huge ones near Saragossa. Still other miners carved marble or cut chunks of soapstone from the mines near Toledo, to be used as shampoo for the ladies.

Cattle grazed in the foothills of the Guadarramas north of Toledo, but these were not for eating. Oxen were work animals. Christians raised pigs, anathema to Moslems and Jews, who frequently disparaged the sinful and disgusting eating habits of their Christian neighbors. Lamb, sheep and goats hung in the market stalls, as did lamb sausages and fish for frying. A much-sought delicacy was a well-baked lamb's head.

Silkworms raised in the south spun the raw materials that were woven into high fashion in the twisting streets of Seville, Jaen and Cordoba. In every city of the country there were streets of weavers, not only of silk but also of linen and wool. There were also streets set aside for leather makers, and fruit and vegetable vendors. Dealers in new clothing, as distinct from those selling secondhand, had their own streets. So it was with shoemakers and shoe repair men, makers of caneware, pots, ceramics, scabbards and belts; sellers of saffron, eggs, sugar, honey and crystal (made according to the formula developed by the Cordoban Abbas ibn Firnas a hundred years earlier). Each had his street, his stall, his organization.

Jewelers multiplied amid the general prosperity. They carved and combined silver, gold, wood, leather, ivory, gems and coral. Out of the clattering workshops in the bazaars would come a stream of bracelets, necklaces, pendants and miniature boxes on which might be carved or painted scenes of the court, of battle, of love and the hunt. The graven image taboo, like the drinking of wine, was one at which all but the most pious winked, smiled or shrugged. For this was a society with room for sinners as well as saints. Men and women tried to harmonize both natures, as did the Caliph himself, who led Friday prayers but still had his wine and enjoyed the wit, political sagacity and love of slaves as well as freed men and women, of Jews and Christians as well as Moslems.

At night when the highway along the Guadalquivir fell still and only a few stragglers hurried over the old Roman bridge, the Caliph would enjoy his jesters and his poets. In the offices of the Alcazar the bureaucrats folded their ledgers. Men took their pleasure in the inns, whorehouses or harems, or in their homes where they sipped rosewater with the one wife they could afford and with whatever children had accumulated. Market people clanged down their shutters over their stalls and night patrols of police began to make their rounds of the alleys in the bazaar. Scurrying behind or before the constable went the thieves, risking the loss of a hand or a life for a bolt of cloth, a sack of fruit, a jug of wine or perhaps a baked lamb's head. They stole, as they begged, as they worked, each following his own traditions. In the days of Abd-er Rahman III there were few obvious signs of gratuitous blood and death. Injustice existed but it was usually deplored. All in all, the Caliphate of Cordoba was a serene corner in a savage world.

That historical generalization is perhaps too glib. It does not adequately picture the time and place. Consider, for example, the irritation of the man in Malaga who was roused from his sleep by a patio party next door to him in which the instruments jangled out of tune and the laughter was too raucous. His complaints—trifling, perhaps—must have been shared by many, as were the compensating appeasements that followed quickly. Both were recorded in an Andalusian cameo that has come down to us intact, although secondhand, as noted by a writer of the time:

"In a garden set within a grand house some twenty young people stood about with cups of wine and bowls of fruit in easy reach. Girls with lyres, drums and flutes in their hands were on their feet but were not playing. A little way apart one girl was seated with her lute in her lap. All eyes and all ears were upon her alone while she lightly touched her instrument and sang verse after verse. . . ."

The one with the lute on her lap was one of these rare women in Andalusia whose talents entitled them to an eccentric affirmation of independence. They were hired for the evening but whether they participated in the usual grand finale—a display of ardent sexual acrobatics—was up to them. Men might swoon for their favors, which they were free to grant or deny. Actually one young Cordoban dandy, moved by the sinuous grace of a dancer, was described—in verse—as covering his head and rocking to and fro like a rabbi entranced by a different sort of vision.

The preliminaries to the more orgiastic climaxes of these parties were often elaborate. Arab historians tell of women in men's clothes prancing around on hobby horses in imitation of a battle designed to end in loving surrender. Although among the respectable classes chastity was enshrined in the high medieval manner, no child, whether raised in an opulent harem or a modest family room, grew up without a thorough education in matters of sex. It was not taught so much as taken in with the air. Sex play was freely observed and anticipated eagerly. Boys experimented at an early age with one another, with the eunuchs, and with the ladies of the harem.

Heterosex and homosex were varying aspects of the joy of life. Actually the most favored prostitutes of Cordoba were boys. Snobs declared that only galley slaves and farmhands would take to bed the women who spent their lives around the taverns, grain markets or whorehouses—where business was brisker but always on the books, and these were open to the tax collector. The dark-eyed boys of the town were often sought out by the more fashionable bisexual gallants.

The Andalusian male in love with a woman performed a graceful courtship dance in which he played the slave of passion while proclaiming himself the master. Women could thus extract all manner of gifts and heady compliments. When they were not obliged to work about the house they could live as the ornaments, idols and prizes of men. With that status went a cradle-to-the-grave protection, guaranteed by law, by religious precept, by custom and by the requirements of male honor.

A woman could be beaten only for the gravest offenses against morality or religion, and then only upon permission of the courts. She could always plead her case before a judge. And even if her husband had good reason to put her aside, he would have to pay her a lifetime pension. It was thought disgraceful to expose a woman to danger. Women were rarely subject to discourtesies and never left alone. They were guarded as a man's most precious possession, but still, they were possessed.

They were not shielded from the boredom of such pervasive security, however. Most had to watch life from the roof garden. They heard its muted sounds in scraps of talk from the street. They shared small talk and frustrations with other women. A visit to the cemetery was a welcome outing. Perhaps they talked with their husbands if the men transcended—as they occasionally did—the limitations of the traditional distribution of powers.

While only the rich could afford polygamy, a man fancying himself in need of fresh stimuli might take a good-looking young slave into the house. Few wives objected because the slave would help with the chores. The slave girl had no objections, because if she produced a son for the man of the house she was freed and treated with the dignity that becomes the mother of a boy. If she gave birth to a girl the master would blame her for the failure but, proclaiming his virility, would be delighted to try again.

In the heyday of the reign of Abd-er Rahman III the walls around women, whether for their protection or their confinement, were rendered less forbidding than in most Islamic countries. Still the walls were there and puritans stood in the wings complaining that time-haloed defenses and taboos were being eroded by liberals. The time was to come soon enough when the puritans would sweep into power and impose upon women, men, children and the state the purity of their doctrine.

One can grasp the color of Cordoban freedom by what the puritans later outlawed and condemned. A manual of reforms advocated by one such moralizing petty official, ibn 'Abdun, proscribes the scandalous practices tolerated by the easy-going Omayyads. No more, he advised, should women be allowed to go to the banks of the river. And certainly they must no more be seen on boats, their painted, unveiled faces visible to men lolling on the shores in summertime, ready to violate them with lustful eyes. Never again, he writes, shall a Moslem woman be permitted to enter a church, because it is well known that, priests are "libertines, fornicators and sodomites."

No women, not even Christians, should be allowed in church, except for religious purposes, because priests, who are known to keep two or more women for their pleasure, may there "eat, drink and fornicate with them." Certainly it would be better, says ibn 'Abdun, if Catholic priests, being subject to fleshly appetites, were to marry as do their brethren in the Eastern Churches. Then women might be safer and husbands could rest more easily. Until priests marry, he goes on, no woman of any faith should be permitted to enter their homes for any reason.

And while on the subject of priests, ibn 'Abdun suggests that they be circumcised like other men. Their objections, he says, are hypocritical, since every January they celebrate the circumcision of Jesus.

The reformer saw dreadful possibilities for lechery at picnics, which were popular in the days of Abd-er Rahman III. Families would hire musicians to play while the picnickers ate and even danced on the hills above the Guadalquivir. Such things lead to perdition, ibn 'Abdun warns. (Whether they did or not and if so, how often, is not a matter of public record.)

The reformer suggests a total suppression of musicians but grudgingly admits that this is probably not feasible, given the light-mindedness bred into the people by a too-secular society. As a compromise he advocates a regulation requiring every musician to have a permit issued by the local magistrate before performing at a picnic. Even then, he insists a constable should be present to keep young men from brawling or consorting with "low-lifes, libertines, men addicted to vice, criminals."

Actually the reformer seems more concerned over the sin that lurks in the hearts of boys than he is over the waywardness of girls. The female—or at least her chastity—must be guarded vigilantly but only because men are so rapacious. Particularly, warns ibn 'Abdun, one must beware of young men "who wear their hair long." Such youths must be seized on sight and shaved. Their hair must be cut, and perhaps one should consider flogging them even before they commit an offense, "because long hair is the mark of criminals and evildoers." At the very least, he adds, they must not be allowed to carry a lance or a sword, because weapons "together with long hair provide the impetus to evil work."

As for young boy prostitutes, they must be beaten whenever found and driven from the city. Like many other would-be reformers, ibn 'Abdun suggests no punishment for the boys' customers.

It would not be fair to ibn 'Abdun to suggest that sexual high jinks are his only concern. He also advocates stricter supervision of markets to guarantee that the milk is not watered, that figs are not prepackaged with the good ones on top concealing rotten ones beneath, that scales are hung on a hook and not held in the seller's hand so that he can tip them. He would forbid glassmakers to make wine goblets and grape sellers to sell too many to any one customer, so as to make it a little less easy to commit the dread sin of drinking alcohol.

The schools, he said, would be improved if none but married men were allowed to teach. (Bachelorhood is always suspect.) Lawyers, like musicians, have no place in society, because, says the preacher, they "make people spend their money in vain." He admits that Andalusians are probably too litigious to make that reform possible. At least, he says, let all lawyers be investigated to make sure they are married, never touch wine, and are not libertines.

The pleasures of Cordoba were thus reflected in the censorious eyes of a zealot who saw the sin only and not the saving graces.

Indeed the look of tenth-century Cordoba might have nourished the suspicions of a puritan. The blank walls of its houses, broken only by an ornamental knocker, a barred window, and a minuscule balcony, offered scarcely a hint of the life within. Closed doors always feed the fertile imaginations of the righteous. (Architectural privacy continues today in those alleys of

Spain that have survived the nineteenth-century predilection for grand boulevards.)

In the poorer parts of town, life swam more easily to the surface. The houses held more people, and laughter and squabbles rang over the walls.

Whatever the size of the house, each was the property of a single family, that is a man—father, husband, lord. As the family multiplied, however, the lord's domain often grew more cramped. A bride entering the family might have no more than a single room to share with her husband and perhaps the first child or two.

Still, she entered the household like a queen on coronation day. The event had been preceded by delicate diplomatic negotiations in which pride, tact and a canny business sense were called for. The dowry had to be bargained to its ultimate figure, the agreement drafted by the scribe, the date set and the horoscopes of the couple properly cast by the astrologer.

Then for a week before the wedding the bride-to-be sat in state in her mother's house, receiving the compliments of women friends, neighbors and relatives, catching only the whiffs of gossip behind the smiles. At last, on the appointed date and hour, clothed in whatever finery could be mustered, seated on an ass with the dowry proudly displayed on another animal, she was escorted by family and friends in a grand parade.

Men and boys stood along the route and cheered. Over the walls came the warbling ululations of women. The bride was a lightly veiled icon being carried through the streets in what Richard Burton (in a footnote to the *Book of The Thousand Nights And A Night*) calls "the majesty of virginity."

The feasting would go on at the house of the groom until the fond farewell to virginity (the bloody stain on the sheet would be proudly exhibited as a trophy). And with it went the bride's majesty as well.

The glory of the wedding day tended to fade amid the chores of the household but the mood of celebration would return with the first signs of pregnancy. Once again there would be the glow of anticipation, though the excitement would be kept quietly bubbling within the walls of the house. When the time of delivery approached the local midwife would be summoned. If the family could afford the expense a doctor might be called, but to have a man trespass in so jealously guarded a garden was unthinkable. He would have violated the lady's modesty by his gaze and touch. Certainly he would have outraged her husband's pride of possession.

There were female doctors available, certified by the court physicians. They were learned, wise and expensive. Then, as in other times and places, female practitioners specialized in gynecology, obstetrics and pediatrics.

When the child was born the mother was again the darling of the house. There were parties to celebrate the arrival of either boy or girl, but the celebration was always grander and noisier for a boy.

Nursing the baby was the duty, if not the delight, of a lower-class mother, but the middle-class lady hired a wet-nurse and the more conspicuously wealthy sent the infant out to a baby farm to be weaned and trained and made acceptable to the delicate sensibilities of the harem. It is not likely that the custom was designed altogether for the convenience of those elegant ladies. Actually it served to restore them to what was regarded as their proper function—the delectation of their men.

The medical means by which lactation was suppressed are not clearly spelled out in the histories, but it is certain that the charms of the women were restored as quickly as possible. The man of the house would hurry to the silversmiths or goldsmiths, generally Jews, to fashion bright baubles for his lady love, who would dutifully dab on fresh makeup from a marble palette and chew pleasantly spiced gum to flavor her breath. She would refresh her spirits with music and her mind with verses recited to her by poets. And so she would ready herself as the most exciting possession of her lord.

Before the infant was packed off to the baby farm or the wet-nurse there would be the formalities of the naming, which always took place on the seventh day after birth. A boy would take the name of his paternal grandfather, to which would be added that of some illustrious ancient Islamic hero, scholar or imam. A girl would be given the name of some pious heroine of ancient days, but it was becoming fashionable in the days of Abd-er Rahman III to endow girls with the secular beauty of flower-names or star-names. In more austere times such prettiness was reserved for the names of slave girls and eunuchs.

The next great occasion for celebration was the circumcision of the son of the house, which was performed on his seventh birthday. Jews who endured the rite of initiation in their infancy quickly forgot the trauma and never knew the glory, but to a Moslem boy of seven the procedure was likely to be more memorable because it was more painful.

How much of a fuss was made at the circumcision depended on the money available. The well-to-do would throw a lavish party with feasting, dancing and poetry.

The occasion also provided the rich man with the opportunity for conspicuous philanthropy. It gave the poor man a taste of once-in-a-lifetime magnificence. And it paid tribute to the egalitarian ghost that always haunts the grandeur of Islam like a beggar at the feast. It was—and still is—customary for a wealthy father to round up poor lads who share his son's birthday. He would have them circumcised along with his son and all their expenses would be paid. Their families would be invited to dine and dance at the banquet with the rich man's other guests. All would be equal in honor.

The romance of the poor man as prince for a day, like the bride who would be queen for a day, was part of the fairy tale of Cordoba.

The poor tended, in any case, to relish vicarious pleasures. They watched the rich play polo on the fields beyond the walls. (The game had been brought over from India.) Or they would take their places on the fringes of the sporting crowd at the bull-baiting rings, where trained dogs tore at the legs and jugulars of fierce and maddened bulls.

A poor man could talk of the exploits of a nobleman's falcons and falconer. He could tell stories over rose tea of the cranes and geese plucked out of the air by this or that miraculous bird of prey.

The Caliph himself preferred to hunt boar with a pack of dogs. His handlers would spread word of the adventures of the chase, but some historians report that whenever a hunt dragged on for days, keeping the Caliph out of touch with Cordoba and the world, there was grumbling at the mosque and the market. A ruler cannot be seen to play too much or too long. The Caliph's subjects were often hard taskmasters.

In the last analysis the supreme game for rich and poor, for slave and free, was war—war in the name of Allah, war against the infidel, glorious holy war that might bring wealth to a poor man, emancipation to a slave, a wife to a bachelor, a concubine to a family man. All this and salvation, too. It was a man's chance to rise in this world and the next.

Death was a possibility but it was not a preoccupation of Andalusia. Death was a passage, nothing more. The dead body—whether of tanner or Caliph, Jew or Moslem, man or woman—was washed, clothed, set in a plain wood box and hurriedly buried with the scantest of ceremonies and no eulogy.

Life had not ended but had merely been transferred to another setting. Family and friends made little public show of their private griefs. Death in Andalusia was like a stone dropped into a deep and quiet pool, rippling the waters for a moment only.

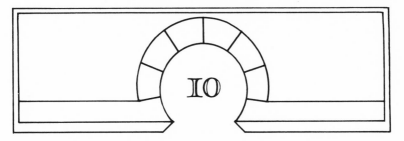

The Kidnaped Rabbi

Jews were a part of Andalusia and apart from it. This social legerdemain was made possible by the liberal spirit emanating from the court of Cordoba. Abd-er Rahman did not find it necessary to integrate everything and everyone into an Islamic world. He himself would not have fitted into a prefabricated category.

His blond hair and blue eyes testified to a heterogeneous genetic blending. In the selection of his multinational, multiracial advisers he paid tribute to the intelligence of people regardless of whether they believed in alien gods or in none. The ethnic variety of his wives and concubines and his wide-ranging taste in art showed him eager to embrace the rich diversity of the world.

In such an Arab state Jews could prosper without feeling the necessity to take on the look and sound of Arabs. When they imitated them they did so freely, out of admiration for the soft beauty of Arabic poetry, the look of Arab architecture or the grace of Arab manners. In the same way Arabs could fancy Jewish ways and adopt them unselfconsciously. There was thus no pressure on Jews in tenth-century Andalusia to retire into a ghetto. There were no laws and scarcely any customs that confined Jews to any place or occupation. When their gates were shut they were the ones who shut them.

The result was that, unlike their kinfolk in other parts of the world, great numbers of Jews owned land and farmed it. Some planted grain on the mesa but still more cultivated the vineyards of the south. If the Jews had a bit of an edge there it was because of the Koranic prejudice against the grape, though in that relaxed era some Moslems owned and worked their vineyards as if they had not been told that the end product was sinful.

On the other hand, even the most devout of Jews found Biblical support for their viniculture. In fact Scripture was interpreted as commanding Jews not only to cultivate the grape but also to work the vineyards with their hands. Jewish landowners occasionally took on some Berber field hands but for the most part they used Jewish workers, who flocked up from North Africa to breathe the relatively free air of Andalusia.

A Jewish preference for agriculture is seen in the flow of questions addressed to the rabbis of Baghdad and later of Cordoba. Problems of land management, property inheritance, relations between neighbors and between farmers and hired hands are far more numerous than those dealing with urban business affairs or with metaphysics.

For example, there is a question from a devout Jewish farmer who pointed out that sometimes "the vineyards are pruned before the Passover and the rains prevent their being plowed and they become impure and are cut down within five days; and when they are again plowed the buds drop off or fall because of the plow and the vineyard is destroyed resulting in heavy losses . . . [which] could be avoided by pruning and plowing during the intermediate days of Passover. . . ."

It is within the spirit of the law, declared the sages, for Jews or non-Jews to work the vineyards during Passover week if that seems necessary.

It is true that many of the Jews that came up from Africa or down from Gaul were likely to be skilled craftsmen or traders, because in many parts of the world the land-proud would not admit Jews to this class. Beyond Andalusia a pattern of "Jewish" occupations was developing, although as yet no one had thought of blaming the Jew for fitting the mold into which he had been cast. Most Andalusian tanners and dyers were Jews, because in North Africa Jews found themselves forced to dirty their hands with jobs disdained by the fastidious Arabs. And since tanneries and dyeing establishments emit disagreeable odors these Jewish artisans were shunted toward the edges of cities where the stench of their trade would not offend too many people. This created a district in which Jews were obliged to live, quite different from the quarters of Cordoba near the great mosque where Jews preferred to live.

In Andalusia some Jews continued the family trade of tanning and dyeing or smithing gold and silver. Others entered agriculture or trade or took to strumming lyres, or navigating or exporting. Still others took up the practice of medicine, a field that for centuries had been almost monopolized throughout the civilized world by Jews and Arabs.

Actually the study of medicine incorporated all that was known of natural history, inherited from the Greeks, Romans, Persians, Indians and Chinese. It included not only an empirically derived pharmacopoeia but also anatomy, animal husbandry and assorted bits of Aristotelean philosophy.

A familiarity with medicine was thought to be a necessary part of the intellectual equipment of any educated man, but rabbis were particularly attracted to the profession as a profitable sideline. It was considered demeaning if not unethical to accept payment for fulfilling the usual rabbinical duties: teaching, preaching, counseling or officiating at religious ceremonies. An impecunious rabbi, however, could support himself handsomely as a physician. He could thus live well without stepping out of character, as he would have if he had chosen to earn his keep as businessman, bricklayer or landowner.

The combination of rabbi and doctor, moreover, helped to impart a certain coherence to Jewish life. If a practitioner's theology was accepted as profound, one tended to follow with more confidence his prescription for a snakebite remedy. And vice versa. The arrangement also allowed the physician to view his patients whole, with all their manifold problems, physical and spiritual. The merger of spiritual and bodily problems became so characteristic of Jewish and Arab medical practice that the conscience was treated almost as if it were an anatomical entity.

Doctors did not ordinarily go to a university for a medical

education, though most had attended a Yeshiva. The medical student was expected to work closely with a well-established practitioner, study his methods and read the books that he had read. He was required to assist his master at surgery (always bloody and frequently fatal), make house calls, observe the important diagnostic signs and commit them to memory. Above all, the apprentice was required to study the bedside manner of his teacher. When he thought he was fit to be a physician he and his mentor would travel to Cordoba, where the court physician would administer a long and grueling examination. If the aspirant passed he was given a royal license to practice and he would be launched in the glow of his teacher's reputation.

If the doctor were also a rabbi—and even in some cases when he was not—his patients would present him with a mixture of medical and moral dilemmas, for in a Jewish community even chemical functions carry the heavy weight of ethical considerations. Practitioners and patients both lived at a foggy crossroads of reason, superstition, tradition and religion. For example, one Andalusian rabbi was asked whether it was permissible to violate the Sabbath in order to prepare an amulet to be worn by a woman in difficult labor.

Before considering the emergency the practitioner had to clarify his thinking on the use of amulets. Most Jewish religious authorities were opposed to such magic, although some had tortured their own logic to accommodate the popular predilection for miraculous and mystical signs. Many Jewish authorities, medical and rabbinical, were agreed, that the recitation of Biblical texts as a therapy for purely physical ills was worse than useless. The words of the Torah, they said, were meant only to cure the soul. Still, there were some who argued that if it comforted the soul it would by that very action also comfort the body. In the end most physician-rabbis shrugged and ruled that a little magic could do no harm. Healing was a pragmatic art, after all.

There were stronger feelings over a suggested prescription for diseases of the loins. This involved the engraving of a lion on a metal plate and its application during a time when the stars were in a happy conjunction. Many physician-rabbis denounced such therapy as heathenish. Others saw it as a transgression of the prohibition against graven images. There were always some, however, who thought that even though the remedy lacked scientific justification, if it had been recommended by reputable scholars of good family, it ought not to be ruled out absolutely.

The timing of the loin therapy ran up against a Jewish antipathy to astrology, although some rabbis nevertheless cast horoscopes in response to the popular fashion. Most thought that the notion of stellar control of human destiny was contrary to the Jewish idea of the powers of God and of man. Were the mechanical motions of the stars and planets more powerful than God's will? Did not the idea suggest a fatalism that contradicted the divine gift of free will to humans? And without free will where would be the celebrated Jewish ethic and that most potent, if invisible, organ of the Jew's anatomy, his conscience?

While such arguments raged amongst the scholars, the average practitioner went about his business utilizing the vast accretion of wisdom handed down by the ancients of assorted cultures, along with a great deal of nonsense from the same sources. They had not only the heritage of Galen and Hippocrates—a mixed bag—but also the 237 books by the renowned Persian contemporary, Abu-Bakr Mohammed ibn-Zakariya al-Razi (simplified by later historians to Rhazes). That prolific Persian closed his monumental literary labors with the self-deprecating caveat: "All that is written in books is worth much less than the experience of the wise doctor."

Despite his modest disclaimer Rhazes gave the physicians of Cordoba some remarkably accurate descriptions of the onset, course and symptomatology of a number of common diseases. He was particularly keen in his discussion of measles and smallpox. Other Arab and Jewish physicians had accurately diagnosed and described tuberculosis, scabies and pericarditis. Therapy, however, lagged behind diagnosis. Bloodletting was routine, and powdered gems were taken internally along with herbs and roots. Whimsy diluted experience in the doctor's theories. Even the brilliant Rhazes taught that one could determine the number of children a woman was likely to bear by counting the wrinkles on her abdomen.

In pharmacology the practitioners were on much more solid ground. The doctors of Andalusia, both Jew and Arab, knew more than anyone before them about distilling the effective ingredients of a plant, crystalizing them and working profound changes in their efficacy by heat and vaporization. Alchemists opened stalls in the markets where they performed chemical transformations with spectacular success.

Autopsies were outlawed by both Moslems and Jews, who thought that the body must be kept intact for Judgment Day. Physicians therefore had to depend on Galen for their ideas of anatomy and guess the rest. With so skimpy a background it was all the more remarkable that their guesswork was so shrewd. For example, they strongly suspected a connection linking the small arteries, veins and lungs.

A Jewish or Arab doctor would sit cross-legged on his cushion, observing in detail the general look and behavior of his patient. The manner of standing, sitting, walking, the attitude of head and hands were all significant. He would examine the site of pain and note the interplay of physical distress with the personality of the patient. He would take the pulse, deducing clues from whether it fluttered wildly, plodded slowly, thumped or barely registered. Above all he relied on a thorough urinalysis using only his well-developed senses. He would note the color of the urine, look for sediment, smell it and, above all, taste it. From such a painstaking examination he would arrive at a diagnosis that might be accurate in the case of diabetes, and somewhat less so with the wide variety of malevolent humors to which the blood was thought to be susceptible.

From a varied pharmacopoeia he would prescribe remedies that included such woodsy ingredients as camphor, cloves and myhrr and the more exotic ambergris, produced in the intestines of whales.

He would scarcely touch any patient and especially not a woman, who was guarded from even a suggestion of intimacy by the most potent taboos. The perils and discomforts of pregnancy were managed by skilled midwives, but in cases of illness the doctor diagnosed and treated women, although he had to proceed gingerly to protect his patient's modesty and his own.

If there were a valid ethical, moral or medical reason to guard the woman against conception the Jewish doctor would turn to the texts of Rhazes, which offered generally sound advice on the care of the breasts and the uterus, and listed a wide variety of contraceptive measures. These included the use of pessaries made of cabbage leaves or the inner skins of pomegranates.

Sal ammoniac and potash were suggested as useful abortifacients because they promoted menstruation. The woman was also advised to leap up promptly after every act of sexual intercourse, and jump violently backward seven or nine times. (The numbers were selected out of the Jewish lore of numerology.) Sneezing and blowing the nose were also thought to discourage conception. The sexual act itself, doctors advised, should be done as vigorously as possible in order to dislodge the semen. "Joking, too, is useful," added Rhazes.

The Cordoban approach to contraception seems quite merry, sophisticated and logical by comparison to tenth-century practices throughout much of Europe. In Germany and Eastern Europe women seeking some contraceptive help were being advised to spit three times into the mouth of a frog, eat bees, wear the testicles of a weasel or drink a concoction that included the ground penis of a wolf.

Complicated surgery, though very risky, was often attempted in Cordoba. The physician might be called upon to perform a tracheotomy or, in rare cases, to clarify the sexual anatomy of a hermaphrodite. Lesser procedures such as cauterizing, cutting or bleeding were usually managed by unlicensed physicians or apprentices.

The ethics and morals of these rabbi-doctors were derived from the Talmud but considerably updated. Rhazes composed a long list of precepts, which late in the century were condensed and refined by Isaac Judaeus, a Jewish physician who made his reputation in Egypt. "Most illnesses," wrote Judaeus, "are cured without the physician's help through the aid of nature." In a further counsel of restraint, Judaeus taught: "If you can cure the patient by dietary means do not turn to drugs." And as to the doctor-patient relationship this tenth-century physician told his colleagues: "Always make the patient feel he will be cured [even] when you are not convinced of it for it aids the healing effects of nature."

All this was before the rise in Cordoba of the great physicians, Avenzoar, Averroes and Maimonides, who tried to add a hitherto unprecedented degree of reason to religion and tradition. Unfortunately they were to preach their logic into a shrieking gale of religious fanaticism. Had they come on the scene while Abd-er Rahman III still ruled in Cordoba the chances are that they would have enjoyed the acclaim of the Andalusian medical profession, who were not then persuaded of the sinfulness of reason.

Young middle-class Jews of Andalusia lived a secular as well as a religious life, seeing no essential conflict between the two. In the Arabic manner they gloried in the sensual delights of love, drink, music and gorgeous landscape. But on suitable occasions these gallants delighted in arguing the profundities of life, a Jewish style of secular prayer. The two faces of Judaism—the mystical and the rational—would confront each other later, but in the tenth century the Jewish mind and soul made a coherent entity in which seeming opposites played creatively against each other. It was a Jewish humanism thriving in a congenial Moslem secular society.

Some Jewish poets wrote of carousals in the high Greco-Roman manner, with wine, food, bright talk and light love. Others wrote passionately of the longing for Zion. And a few, like Dunash Ha-Levi ben Labrat, simultaneously celebrated sacred and profane love, though being careful to let the first seem to take prominence. An example is Dunash's verse on receiving an invitation to a party. He anticipates the fun but adds a stern

declination that does not altogether succeed in erasing the seductive charm of the party he missed:

> The singers are accompanied
> By cithern and viol,
> The ripple of the fountains
> The murmur of the lute . . .
>
> We shall drink in the gardens
> Surrounded by lilies,
> And with songs of praise
> Ease our weary bones.
>
> We shall eat sweetmeats
> And drink from bowls,
> Pretend we are giants,
> And drink from the vats . . .

The poet turns away, like a reproving prophet at the feast:

> You no longer think
> On the law of God.
> You can be happy,
> And there are foxes in Zion.

One cannot be sure that Dunash ben Labrat did not in the
end accept the invitation. Many young Jews remembered Zion
when a romantic melancholy mood was on them but saw no
reason why this should keep them from the delights of Cordoban gardens, feasts and flowers. A touch of the spirit seemed to
help the appetite, as in the case of another rhapsodic Jewish
poet who dreamed of rising before dawn and taking a cup "of
spiced pomegranate juice from the perfumed hand of a girl
who will sing songs. . . ."

Their God-haunted laments were sometimes leavened by
playful trivia, such as the Catulluslike lines of a host disappointed with a guest's thank-you present: "And what's the
good of cheese when I am dry with thirst."

Even when they wrote of godly things they used similes as

sensual as those of the Song of Solomon. Sexual imagery in sacred contexts was common in the tenth century, though such
figures of speech reached their epitome a little later among Ca-
balists such as Isaac de Acre, who wrote:

"The Torah can be compared to a beautiful and heavenly
maiden imprisoned in an isolated chamber of a palace, who has
a secret lover known only to herself. For love of her he stands at
her door seeking in all manner of ways to catch a glimpse of
her. She, aware that he keeps his vigil at the palace, opens a little door to her secret chamber, shows for a moment her face to
her lover and then retreats to hide herself once more. He
alone—none but he—is aware of what has happened—but he
knows that she has shown herself to him for an instant because
she loves him and so his heart, his soul and all his being is
drawn toward her."

It was a time of high-flown fancies nourished by prophets
who wandered out of the deserts of Arabia and the lands of
black Africa, bringing revelations to the Jews of Cordoba concerning their exotic kinfolk. To underscore their messages of
pride, rebellion or nostalgia, many of these travelers proclaimed strange pedigrees. That phenomenal story-teller
Eldad, for example, with his white hair and his skin blasted by
desert winds, stood up in the synagogues of Cordoba, Seville
and Lucena to tell of his descent from the lost tribe of Dan. Actually, he insisted, the missing tribes were not lost at all but
were living in kingdoms of their own, free and independent,
ruling in their own right and not by the sufferance of a Caliph,
however kind.

This particular prophet had been a prosperous merchant
doing business at an Arabian crossroads, where travelers fed
but did not satisfy his appetite for romance. No one knows his
real name but it was certainly not the one he used in his travels,
Eldad. He brooded on reports of Jews living in a never-never
land of their own beyond the mountains or over the seas. As
the reality of Jewish life in Arabia became more dismaying his
fancies came to involve him utterly.

When he heard of the arrival of a group of Ethiopian Jews,

Falashas, who had been ransomed from Arab slave dealers he spent days interrogating them. Ethiopia was a land of fables. Medieval Christians spoke of it as the kingdom of Prester John, a priestly knight or knightly priest, whichever characteristic best suited the episode being told. Scholars had written of Ethiopian warriors who for a brief time had ruled Egypt. Now here were living Jews from that much-sung and little-known land.

Cut off from the world, locked in a mountainous country beyond the trade routes, the Jews of Ethiopia knew nothing of rabbinical teaching. They kept the Sabbath but lit no candles on Friday night. They offered sacrifices in the form of cakes made of fine flour. They were descended from the lost tribe of Dan and they were founding a Jewish dynasty that was to rule their land. This was not only delicious romance but heady politics, offering intoxicating visions of Jewish independence.

Whether by conscious fraud or innocent self-deception, this crossroads merchant became Eldad, a prophet of the tribe of Dan. He cultivated an eccentric accent in both Arabic and Hebrew, suggesting an exotic origin. He sprinkled his talk with antiquated Biblical turns of phrase. Finally he left his home and set out to wander among the Jews of the world. He was greeted sometimes with cordiality and at other times with skepticism. He held his listeners by yarns about his own hairbreadth escapes from cannibals and other exotic dangers. He created a history of Ethiopia, based on what he had picked up from the Falashas but considerably embellished.

Before Eldad left Cordoba to vanish in the deserts of Arabia he gave the rabbis one useful item of news. He told them that the Falashas had written their own Talmud, a collection of commentaries and explanations of the Torah. Though he never produced a copy he quoted from it convincingly. The rabbis could thus assure their audiences that even so remote and isolated a group of Jews as those in Ethiopia needed a Talmud so urgently that they had to invent one.

The rabbis would throw this story at the heads of the Karaites. These were schismatics—a terrible word for any establishment—who had come up out of Arabia preaching a fundamentalist doctrine that the divinely inspired Bible needed no rabbinical explanation, that every Jew, however lowly, could find all the wisdom he needed in the five books of the Torah. They saw no need for a Talmud or for rabbis. They would thus have overturned the law by which Jews everywhere governed their lives from religious ceremonies down to the management of property and the pursuit of agriculture. Judaism, like Islam, was a way of life.

The Karaites stalked the Jewish world like the wrath of God, threatening with damnation all who hungered for new insights, whether to cure a stomachache or find a fresh path to heaven. One of them, Solomon ben Yeruclaim, thundered: "Woe to him who leaves the Book of God and seeks others. Woe to him who passes his time with strange sciences and who turns his back upon the pure truth of God!"

Though the Karaites had their own music and their lighter moments, their general effect was grim. They separated themselves from "contaminated Jews" by a variety of practices. Some of them found a snatch of Holy Writ to justify incorporating into Judaism the oriental doctrine of the transmigration of souls. Others held to the belief that Jews must become vegetarians until the arrival of the Messiah. On Sabbath eve they sat in darkness because their strict reading of the Bible led them to believe that the injunction against lighting fires required that all flames, including those of candles lit before the Sabbath, must be extinguished.

Even more difficult to live with was the structure of kinship that they erected over the simple but vivid description of marriage in Genesis, according to which man and wife "shall be one flesh." Taking poetry literally, as they were always prone to do, the Karaites argued that there was no difference between blood relatives and in-laws, since the marriage vow had merged the partners and their families. Marriage was thus excluded even among the most distant relatives on the family tree. The temptations of incest sprouted everywhere. The rule would have made procreation almost impossible. But the Karaite leaders drew a line, without any discernible logic, permitting marriages between those whose only connection was a legal knot tied at least four or more generations earlier.

Though the Karaites were to thrive in Asia and in Eastern Europe, they were as attractive as a hair shirt to most comfortably situated Andalusian Jews. Still, there were some who saw in the movement an egalitarian approach that would deflate those aristocrats who sat in the synagogue patio proudly displaying their knowledge of the law. The Karaites granted that the Talmud and the rabbis might help to settle a few minor questions related to the precise timing of holidays or other such practical matters that might be a bit obscure in the Torah. This was not because of any authority possessed by those mortals who wrote the commentaries, the Karaites said, but "since all coins are counterfeit one might as well use the one at hand."

The synagogue that served as an arena for such ideological battles was not a Holy of Holies reserved for talking to God on ceremonial occasions; it was the center of everyday life. For the Jews of Andalusia it was their court, their town hall and their forum. It was not a building but a compound of structures, usually tall and elegant, with the Arab predilection for chaste white marble, delicate filigree, pink columns and windows arched like horseshoes.

One walked through a gate into a spacious patio. On a weekday morning one might see the community's tax collectors sitting cross-legged in a shady portico. They would be backed by clerks with their files, and confronting them would be a crowd of complaining taxpayers. People would come and go as if in the central square of a city. At one side of the courtyard there would be a hall in which community members might celebrate births, marriages, deaths and other rites of passage. That same building would also accommodate visiting Jews—strangers who would pay for their keep in travelers' tales, in scholarship, wit or poetry.

On the other side of the courtyard would stand the school where children, beginning at the age of six or seven, would learn to read and write. They would also memorize long passages of Scripture, which they would recite in tremulous sing-

song chants. At the age of ten or so the boys would be gradu-
ated to a secondary school, where more experienced teachers
would expound the greater complexities of the Talmud, with
limited excursions into other matters, such as arithmetic. Most
boys completed their formal education at the age of sixteen or
seventeen but the more privileged or the more talented went on
to a university, such as that in Cordoba, where all that was
then known of history, science and theology would be open to
them.

The school that shared the courtyard with the synagogue
was actually treated with the most awesome respect, in line
with the Jewish reverence for education. It was called the
House of the Book, and venerated even more than the Temple
itself. Adults would gather there to study the more abstruse
points of law and theology. The ruling council of elders would
meet in a schoolroom to act on all problems of the community,
from garbage disposal to the ransoming of Jewish slaves, to im-
proving relations with the Caliph. To their meetings people
would flock with questions, petitions, complaints, all respect-
fully worded but nonetheless pressed with relentless energy. If
the school was otherwise occupied and the patio too crowded
with taxpayers or with litigants arguing before a judge, the
council would gather in the synagogue itself.

Through the high arched windows, sunlight would enter in
long golden shafts, touching the raised platform where on Sabbath mornings the reader of the week would intone a section of
the Torah, the rabbi would preach and the cantor would sing.
Around the walls were ranged a variety of pews, divans, high-
backed chairs and low stools. Each such accommodation was
designed by the owner to fit his taste. Families would pay for
their places in the synagogue and would then have seats built
to their design. The architectural effect was less than harmoni-
ous and the social effect tended to be downright destructive.
Families were forever wrangling over precedence. The elders of
the synagogue distributed the places according to the social
standing of the families who applied, with an aristocratic con-
sideration of lineage as well as wealth.

The competition for synagogue seats often grew bitter. Men were known to abuse one another verbally or beat one another over the head to assert their rights. The most revered sage could scarcely succeed in calling them to some decorum.

Those who, for one reason or another, were not included in the original distribution of wall space stood or roamed about during the services, as did the children. Spaces were also sold for the women, who were shielded by lattice work so as not to distract the men from their serious business with God. Some synagogues ruled that any unused seat would have to be rented by the owner at a reasonable price to those who needed it. When no more space was available the disappointed applicants usually went off and founded a new synagogue. Often they joined with friends or colleagues in the venture. In large cities separate synagogues were built by and for weavers, tanners, silversmiths, goldsmiths and members of societies for good works or mutual burial.

It was in a particularly aristocratic synagogue in Cordoba in the year 956 that the much-revered rabbi Nathan was lecturing on a difficult Talmudic question to a coterie of young students. The rabbi and his admirers played a subtle game in which the leader held his authority by mental agility and an accumulation of weighty references and precedents, while his disciples, with all due respect, baited him with tricky questions and fussy logic-chopping. If the rabbi was stumped to a point of embarrassment he would quickly fall from power.

Rabbi Nathan was handling his followers with his customary display of erudition when a man dressed in tatters leaped up from the corner where he sat and challenged the rabbi's premises, references and reasoning. The rabbi was thunderstruck and his followers even more so. They fired their most pointed questions at the stranger. He answered them easily and gracefully, turning aside the sharpest points designed to pierce his aplomb. He held his own for hours. He was polished, witty and profound.

At last Rabbi Nathan stopped the contest. He turned to the disciples that followed him and declared with time-honored gallantry: "I am no longer the rabbi here, no longer the judge. This stranger, dressed in a sack, is my master. From this day on I am his disciple."

The man was immediately taken up by the students in great excitement. He was fitted out in proper clothes and given a suitable retinue to escort him around the town, although no one knew more about him than that he was a rabbi fished from the sea and that his name was Moses ben Hanoch. In fact he had recently been ransomed by the community from a pirate captain. Ransoms were being paid all the time and few kept track of the less-distinguished strangers once they were free. They sat around the synagogue living on the stories they told, some seeking a way to go home, some a way to stay in Cordoba, some content merely to fend off dreadful memories with the protective presence of their own people.

Until he leaped up to refute Rabbi Nathan with a burst of eloquence the stranger in the sack was such a man. After Nathan yielded to him as his superior in scholarship and rhetoric the story of Moses ben Hanoch was pieced together.

He was one of four rabbis who had been sent to raise funds from the Mediterranean Jewish communities for support of the academies of Pumbedita and Sura in Iraq, which had been waning in authority and verging on bankruptcy. The four, plus the young wife of Moses ben Hanoch and their infant son, Hanoch ben Moses, toured the Jewish towns along the Italian coast. It was while they were sailing off the Port of Bari that a pirate ship bore down on them. Some historians suggest that it may have been a Cordoban privateer commissioned by Abd-er Rahman III to prey on North African ships of the rival Fatimid Caliph. Such privateers were expected to indulge in a bit of piracy now and then as a profitable sideline. And holding rabbis for ransom was usually most profitable.

In any case the warship, captained by one ibn Rumakis (or Damakis as some historians say) scooped up the four rabbis and set a course for the likeliest ports in which to sell sages to wealthy Jews. One of the rabbis was sold in Cairo, another in Kairouan and a third in Narbonne, so that Moses ben Hanoch, his wife and son were the only captives left. They were sailing toward Andalusia when the captain began to take a heated interest in the young and beautiful but chaste wife of the rabbi. She fended him off as well as she could but grew desperate as his ardor and authority made an eventual conquest seem inevitable. She told her husband nothing of the passionate pursuit.

If the rabbi had been more worldly he might have guessed the reason for his wife's sudden interest in a ticklish theological question. On the Day of Judgment would God resurrect all the dead—even suicides? she asked her husband. It could not have occurred to him at that moment that his wife was the object of anyone's lust. Such notions did not readily find their way to the mind of Moses ben Hanoch. He became intrigued with the intellectual problem his wife had set before him. It was as if she had given him a puzzle in geometry—the science that scholars then called "The Mishna of Euclid."

He smiled benignly as with tortuous ifs and buts he argued toward a triumphant answer. No, he finally told his wife, the manner of dying would be regarded as irrelevant on Judgment Day. Whereupon—when safely out of her husband's sight, one supposes—the chaste lady leaped overboard and was drowned.

In time the widower rabbi and his little son were delivered to Cordoba and duly paid for. Dressed in rags and in a state of deep depression, he seemed no great prize, and the pirate captain was prepared to sell him cheap. However, after all Cordoba began to buzz about the brilliant coup of the ragged rabbi, the captain came to the synagogue to complain that he had been cheated of a fair price because the rabbi had concealed his talents. He was sent away empty-handed, and the Cordoban Jews celebrated the coming of a new sage.

For a thousand years historians have been telling and retelling this story as confirmed fact. Only recently have a few twentieth-century scholars expressed some doubts concerning the suicide of the beautiful wife of Rabbi Moses ben Hanoch. They do not dispute nor otherwise explain the rabbi's arrival in Cordoba in rags with no wife but with an infant son.

In time the mild-mannered rabbi took the place of honor to

which his scholarship entitled him. It was useless to dream of returning to Pumbedita when Cordoba was at his feet. Jews from all parts of the Caliphate, from Narbonne, Africa and over the mountains in Gaul, began to send their problems to Moses ben Hanoch in Cordoba instead of to the older academics of Babylon.

The spreading fame of the new rabbi shed added luster on the Caliphate. Abd-er Rahman saw in the emancipation of Cordoban Jews from their spiritual dependence on Arabia a happy parallel with his own assumption of the Caliph's title and his independence from Moslem capitals. Now both Moslem and Jew in Andalusia were free from foreign overlordship, spiritual or military.

The authority of Moses ben Hanoch, chief rabbi of Cordoba, was hailed and protected by the Caliph's friend, adviser, diplomat, physician and poet, then considered to be the world's most powerful Jew. In the words of a medieval writer it was he who "opened the gates of cities not by swords or arrows but by his eloquence and the sweet clarity of his thoughts." His name was Abu-Yusuf Hasdai ben Isaac ibn Shaprut.

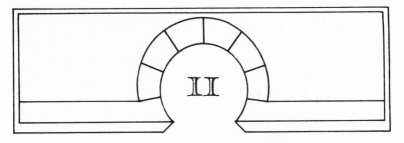

Doctor and Diplomat

Hasdai ibn Shaprut came of "good family," a phrase that suggested to tenth-century Jews a lineage of intellectual distinction, generosity, piety and wealth, in that order of importance. He exhibited the self-confidence of the well-born by a display of charm and good manners that may have carried a hint of condescension, although no such failing is recorded by his worshipful chroniclers.

He was a worldly young man, respectful of religious tradition but not conspicuously pious. He was not as concerned with the Talmud as he was with the poetry and politics of his time and with the new rationality that was quickening the heart of the Caliphate.

His father, Isaac, celebrated for his piety and philanthropy, had been a pillar of the Jewish establishment in Jaen. He had collected a library of some distinction and was known as a patron of literature. The writers and scholars whom he subsidized were not the poets who used the sacred language of Hebrew to celebrate wine and women or who imitated the Arabic cadences and indulged in linguistic acrobatics. The beneficiaries of Isaac ibn Shaprut had to keep their minds on sacred themes and adapt their verse to the ritual of the synagogue.

The venerable Isaac, for reasons that are now unknown, moved his family from Jaen to Cordoba, where, some time between the years 910 and 915, Hasdai was born. It was about the time that Abd-er Rahman III came to the throne.

The elder Shaprut continued to bestow his wealth on worthy charities—building a synagogue here, a library there—but still put aside enough to give Hasdai proper tutors and to launch him upon a suitably intellectual career. Hasdai grew up, however, in a society that had burst the provincial and tribal bounds his father knew. The young man reveled in a legacy of Baghdad, Byzantium, ancient Greece, Rome, Egypt, India and China along with the glories of the Torah and Talmud.

Heinrich Graetz, the authoritative nineteenth-century historian of the Jews, becomes almost sprightly in speaking of Hasdai:

"His easy, pliant and genial nature was free both from the heaviness of the Orientals and the gloomy earnestness of the Jews. His actions and expressions make us look upon him as a European, and through him, so to speak, Jewish history receives a European character."

Hasdai cultivated not only a literary Hebrew but an equally stylish Arabic. A couple of priests taught him Latin and so opened his way to the study of natural sciences and medicine. He could also speak and write the popular language called Romance, a modified Latin on its way to becoming Spanish and absorbing a good deal of Arabic en route. He was, in short, a medieval man with a premature Renaissance appetite for the glories of the world.

There seems to be no record of how Hasdai looked, since those who wrote about him were content to describe mainly the brilliance of his mind and the gentility of his manners. He had few critics, and those few were seemingly motivated by personal clashes they might have had with him after his power somewhat subverted his character.

In his youth he must have been viewed by many families as eminently suitable marriage material but—and this was almost un-Jewish of him—apparently he stayed a bachelor all his life. Since his charm was winning and his style gallant, and since he was far from shy or overly bound by convention, one must assume that he loved and was loved not only as a leader but as a man. With whom and how he took such pleasures is unrecorded.

He developed his interest in medicine very early in his student years. He completed his theoretical studies, based on Galen though not limited to him. He then worked as an apprentice and finally passed the requisite examination prepared by the court physicians. He became quite popular as a Cordoban general practitioner but set himself the goal of rediscovering a seemingly miraculous pharmaceutical panacea that had been known to the ancients but had long been lost.

The original formula, it was said, was devised by Mithradates VI, who ruled the kingdom of Pontus on the shores of the Black Sea until he was conquered by Pompey in the first century B.C. This king was obsessed by a fear of poisons, whether in the fangs of snakes or dropped into his food by assassins. In his efforts to find an antidote he experimented freely on his slaves, whose ranks, one supposes, needed constant replenishment.

The king developed what appeared to be a successful formula for an antidote to common poisons. It came to be called Mithradatum. This had a considerable vogue throughout the Mediterranean world among those in power who were haunted by a fear of poison. Some two hundred years later Nero's medical adviser Andromachus improved on the old formula by adding a number of ingredients, including the chopped meat of venomous snakes. It was this last rather shocking addition that gave the new antidote the name *theriaca,* meaning "wild beast."

Galen and subsequent investigators threw more ingredients into the pot until one had to have at hand more than one hundred substances to manufacture the improved theriaca. Its reputed powers also grew, so that municipalities began producing it in quantity and advocating its use not only for snakebite and subtler poisons but also for asthma, impotence and the plague, among other dire disorders.

(Theriaca as rediscovered by Hasdai came ultimately to include opium and survived as a panacea until late in the nineteenth century, when European and American pharmacists reluctantly relinquished it for greater wonder drugs.)

When Hasdai ibn Shaprut began his practice in Cordoba the secrets of Nero and subsequent panacea hunters had been lost or garbled. Hasdai used his linguistic studies to unravel fragments of old scrolls and in the end came up with a formula for theriaca that, with some confidence, he offered as probably very close to the ancient model. Other physicians agreed that by ingenious associations and etymologies he had correctly identified the herbs and potions listed in an old formulae. It was acclaimed as a breakthrough of enormous clinical significance.

Abd-er Rahman sent for Hasdai, of course, and, being impressed with the young man, appointed him to serve as one of the court physicians. The stocky Caliph, still lithe and active though in his fifties, and the genial, soft-spoken Jewish physician, then in his thirties, had reason to like each other. Neither was dogmatic about his religion and neither saw in the other a man beyond the pale. They could converse not only concerning the advances of medicine and of science in general but also of politics and art.

In view of Abd-er Rahman's declared policy of recruiting political aides from outside the preserves of Arab aristocracy, it is not surprising that he found a post for Hasdai. Certainly a Caliph who could make room at the top for Eastern European slaves would not hesitate to appoint a Jew who was as much a product of Cordoba as he was himself. He gave Hasdai the important post of director of customs, in charge of collecting revenue from every ship entering or leaving the ports of the Caliphate. As a major source of income for the government the department had to present a shining example of efficiency and honesty. Corruption in an agency given into the hands of a Jew would be embarrassing for the Caliph and dangerous for the Jew.

Hasdai took the job and carried it off with his customary even-tempered aplomb, conducting the business with a grace, formality and eloquence much valued by the Caliph in his bureaucrats.

Hasdai was also assigned to be spokesman, ombudsman and governor of his people. The Caliph granted him viceregal authority to settle all disputes and develop the necessary statutes to regulate Jewish life. The Jews, who took his advancement as a tribute to themselves, responded by calling him prince and flooding him with complaints and demands.

His title of Nasi or prince, although not a hereditary one, was taken seriously enough by the Jews of Cordoba so that Hasdai was accorded a kind of royal homage. In turn he displayed a noble largesse, scattering alms as if he were a great lord. It became a minor fashion to write poetry in his honor, flattering him as a power in his own right and as conduit to and from a greater power. It is possible that the Jews of Cordoba felt themselves more of a nation with a prince of their own, just as did the Jews of Narbonne. By temperament and history Jews tend to be royalists as well as rebels.

The Caliph found still another use for Hasdai's talents. So long as Cordoba dealt only with Andalusian rebels or with Arab and Berber states in North Africa or with the old Caliphates of Babylon, a knowledge of Arabic, graced by the customary literary flourishes, was enough. Now, however, the Caliph of Cordoba had to deal with the Christian kingdoms in the north and beyond the mountains. For such a correspondence only Latin would do.

Though not averse to drawing on Christian talent, the Caliph was wary of priests as he was of mullahs and rabbis. For Abd-er Rahman politics was a secular game. The mullahs grumbled at that, for it was contrary to orthodox Islamic principles, but they would fly into a storm at the spectacle of an infidel priest conducting their foreign affairs. The Caliph therefore turned to Hasdai, who was discreet, perceptive, worldly and gifted with an elegant Latin style. He offered the Caliph sound advice and an enormous fund of background information on geography, politics, poetry, linguistics and natural science. It was also helpful to have him available for consultation by the other doctors on the palace staff. And it added to the prestige of the court to have in attendance the renowned rediscoverer of theriaca.

When diplomatic overtures came from Byzantium Hasdai was obviously the man to handle the affair. The Byzantine emperor of the time was Constantine VII, called Porphyrogenitus because he was born in a chamber decked out in royal purple. He was never very interested in imperial power, preferring to have himself admired as a scholar and an artist. To support that image he gathered around him a staff of erudite men and set them to write encyclopedias and histories. The only aspect of empire that seemed to interest him was the theatrical, the ritualistic. He himself wrote *The Book of Ceremonies* to instruct his diplomats and courtiers on etiquette. It was perhaps the only subject on which they took their emperor seriously.

What impelled Byzantium to think of Cordoba at all was the growing nuisance of the Fatimid navy, which was preying on Byzantine shipping from North African bases. Byzantine diplomats reasoned that the best way to stop a Fatimid was with an Omayyad. Accordingly they set their emperor to woo Abd-er Rahman III. Diplomacy of any sort moved slowly in those years but Byzantine diplomacy, freighted with the emperor's delight in the ceremonial dance, was particularly ponderous.

In 947 a Byzantine eunuch arrived in Cordoba attended by a glittering retinue and bearing gifts to Abd-er Rahman but empowered only to invite the Caliph to send an emissary to Constantinople for friendly discussions and an exercise in protocol. The eunuch displayed the finery of his emperor and in turn beheld the finery of the Caliph. He then proceeded northward on a similar ceremonial mission to Otto the Great, the emperor rising from the ruins of the German part of the Carolingian empire. Fatimid pirates had made their way up from Italy, making the Alpine passes hazardous and bringing Otto into common cause with Byzantium.

In the following summer—948—a delegation from the Caliph led by a Latin-speaking Catholic priest sailed from Cordoba to Constantinople carrying gifts to the Byzantine emperor and an invitation to send a mission to Cordoba. It took the priest some three months to make the journey and, what with resting, feasting, ceremonial audiences and sight-seeing, it was the end of the year before he returned to Cordoba.

In the spring of 949 three Byzantine warships arrived at the Andalusian port of Pechina (subsequently to be called Almería). The Caliph dispatched the usual eunuch and retinue, heavily laden with gifts, to the port to greet the ambassadors. The visitors came up by easy stages to Cordoba, where the city turned out in a gala display as the Byzantine party was escorted to the palace of one of the numerous princes of the realm.

Abd-er Rahman and the court, which usually included Hasdai, galloped down from Madinat al-Zahra on streets covered with red carpets, with the Sudanese guard flashing scimitars, with the rumbling of tambours and the strumming of lutes. The Caliph met the Byzantine envoys in the *madjlis* of the Alcazar across the road from the Great Mosque.

With a superb sense of theater Abd-er Rahman was clad in a simple white robe of coarse material. He sat cross-legged on the floor, a scimitar beside him. The contrast with his opulent guard and the carpeted road was overwhelming, like a pure diamond in a gaudy setting.

The courtesies however, must have been as elaborate as Constantine Porphyrogenitus could have wished. The envoys knelt and handed to the Caliph an elaborately carved silver box with a lid of solid gold. Inside was a blue parchment scroll bearing a heavy gold seal. On one side of the seal was a miniature portrait of the emperor himself with his son. The other side—and it was hard to know which was heads and which was tails—bore the face of Jesus.

Unrolled, the blue scroll was seen to bear a message in gold Greek letters that not even the scholarly Hasdai could translate. The meaning of the letter, it turned out, was as nothing compared with the artistry of the presentation. It was an illuminated bill of lading—a list of the gifts the envoys had brought. In addition to the usual bolts of silk and bars of gold and rare gems there were the presents that best characterized the giver—rare literary works masterfully copied. One of those was a work by Paulus Orosius, a fifth-century churchman from Tarragona. His *History* was an effort to refute the notion that the empire had declined because the old Roman gods had been outraged by official acceptance of Christianity. The subject was of only academic interest to Moslems and Jews, although the author was an Iberian.

Another great work in the envoys' baggage was received with far greater excitement although it was in Greek, much less accessible than Latin. It was the leading medical classic of its time, a gigantic pharmacological text presenting some six hundred plants in handsome illustration and elegant description. It listed the properties of each, the indications for use, the suggested dosages and possible side effects. It was *De Materia Medica*, a work of the first-century Greek physician Pedanius Dioscorides, who not only compiled most of what was then known about medicinal herbs but also added the findings of his own field research, arrived at in the spare moments of a military career. The Arabs had not neglected it. Actually the Abbasid Caliph of Baghdad had engaged some Christian scholars to translate it, but since these monks were neither physicians nor herbalists they were at a loss to find equivalents of many of the Greek plants and therapies mentioned by Dioscorides. Because there were wide gaps and glaring inaccuracies in the version that had come out of Baghdad, all of Cordoba's medical community hankered after an authentic version of *De Materia Medica*.

The Caliph and Byzantine envoys watched the excitement of the doctors, Arab, Christian and Jewish, who stared in wonder and frustration at the undecipherable Greek characters. Then the Caliph brought on his poets, who were to improvise for the guests, some of whom may have understood enough Arabic to appreciate the word-juggling they were about to hear.

Actually the court's most brilliant poets, including one who had been lured at enormous expense from Baghdad, had an off day, performing lamely at what was to be an elaborate display of Cordoban literary skill. Overawed into silence by the grandeur of the company and the challenge of the day, they were about to disgrace their Caliph when Sa'id al-Balluk, an old teacher, lawyer and poet of a Berber family, rose and rattled off a long discourse on the glories of Cordoba—all in impeccable rhyme and meter and in the most florid Arab style of imagery and metaphor. The performance won the lasting gratitude of the Caliph, who afterwards appointed him to a lifetime post as a judge.

The caustic Sa'id later delivered with impunity some very harsh criticism of the Madinat al-Zahra. When the Caliph asked him to comment on the gold-and-silver roofs of the royal buildings the aging curmudgeon said: "I would never have believed that some demon could have debased you to the level of the infidels." Instead of lopping off the old man's head, the Caliph accepted the strongly worded suggestion, ordered the gold and silver removed and substituted a more modest roof. All that was still in the future when Sa'id proved himself a literary hero at the reception of the Byzantine ambassadors.

In time the Byzantine envoys left for home, bearing the Caliph's request that the emperor lend them a scholar who could translate Greek into Latin. What the Caliph may have communicated to Byzantium concerning the Fatimid pirates, the ostensible occasion of the embassy, is not clear from the history books.

The piracy crisis was replaced in time by other and graver political questions, but the preparation of *De Materia Medica* in a form in which it could be passed on to subsequent generations was a matter of far more significance. That seems to have been the view of the scholarly emperor Constantine Porphyrogenitus.

In 952, some five years after the first Byzantine mission was sent to Cordoba, a monk named Nicolas arrived on loan from Constantine to help translate Dioscorides. Hasdai organized a team of physicians and copyists and herbalists to carry out whatever research was necessary but took upon himself the prime job of collaborating with the monk on a definitive edition of *De Materia Medica* in Latin and Arabic.

To Abd-er Rahman the translation would be a significant achievement of his Caliphate, no matter that it was done by a Christian monk and a Jewish scholar.

The matter of pirates continued to trouble the European powers, including the new German entity springing up in

Northern and Central Europe. Otto I, known subsequently as the Great, was in the process of building on the fragments of the Carolingian empire a structure that would eventually appear in history as the Holy Roman Empire. He had not yet succeeded in maneuvering the pope into crowning him, but Otto was well on his way when he sent an envoy to Cordoba asking that the Caliph do whatever was necessary to control whatever pirate bands were operating from Spanish bases.

Otto was a tough man and certainly he played a very tough political game with the pope, but he was nevertheless a devoted churchman. In his vast, disordered and contentious realm the only literates were the high ecclesiastics from whom he drew his counselors.

When in 950 an Arabized Christian bishop from Cordoba caught up with the emperor, probably near Mainz, he was received royally. It seemed a gracious gesture on the part of the Caliph of Cordoba to use a bishop as a messenger to the chief protector of the Church. The letter itself, however, was a major diplomatic gaffe, which is scarcely explicable except as an example of bureaucratic arrogance and a lapse of vigilance at the executive level. It contained references to Christianity that outraged the churchly advisers to the German monarch.

Otto was so taken up with wars and politics in Germany and Italy, and among the Eastern tribes, that he took almost three years to respond. Astonishingly his temper had not improved in the interim. Neither had that of his advisers. They drafted a stinging response full of ingenious insults to Islam. It was strongly suggested that such blasphemy might well be dangerous to the messenger, who might have to be offered as a sacrifice.

Otto asked the bishop of Metz to find a volunteer. He in turn asked the abbot of the Benedictine monastery of Gorze to select a couple of hardy potential martyrs. Two monks were thereupon proposed as candidates for the sacrifice. One of them became too panicky to be allowed out of the monastery. The other was the prior who had helped to found the monastery. Brother John of Gorze was a passionate man, burning with re-

ligious zeal, but he was also a well-traveled man, who had been
to Italy and France, who knew how to deliver even so hot a
message with the necessary niceties. He went off bearing gifts to
the Caliph, for it would have greatly demeaned Otto to send
even his insults in a plain scroll.

With him went another monk, no doubt persuaded by
John's grim determination, a businessman from Verdun, and
two Jews, who enter and vanish from history with little more
than their names—Saul and Joseph. Why John of Gorze included these Jews in his delegation is a matter for speculation. Were they navigators, translators, advisers on Arab
protocol? It is not known. Also traveling with the delegation
were some remnants of the Caliph's party of emissaries who
had come to Germany three years earlier. The bishop who
carried that ill-worded message to Otto had died waiting
for an answer.

The strangely assorted group, on what must have seemed a
doomed mission, traveled by mule and ship in the summer of
953. It is a pity that their voyage was not recorded in greater
detail than John of Gorze saw fit. They must have carried on a
fascinating dialogue, touching perhaps on faith, morals, politics and martyrdom as well as on the sights and sounds of medieval Europe and the price of wolfbane.

They arrived in Cordoba in the fall of the year and were
taken to a princely villa where they were left to while away
their time in lavish idleness. The Caliph's representatives, who
saw the group from time to time, gently deflected Brother
John's increasingly irritated protests by reminding him that,
after all, the Caliph had been kept waiting three years for an
answer from Otto. Surely, they suggested, John could put up
with a few months spent in the best accommodations Cordoba
had to offer.

Actually the Caliph was stalling for time, because word had
leaked that the message John carried was so offensive to Islam
as to demand, at the very minimum, the decapitation of the
messenger, and perhaps even war against Otto. Clearly, it was
felt, it would be better for the peace of the world if such letters

were never written. Once written, it would be best if they were not read.

The undoing of Otto's message was a matter calling for exquisite tact. The Caliph put the affair in the hands of Hasdai. Although in the beginning Brother John refused to divulge the contents of Otto's letter, he eventually yielded to Hasdai's blend of argument, friendly advice and delicate references to the inevitable consequences of blasphemy under the stern Islamic code. He confirmed the worst: The letter was highly explosive.

The year 953 came to an end with John and his party allowed to celebrate the Christmas holidays at a nearby church, after which they returned to the gentle life of an Andalusian court in a sumptuous villa amid luxuries that must have shocked an austere monk.

In the spring of 954, a bishop came to the villa to advise the monk that everyone would breathe much more easily if he would find a way to avoid delivering the message. One's faith may be inviolable, but surely one can fit one's instructions to circumstances, the bishop pleaded. Indeed, Mozarabes—those Christians clad in burnooses to mark their adaptation to an Islamic world—had to make these adjustments all the time. They were necessary adjustments sanctioned by the Church.

Brother John furiously rejected such compromise. He was ordered to deliver a message he knew would doom him. He would not shrink from the fate he expected.

Early in 955, as John was on his way to church, a message was put into his hand pointing out that he held the fate of all the Christians in Andalusia. The Caliph's duty to Islam might be seen as requiring not only John's head, it was pointed out, but the heads of all available Christians, if the letter were delivered. On the other hand, the unsigned note informed the monk, if Otto's inflammatory message were not officially transmitted, the Caliph would be pleased to enhance the lives of Christians in his realm.

John's logic is not altogether clear, but he drew an analogy between such Christian advice and that of Haman, who urged his king to let him slaughter the Jews. Was this odd reference attributable to the frequent visits to the villa of Hasdai ibn Shaprut? Perhaps, because it is known that the monk had conceived an admiration and a deep affection for this Jewish negotiator. Nevertheless, Hasdai had so far failed to persuade John to a solution that would be less ideological and more politic.

As the third year of John's strange embassy opened, the question of war or peace, of life or martyrdom, was being weighed in the monk's uncluttered simplicity of mind. The Caliph and the emperor would have preferred to bend their supple consciences around the hard realities of politics, but John, having no responsibility for the world or for anything but his soul, could afford the luxury of inflexibility.

In the end the Caliph chose a direct approach. He sent a message to John asking for advice on how to solve the dilemma of the message nobody wanted to hear. John, possibly because he was worn out by the luxurious idleness of his days, possibly because the sweet reasonableness of Hasdai had at last made some impression on him, decided to relax his rigid spirit. He suggested that the Caliph send an ambassador to Otto asking him to dispatch new instructions to his faithful servant, John.

A Christian layman who spoke fluent Latin volunteered for the mission. For greater protection he was ordained not only as a priest but also as a bishop. The Church in Cordoba was as eager as the Caliph to evade the terrible consequence of the monk's message. They organized an impressive retinue and sent the bishop-messenger on his way on a June morning in 955.

It took the bishop ten weeks to reach John's monastery of Gorze. He made it to Metz before the snow fell and had to stay there until the spring. Then the travelers, along with the abbott of Gorze and another bishop picked up along the way, went on to Frankfurt where, after the usual delays for protocol, they were granted an audience with Otto.

The original insult had long been forgotten and the emperor, dreaming of adventures in Italy, saw every reason to make a friend of the Caliph. He sent off a new ambassador with instructions to thank Brother John for his loyalty and his heroic steadfastness of purpose. The monk was now to destroy the collection of insults and to see if he could draft a treaty of friendship with the Caliph, stipulating an end to piracy in the mountains, and also a beneficent neutrality in the event that Otto's armies should embark on a parade through Italy. The new instructions arrived in June 956.

John, possibly with more relief than he would have cared to admit, accepted his new orders and, three years late, was given a royal reception at the Madinat al-Zahra. He rode on the customary royal red carpet to the palace. Before him and behind him galloped the ceremonial cavaliers of the Caliphate, the Sudanese guards on Arabian horses, letting their cloaks fly and flourishing their scimitars aloft. The monk noted that the Caliph's light cavalry were mounted quite handsomely and effectively on mules.

John of Gorze, clad in somber brown robe and cowl, walked into the royal audience chamber where Abd-er Rahman sat enthroned amid gold, pink and blue columns, facing his pools, his trees, his orchards, his fields and beyond them the Guadalquivir. The monk presented Otto's message of peace and affection as if there had never been a correspondence of curses.

The Christian monk could now cultivate the friendship of Hasdai, the Jewish courtier of the Caliph, less guardedly and in greater leisure. It is not known precisely what was accomplished by John's mission, but in the years that followed, the Caliphate did nothing to harass the German emperor, and the Christians of Andalusia continued to enjoy the peace that comes from compromise.

Actually, in that final year of Brother John's mission—before he returned to Gorze to become abbot and to write his memoirs—Hasdai could not have been as available for chatting as either would have liked. The Caliph had found another task for his doctor-diplomat, this one with one of the quarrelsome Christian kings on the northern borders.

Early in his reign the Caliph had been obliged to fight Ordoño II of Leon. Periodically that minor monarch would sweep down from his walled dominions to ravage the country-side. Afterwards he would nail to the gates the heads of his Moslem foes and dedicate a new church—or rededicate an old one—by way of sanctifying the bloodshed and legitimizing the loot.

Later on, in 939, when Ramiro II of Leon formed an alliance with the wily queen-regent Theuda of Navarre, Abd-er Rah-man came close to catastrophe at the battle of Simancas. The Caliph's armies were led by one of his favorite Slav generals, Najda, to whom the purebred Arab princelings had been forced to salaam. It is safe enough to humiliate dependent princes in peacetime but a mistake to send them, still brooding, into battle. At Simancas, the princes and nobles deserted their Slav commander and led a general rout. When they saw Najda killed they tried to stem the panic, but it was too late and in the disorder whole regiments of the Caliph's armies were wiped out. The outcome of the battle at Simancas, it was said, gave heart to Christians as far away as England and the German forests.

It might have signaled the end of Moslem rule if at that time the Christian forces had been capable of political unity and military discipline. As it was, Leon, Navarre and Castile were soon embroiled in deadly internecine warfare. The Caliph, for the sake of his own prestige, and to keep the Christian warriors from straying into Moslem territory, kept up the pressure on his northern frontier. His generals, mainly Slavs now and with-out even a show of Arab lieutenants, sent back to Cordoba a stream of souvenirs—crosses, church bells and occasionally the heads of fallen Christians.

In 955, Ordoño III of Leon and Abd-er Rahman simultan-eously felt an urgent need for peace on the frontier. The Caliph was faced with a threat of invasion from the Fatimids of North Africa and Ordoño desired a respite so that he could be free to demolish his half-brother, Sancho of Navarre.

The Caliph thereupon broke into Hasdai's routine of pleas-ant chats with John of Gorze and of playing the prince among the Jews of Cordoba and Lucena. Hasdai was dispatched on his first foreign mission—to make peace with Leon. He accomplished the affair smoothly enough but no great diplomatic bargaining was necessary. Both sides were so eager for peace that it was a simple matter to negotiate a kind of mutual disarmament.

Ordoño readily agreed to Hasdai's proposals for eliminating certain fortifications that had always constituted jumping-off points for incursions into the Caliphate. Hasdai thus brought home a treaty that left the Caliph free to organize a defense against the North African threat.

A war fever then gripped the Caliphate, from the fashionable salons of the capital to the Jewish synagogues. There loyalty to Abd-er Rahman and to Hasdai was loud, vigorous and heartfelt, for Jews could scarcely imagine that an alternative regime would prove as safe or as pleasant.

Recruiters beat the drums up and down Andalusia to build a navy and an army that would once and for all settle the threat from the rival Caliphs across the straits.

All was in order in 955 when Ordoño III died and left the throne available to his sworn enemy and half-brother, Sancho the Fat. This was a most unfortunate prince who had the ambitions of a gallant hero encased in grotesque rolls of lard, which rendered him ridiculous. His attempts to subdue the scornful nobility of Leon usually led to hilarious laughter. He could not mount a horse without an embarrassing amount of engineering and finally had to give up riding altogether. That made it difficult to lead his men in battle or on parade. As a matter of fact, he found it awkward even to walk without leaning on an attendant.

Sancho attempted to assert himself by disowning the treaty his late half-brother had signed with the Caliph. He resolutely refused to leave unfortified the frontier positions specified in the treaty that Hasdai had secured. There was nothing for the Caliph to do but to send part of his carefully assembled forces from their southern bases north to chastise Sancho the Fat.

The Caliph's army did that effectively, but their victory only served to undermine whatever tatters of power were left to the wretched Sancho. His cousin, the king of Castile, contrived to stir up a faction of the army that, in the spring of 958, sent the king rolling eastward toward Pamplona.

Oddly enough the kingmakers of Leon, with some help from Castile, foisted upon the kingdom a far more deformed character than Sancho the Fat. He was Ordoño IV, otherwise known as El Malo—the Wicked. He was singularly unattractive, but a hunchbacked king with a malevolent face could evoke a chilling horror not incompatible with majesty. His subjects did not laugh at him as they did at Sancho.

The fat prince went home to Pamplona where his uncle Garcia and his grandmother Theuda ran the kingdom of Navarre. Theuda had gotten used to ruling the country while serving as regent for her son Garcia. She used to don armor and take to the field at the head of her armies. She was not overwhelmingly successful as a general—having had to acknowledge the suzerainty of the Caliphate on at least one occasion—but her bravery was never in doubt. And as governor and politician she was generally acknowledged to be one of the most capable of all the Christian rulers of Spain. For a woman who could govern Navarre in those days when treachery and a lack of scruple were the requisites of leadership, there was no difficulty in ruling her son Garcia. As he advanced to middle age and she to old age she allowed the nominal king to sign state documents, as long as she countersigned them. For a quarter of a century Theuda had led her kingdom, avoiding all threats to the throne, including financial bankruptcy. She was an effective ruler.

Clearly she had a sentimental side, for she was inordinately fond of her unfortunate grandson Sancho. She was determined to restore him to the throne of Leon, although apparently that would take considerable doing, since it would mean that Navarre would have to confront Castile as well as the people of Leon, who tended to laugh at the spectacle of their ponderous prince being groomed for his post by his aging grandmother.

Theuda saw that Sancho's problem was not gluttony, or at least not solely that. The queen mother was a level-headed lady who did not believe that her grandson had been transformed into an elephantine freak by malevolent spirits or as a punishment for his family's or his own iniquities. It was, she surmised, a medical matter. She needed, then, a doctor and an army. For either or both there was only one place to turn—Cordoba. Everyone knew that the Jews and Arabs had a near-monopoly of medical skills. And the armies of Cordoba were the only ones to strike terror in the heart of a Christian city-state. Of course, there was the question of seeming to crawl into bed with the anti-Christ, but such sins can be atoned for in time. It was also true that Moslems had burned and plundered Navarrese villages, but so had the Christians of Castile and Leon. If one does not make peace with one enemy one must with another and, after all, with whom can one make peace if not with an enemy?

The queen sent a mission to Cordoba bearing the usual gifts and sweet words. Her ambassadors stipulated the queen's concerns—medical attention for her oversized grandson and perhaps some assistance that the Caliph might be kind enough to offer to remedy the terrible injustice that had driven the poor young man from his throne.

The Caliph sent word that a physician and a statesman would be sent to confer with Her Majesty at Pamplona. There was only one physician-statesman in the court of Cordoba, and that was Hasdai.

The Caliph's envoy went off to Pamplona, where he proceeded to display a consummate knowledge of why men grow fat and how aging queens can be played upon as on a lute. He examined Sancho the Fat and talked with him at length. Finally he declared that in his professional view something could be done to reduce the dethroned monarch to something approaching human proportions.

Unfortunately, however, it would be difficult to affect such a transformation in Pamplona. In Cordoba, he pointed out, he had his medications, implements, advisers and texts. Before Sancho came, however, it would be well to settle a few controversies that would otherwise trouble the minds of patient and physician, the doctor suggested. Would Sancho reaffirm a pledge made by his predecessors to dismantle the fortifications on the frontier? Sancho temporized but in the end complied with the doctor's orders.

Then, over lunches and dinners and in conversations while walking and riding, Hasdai hinted that once Sancho was of a size to fit a throne, a Moslem army might be available to put him into it. Such affairs would require the presence of the queen, he pointed out, and suggested that she accompany her grandson when he came to Cordoba for the cure. The queen felt neatly boxed in. Never before had a Christian been obliged to so openly solicit the help of an infidel to take a Christian throne.

Hasdai appreciated the delicacy of the queen's position, but he might have pointed out that to the Caliph the very Christian queen of Navarre was as much an infidel as he was to her. For him, as for her, the precedent would be far-reaching. Yet the exigencies of the queen's situation demanded extraordinary boldness.

With the queen wavering, Hasdai pressed his luck and suggested that since it would be a royal state visit with a critical agenda for discussion, it would be proper to allow her son Garcia, the king of Navarre, to come as well. No doubt he expatiated on the delights of Cordoba, the red carpets, the Madinat al-Zahra, the glories of the Caliphate. And, above all, he stressed the political astuteness Her Majesty would demonstrate by such a move. Without such queenly brilliance, he suggested, Sancho might well regain his figure, but probably not his throne.

A Jewish commentator of the time reported that the "haughty" queen had been conquered "by the charm of his [Hasdai's] words, the ripeness of his wisdom, the power of his cunning and his manifold wiles." In the autumn of that same year, 958, the queen mother, with her royal son and grandson in tow, took the road from Pamplona to Cordoba.

It was a long procession that wound diagonally across the Iberian peninsula. Sancho, who could not straddle a horse, was carried on a litter or walked leaning on his new-found friend and physician, Hasdai. The queen, in her seventies, and her middle-aged, dutiful son, the king of Navarre, rode an assortment of vehicles that preserved as much as possible of the royal dignity. A collection of priests and nobles, soldiers, servants and muleteers brought up the rear.

They plodded along for five hundred miles, up the Sierra de Guadarrama and down onto the great central plains, then up again into the Sierra Morena and at last down to the valley of the Guadalquivir, where the Caliph's honor guard came to meet them and bring them to the capital.

All along the route, in cities and villages people came to stare at the royal Christians and the black-robed priests on their way to petition the Caliph of Cordoba. Few could have missed the high irony that the whole affair seemed to be managed by a beguiling Jew.

Once again the Caliph's troops came out in full regalia. Once again the poets composed elaborate commemorative rhymes, all probably lost on the guests of honor, though Hasdai was on hand to interpret from Arabic to Romance or (for the benefit of the clergy) to Latin.

The Moslems of Cordoba came out in huge throngs to watch the royal infidels being overawed by Moslem magnificence. The Jews of Cordoba were even more ecstatic, for the diplomatic coup had been brought off by their own princeling. They knew that as Hasdai mounted to glory his people would undoubtedly rise in the favor of the Caliph. Their writers went to work in a glow of euphoria, of which this is a fair sample:

"Bow down, O ye mountains, to Judah's chief . . . God hath given him to us as our chief; he standeth at the right hand of the King, who calleth him Prince, and hath exalted him above the mighty. . . . Without sword or arrows, by the word of his mouth alone he hath taken by storm the fenced cities of the devourers of accursed flesh."

It is not likely that for his royal guests Hasdai translated that last unkind reference to the Christian taste for pork.

When he was not needed to soothe the queen mother or otherwise engage in the ritual dances of diplomacy Hasdai and a team of doctors went to work on Sancho. Unfortunately the methods they used to render the fat from the prince have not been transmitted to later generations of doctors.

Very little has come down from medieval sources on the treatment of obesity. Often fat was considered a status symbol beyond the reach of the poor. Although the ancients had deplored it as a cause of shortness of breath, if not of life, it was not considered a major medical problem.

It is likely that although Hasdai and his colleagues dressed up their cure with herbal concoctions—perhaps appetite depressants—they attained their success by a rigidly enforced diet and a regimen of exercise that kept the caloric intake substantially below the outgo.

Whatever the method, within six months Hasdai had Sancho in very presentable shape. Historians depict the prince restored to the slim proportions of early youth but that may be an exaggeration. In that age of wonder chroniclers insisted on describing the merely remarkable as absolutely miraculous. It seems to be true that Sancho, at the end of his treatment, could not only walk unaided but also mount a reasonably sized horse and cut an acceptable cavalier figure.

In 959 a Moslem army with Sancho in its midst captured Zamora and then most of the Asturian countryside of the kingdom of Leon. In the autumn of 960 the capital city of Leon fell to the Caliph's armies and Sancho was securely seated on his throne. He was pleased to note that his subjects and courtiers had stopped laughing. He sent delegations to all the neighboring states, to announce that the kingdom had been restored to the previous management. And special envoys went off to express eternal gratitude to Cordoba, to the Caliph and to his ingenious doctor-diplomat Hasdai for all that they had done for him.

The gratitude proved less than eternal, and a few years later a Moslem army was required to lay waste a few cities and burn the crops to remind him of his solemn promise to remove the ten menacing fortifications. But that was after the reign of Abd-er Rahman III.

It was barely a year after Sancho the Fat was restored to the throne of Leon that the Caliph fell ill. His physicians, undoubtedly including Hasdai, gathered at his bedside and, with the customary bleedings and the skillful blendings of samples from the herbal gardens of the palace, he rallied.

When the winds of autumn swept down the valley of the Guadalquivir, however, the Caliph began to fail once more and on October 16, 961, the grandest European monarch of his time, the first Caliph of Cordoba, died. He was just seventy years old and had reigned for forty-nine years.

He left a country in what passed for a serene peace in those years. Both the Christian and Fatimid enemies were held at bay, and no rebels were rising in Andalusia. To succeed him there was his son Hakam, a man approaching middle age with a passion for peace, literature and, they say, comely boys.

The Caliphate, when the Caliph left it, was one of the world's bright glories, gilded by the refinements of wealth and fashion. Ladies, high-born or middle class, took their daily baths while masseuses anointed them and taught them how to pinch their waists and apply their makeup with telling effect. Fruit was never more abundant or cheaper than in the year of the Caliph's death. Prosperity dazzled visitors and left the residents satisfied with themselves and their state. Every man and woman, it seemed, had a mule to ride, and they made a constant cheery clatter on the cobbled streets.

Making possible all this comfort was that supreme stabilizer of social order, a competent civil service, which, it was hoped, would always carry on the day-to-day tasks of government, regardless of palace coups and harem politics.

Except for the most remotely situated farmers, nearly everyone in the Caliphate could read and write. And this on a continent where literacy was rare even among nobles.

At such felicitous times only professional doom-sayers listen for rumbles beneath their feet and sniff the wind suspiciously. When the honor guards took the body of Abd-er Rahman III on a bare plank from his pleasure palace, the Madinat al-

Zahra, through the streets to the tomb of his ancestors in the Alcazar at Cordoba, there were no grim prophets to note that the evening of the Caliphate was creeping in beneath the blaze of afternoon.

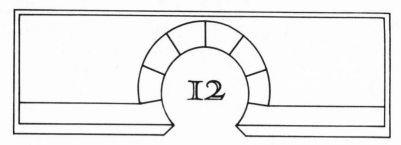

The Dictatorship of Dogma

During the first nine years of his reign Hakam II had to neglect his library and other gentle pursuits to attend to the unfinished military business left by his father. Among these preoccupations was the persistent itch caused by Sancho, the ex-Fat. After the death of Abd-er Rahman III Sancho thought it safe to renege on his promises to disarm the frontier.

On the advice of his counselors—Hasdai, no doubt, among others—the new Caliph employed a subtle gambit to keep Sancho in line without dispatching an expeditionary force. He played Ordoño the Wicked as a pawn. That pretender to the Leonese throne was actually a son-in-law of Sancho's, but he would cheerfully have assassinated his wife's father to regain a throne.

Ordoño had come to Cordoba to court the Caliph as Sancho and his grandmother had come earlier. Ordoño made a point of displaying his awe at the pomp of the royal welcome accorded him and at the magnificence of the Caliph's court. He fawned over influential politicians and knelt to kiss the carpet before the throne in the Madinat al-Zahra. Seemingly without embarrassment he declared himself the dutiful slave of the "Commander of the Faithful," who was known in Christian lands as the arch-infidel and anti-Christ.

The Caliph loaded Ordoño with extravagant gifts and sent him off with the promise of an army to humble the treacherous Sancho. The Wicked was certain that he had replaced the Fat in the Caliph's favor and the word of that switch quickly reached Leon. At once Sancho sent messages to Cordoba proclaiming his eternal friendship. Simultaneously he set about dismantling the ten fortresses that the Caliphate had always found objectionable.

The Caliph thereupon postponed mobilizing an army for Ordoño the Wicked but kept him dangling in Cordoba where, after a year or so, he died, much embittered by the treacheries of the world. With the pretender gone Sancho again began to conspire with his fellow monarchs on the frontier against the power of the Caliph. It took four years for Hakam's generals to bring the kings bowing and scraping once again to Cordoba.

In 966 Sancho's career, which had exalted treachery as a tactic, ended in betrayal. A general of a rival Christian kingdom had proposed a truce and in the ensuing discussions offered Sancho a bit of refreshment. Sancho did not detect until it was too late the poison in which the fruit had been dipped. He spent three excruciatingly painful days before succumbing.

Thereafter the frontier kings tore each other apart, leaving Hakam in peace to indulge his bibliophilic passions. He dispatched agents to all parts of the world to buy manuscripts dealing with mathematics, natural science, art and history. Where the scrolls themselves were not for sale he hired scribes to copy them. Hakam had begun to pursue this hobby as a prince. By the time he was firmly established as Caliph his library included some four hundred thousand works. The catalogue alone ran to forty-four volumes.

Hakam II gave Cordoba its last sunny years. The gentle Caliph not only organized the royal library in the palace but also fostered a national preoccupation with education. Primary school children learned to read and write with a proper understanding of grammar and style, even if the approved taste ran to somewhat overblown rhetoric. The beggars of Cordoba were functionally literate and workmen could enjoy the satiric verse that poured from the palace poets.

Out of the Caliph's private purse came the funds for twenty-seven advanced public schools—all tuition-free—to give the

promising children of the poor a better-than-average education. The road to political and commercial advantage for middle-class Cordobans ran not so much through military as
through academic channels. Lecturers at the University of
Cordoba came from Baghdad and Damascus to discuss the fine
points of Arabic poetry, philosophy, music and law. All this
served to dilute Koranic precepts with secular aesthetic considerations.

Hakam's fervor for education found echoes in the administration of the viceroy of the Jews, Hasdai ibn Shaprut, who of-
ficiated in the palace and in synagogue compounds as he had
in the days of Abd-er Rahman III. He continued to be available to Hakam II as physician, adviser and friend.

Hasdai had long before learned to settle for the reality of influence rather than the show of a formal title. Even in the heyday of Omayyad toleration there were always Moslem funda-
mentalists whose hackles would rise at the idea of a Jew or
Christian holding the rank of prime minister or foreign minister.

Actually the glory surrounding a prince of Israel was enough
to gratify a far vainer man than Hasdai ibn Shaprut. His most
casual look might make or break a poet or a rabbi. His influence, if not his legal power, could set taxes, sway the opinions of
the elders on community operations or the merits of delicate lit-
igation. And, on occasion it could set a militia in motion. It was
odd that these powers should be freely given to a man with
such decisively secular interests by a community for which justice, politics and art had their source and authority in the
Torah. Still, it was symptomatic of those times when absolut-
ism—in ideas, at least—was yielding to the subversive charm of
civilized discourse.

This prince of Jews was no more a Talmudic scholar than
Hakam II was a mullah. Both men, along with the father of
their liberties, Abd-er Rahman III, prefigured the Renaissance
that would one day focus art and science on humanity and the
wonderful, terrible reality of the world, rather than on angels
and the Day of Judgment.

Like the Caliph, Hasdai sent scouts to Italy, Byzantium,

Cairo and Damascus. There they would buy or copy literary Judaica. And, like the Caliph, he presided over his own coterie of poets and historians, who gathered regularly in his patio or drawing room. There they would hone their critical wit on one another's work or listen to a plangent lute accompanying light love songs written in an elegant Hebrew or Arabic.

There were Hebrew salons and Arabic salons but guests were freely interchanged between the two. Only in occasional hymns to lost Zion or in references to Allah and the Prophet were there substantive differences in theme. Songs sung in both quarters glorified dark-eyed shepherdesses and the soul-wrenching sight of olive and almond trees on a hillside in the morning.

Such a literary court inevitably produced bursts of elaborate sycophancy. Again like the Caliph, Hasdai came to expect outrageous flattery from his courtiers. The praises he heard in his lifetime rivaled the encomia composed after his death. This is an example:

"With the dew of his grace that prince restored to life those who were dying of folly . . . for his kindness has made the tongues of the dumb to break out in song. . . . So that they gathered about him with sweet songs bright as the stars on high."

Hasdai required a sizeable staff to handle his correspondence, review petitions, dispense the necessary scholarships for worthy students, follow the political events with reference to the welfare of Jews in Andalusia or Italy or Byzantium, and help to gratify his wide-ranging aesthetic enthusiasms. He had secretaries who could handle these affairs in a suitably elegant Arabic, but for his Hebrew letters he had Menahem ben Jacob ibn Saruq.

Menahem was a country boy with lofty dreams. He came from Tortosa, on the eastern coast, south of Tarragona, where few Jews argued, few scholars taught and books were rare. When his father died Menahem seized the occasion to break away from Tortosa and head for the excitement of Cordoba. It was not the food, drink, women and adventure of the capital that drew Menahem. This strange young man was intoxicated by the idea of serious study with pious masters whom he could follow through the lovely mazes of the Talmud.

In Cordoba Menahem soon found himself the protégé of the Shaprut family. Some chroniclers say it was Hasdai's older brother Abun who discovered him while others insist it was Isaac, the father of the clan. No matter who found this lad in all his innocence, he soon became the family's pet poet. He was called on to commemorate every family event in impeccably proper verse exemplifying traditional virtues.

After some years with the Shapruts Menahem went back to Tortosa, where he married and settled into a modest business career. He had had his fling but still he hankered after the intellectual challenge of Cordoba. While living with the Shapruts he had begun to explore the complex origins of Hebrew words.

Years later, when Hasdai had become the fountainhead and arbiter of Andalusian-Jewish culture, Menahem received an offer to again take up his post with the family. The pay would be handsome, and the duties would allow him time to pursue his linguistic studies, which indeed would be encouraged. He would be the Hebrew secretary of the renowned doctor-diplomat Prince Hasdai ibn Shaprut. He could not resist. He and his family moved to Cordoba, where he happily resumed life in the court of the Jewish royal family.

He began his serious work on Hebrew etymology, which he called the *Book of Interpretations*. In it he traced the roots of the language and illustrated the evolution of the meanings of words by lines of ancient verse. All this he did in whatever time could be spared from Hasdai's growing volume of correspondence to all parts of Andalusia and the world beyond.

Periodically he would dash off a poem in praise of Hasdai, and when the venerable Isaac ibn Shaprut died, Menahem was ready with a series of elegies suitable for recitation in synagogues along with the prayers for the dead. And on the very day that Hasdai's mother died there was Menahem at midnight busy on a suitable lamentation. This endeared him to Hasdai, at least for the moment.

The most celebrated correspondence in which Menahem's hand can be clearly seen is Hasdai's letter to the king of the

Khazars. This was the unhappy nation placed by geography and history as a buffer between the Vikings raiding from the north and the Persians driving up from the south. One is tempted to read some purposive irony in the circumstances that converted to Judaism this most vulnerable of all kingdoms at a crossroads of ambitions and conquest.

Some in Cordoba had thought that the tale of a Jewish kingdom in the Caucasus had been an invention of Eldad, that traveling maker of myths. (Scholars now suggest that perhaps Eldad himself was a Khazar.) Merchants less imaginative than Eldad, who had traveled the Khorosan caravan route, had repeatedly confirmed the existence of the Jewish state in the Crimea, and when an ambassador from Byzantium came to Cordoba he told Hasdai that there could be no doubt of the Jewish kingdom, situated some fifteen days by ship from Constantinople.

Hasdai prepared to send his own envoy to Khazaria and accordingly addressed a letter to that distant king. We know that at least the first draft of it was written by Menahem, because, in the playful literary mannerisms of the times, the secretary wove his signature into the historic documents by means of an acrostic. The first initials of the opening words spell out Hasdai's name, followed by Menahem's.

The letter pays the customary florid tribute to the king of the Khazars, congratulating him on a military victory over "the sinful kingdom," a phrase frequently used to describe Byzantium. Hasdai exclaims delightedly at a Jewish victory, remarking on the miracle, "That survivors should prevail over the mighty!"

He describes the situation in Andalusia, noting the precise latitude of Cordoba, comparing it with that of Constantinople and with what he supposes is that of the Khazars' capital. He describes the glories of Abd-er Rahman III and the peace enjoyed by Jews in Andalusia. With a great many rhetorical bows suggesting abject humility, Hasdai tells of his own authority, noting that he is in charge of foreign trade, among other matters.

He then puts a series of questions about the geography of

Khazaria, its military strength, the method of appointing judges, whether in wartime the king still observes the Sabbath, and whether anyone in Khazaria has yet figured out how many more years it may be before "the final redemption."

The letter has been the subject of scholarly controversy but is now generally regarded as authentic. A little more than a century after it was written Judah Halevi, that Jewish poet of Cordoba's twilight agonies, wrote his eloquent narrative (in Arabic, incidentally) of the conversion of the Khazars to Judaism. Since then historians and archeologists have confirmed the existence of Khazaria and traced its rise and fall. Some say the Polish Jews or the Hungarian Jews or indeed the Jews of all Eastern Europe sprang from the dispersed Khazars, but that is generally regarded as pure speculation.

Hasdai entrusted the letter that he and Menahem had so painstakingly put together to a messenger named Isaac ben Nathan, who went off to Constantinople. He stayed there for six months until the emperor and his court persuaded him that the overland route to Khazaria would be much too risky and that the Black Sea was fearful and unpredictable.

When word reached Hasdai of the failure of Isaac's mission, he thought of sending the letter to Jerusalem. There friendly Jews would carry it to Armenia, from where it could be picked up by still another relay for the last lap to the land of the Khazars. Hasdai might have tried that circuitous route if two sympathetic Jews, named Saul and Joseph, had not turned up in a delegation to the Caliph from the king of the Gebalim, an Eastern European people. They offered to pass it on to Hungarians who would take it to Bulgarians who would deliver it at last— after a year or so, perhaps—to King Joseph of the Khazars. Hasdai chose Saul and Joseph as the likeliest couriers.

A version of King Joseph's reply has been troubling historians for almost a thousand years. The message is under a cloud of scholars' doubts. Some have been skeptical even concerning the existence of King Joseph. The internal evidence of the response from Khazaria gives them pause. There seem to be Arabisms in the style, which would be most unlikely in the royal

Khazar. There is also an absence of detail on Jewish life in Khazaria. And there is too much anti-Islamic propaganda. The doubters suggest that a Spanish Jew with a flair for Arabic rhetoric might have faked the document long after the event.

Much of this long-drawn-out correspondence took place during the reign of Abd-er Rahman III, a period when Menahem seemed secure in the affections of Hasdai. There can be no doubt, however, that Hasdai was more closely attuned to the livelier souls in his entourage. Among these was a man with a Berber name who came from Fez by way of Baghdad or Baghdad by way of Fez (depending on which historian one cares to follow). Dunash ben Labrat had come to Cordoba because that was where he could write poetry that would go beyond the obligatory synagogue themes of the coming of the Messiah, of penitence and hope of deliverance in a restored Zion.

Dunash made his living in Cordoba as a cantor, frequently composing his own chants, both music and text. To Hasdai's literary circle he brought more than a voice and a collection of hymns. He also offered songs to the joy of life, to wine and music and love. Just to be on the safe side, however, he made sure to add a proper note of censoriousness at the end of his catalogue of delights. All this is vain without Zion, he would say in effect. This, no doubt, shielded him from rabbis who might tolerate a touch of light love in folk singers but not in serious poets.

Although the secular sweep and humor of Dunash's verse excited the youngsters in the literary salons, what interested his older colleagues were his technical innovations. He borrowed from the Arabs their use of meter, which gave a new sensuous rhythm to Hebrew poetry. One tended to sing rather than proclaim the verses of Dunash. He also adapted the structure of Arabic verse, thereby giving Hebrew poetry an added measure of discipline and coherence.

This willingness to learn and to borrow from the Arabs was in violent contrast with the thinking of Menahem, who studied the Hebrew language as if each root and stem came direct from God. He finished his book of linguistic studies without ever venturing to make a single comparison between sacred Hebrew and profane Arabic. To borrow from the Arabic in order to explain Hebrew would be to insult the word of God.

Except for this singularly unscientific approach his book was a model of painstaking scholarship and it gained Menahem the respect of rabbis and the defenders of tradition. Hasdai commended the work but he was far more interested in the poetic experimentation of Dunash and other secular writers of his circle. This waning of his rival's influence was not enough for Dunash, who regularly assailed Menahem with devastating wit.

Quite possibly the rivalry existed solely in the envious and ambitious mind of Dunash, who actually had no reason to worry. The pedantic Menahem had never been an intimate friend of Hasdai's. Nevertheless Dunash and his friends conspired energetically against the little scholar from the provinces, as if he were a major power in their way. Precisely what rumors were circulated, what accusations made, what insinuations dropped into the ear of Hasdai are not known, but there were suggestions of grave scandal.

Some say the charges concerned a possible Karaite tendency. This was an anti-Talmudic heresy, anathema to most rabbis and possibly to Hasdai, for it was characterized in some eyes by a narrow fundamentalism. Perhaps the rumors concerned an alleged infidelity to the ibn Shaprut clan. In any case the indictment must have been horrifying, for it drove Hasdai to his only recorded act of mean-spirited violence.

Reportedly he sent some of his guard—for even a Jewish prince of scholars had a military arm—to his secretary's house on the Sabbath. There the guardsmen, all Jews, stripped the poor scholar, beat him, tore handfuls of hair out of his head and ran him out of Cordoba.

From his home in Tortosa Menahem wrote a letter of protest to Hasdai, declaring his innocence of whatever was charged against him and demanding a fair trial. Hasdai answered like one of the cynical wits of his princely court:

"If you have sinned, I have made it possible for you to receive punishment. If you have not sinned, I have made it possible for you to attain life in the world to come."

Dunash proceeded to scrutinize every entry in Menahem's lexicon and to blast the grammar, the philology, the philosophy and the religion explicit and implicit in the work. His criticism was spleenful but performed with surgical skill. For a thousand years scholars would argue over whether Menahem or Dunash was right on this or that root or historical allusion. In Cordoba, when the issue was fresh and hot, the opposing camps spiced their theses with the most violent invective.

The family pet and tame poet Menahem was at last driven to assert himself against his prince in a letter of protest. In leveling a moral judgment on what happened next in the story of the faithful Menahem and his master one must bear in mind that a prince may only wish a despicable act to occur and some ambitious courtier will see that it is done. One cannot be certain that Hasdai sent a squad of armed men from Cordoba to Tortosa to further punish Menahem, but there is little doubt that such a squad did arrive in Tortosa and carried out just such a mission.

Wrapping their vengeance in pretended outrage against Menahem's alleged leanings toward the Karaites, the squad broke in on their victim's family in the middle of the Passover holidays. They tossed Menahem into jail and then tore his house apart. When Menahem emerged from jail he dispatched a letter to Hasdai, outlining his grievances in the tone of an angry rebel rather than that of a devoted servant complaining of an undeserved kick from a much-loved master. He reminded Hasdai of the Biblical egalitarianism in which princes and plebeians alike evolve from dust to dust, however variously they may spend their time en route.

Menahem recited the story of his services to the family of ibn Shaprut, the promises made by the prince, and the dismal end in the Passover raid on his home in Tortosa. His indignation, it was noted, had vastly improved his literary style.

What or whether Hasdai responded is unknown. The affair was far from the most pressing in his life. Within the Jewish community of Cordoba he had to arbitrate the succession to the important post of chief rabbi after the death of that brilliant, unassuming sage who had been ransomed from pirates, Moses ben Hanoch.

The rabbi's son Hanoch ben Moses, who had been ransomed as an infant, was now of an age to succeed to the post of grand rabbi. He too was mild-mannered, though firm in his views, wise and in all respects a man likely to continue his father's traditions. He, too, would be a gentle sage who would ponder the fine points of the Talmud and answer questions with a careful eye to precedent, to the written and spoken law.

A rival for the post was far more dynamic, worldly and ambitious. He came from a family that had been in the Spanish peninsula for many generations and had intermarried with Arabs without ever departing from the faith. His name, Joseph ben Isaac ibn Abitur, was essentially Arabic—a contraction of ibn Abi Thaur, meaning literally "son of the father of the ox." In the Romance tongue the family was known as Santas, sometimes mischievously pronounced Satanas.

He was the star among the students of Moses ben Hanoch. Even as a humble assistant he wrote brilliant *responsa* to questions that came to the venerable rabbi from all over the Mediterranean basin. He also wrote hymns and poems of atonement marked by a passion for God and an angry sorrow for the fate of the "people of God," who, he said "stand today like a mendicant beggar."

His religion was marked by a strong strain of proud nationalism but also by a delight in word-play that was characteristically Arabic. Often he wrote clever acrostics in which the initial letters of each line of verse would combine to form his name or a message or a Biblical quotation. In some poems, each line of verse would begin with the same letter, and the initial letters would proceed from verse to verse in alphabetical order.

In his pride, his wit and the broad range of his interests, spiritual and secular, he would seem to have been far closer in style to the spirit of the tenth century than the equally brilliant but other-worldly Hanoch ben Moses. One would have thought that Hasdai, a man of tenth-century breadth, would have preferred Joseph ben Isaac ibn Abitur, as he preferred Dunash to Menahem. In trying to understand why Hasdai chose Hanoch ben Moses one must imagine the fears that accompany princely power. It may be that Hasdai had come to think as a Caliph thinks: "Beware the man too like yourself." Imaginative rulers have often chosen their staffs from among those who offered not even the potential of competition.

In any case Hasdai chose Hanoch and thereby set in motion a controversy that was to rage among the Jews of Cordoba long after Hasdai's death. It was to set the Jews clamoring for a decision from the Caliph himself on the succession of the rabbinate and it was to end in a formal excommunication and exile of that brilliant, power-hungry, politicized rabbi, Joseph ibn Abitur.

Hasdai presided over a shadow-court within the Caliphate, pacifying by wise domestic policy the turbulent factions in the Jewish community and operating his own foreign affairs department and intelligence service. His agents gathered not only the literary finds that delighted Hasdai but also detailed reports on the way of life, the prosperity and the safety of Jews everywhere, from Ethiopia to the kingdoms of Italy to the towns of Germany to Khazaria. Hasdai played a subtle diplomatic game in the court of the Caliphate, seeking to manipulate the world scene simultaneously for the benefit of the Caliph and for the Jews of the world.

Actually Hasdai must have missed the sophisticated and adventurous Abd-er Rahman. Hakam II was so preoccupied with the building of his library that he had little enthusiasm left for other more characteristically caliphal functions. He was not a politician, though he went through the motions, and he was not a military genius, though he did tolerably well when he had to.

Neither he nor Hasdai seem to have been fully aware of the explosive potential gathering in the countryside. On the one hand were the Berber farmers, tilling their small plots of land, living and eating well enough but not luxuriously, listening to the mullahs extol the virtues of austerity and boast of their humility. On the other hand were the urban Arabs and their imitators, parading their fashions, their cosmopolitan ideas, their rarefied tastes in the marketplaces and mosques.

No one seemed to hear the premonitory rumbles that signal those moral earthquakes that periodically shake the Islamic world. It is safe to assume that such tremors were discernible, but if so they were dismissed as the chronic condition of Islamic society, perhaps of any society.

Seemingly more pressing was the danger that came from the harem. Hakam was thought to favor young men as his companions in love, and even with them he was rumored to be not overly energetic. This was not the sort of caliphal temperament that is well tolerated by the public. The Islamic ruler was expected to demonstrate his virility not only on the battlefield but in bed. A little pederasty was to be expected but the proof of a man was in his children—particularly his sons. When Hakam ascended the throne in his mid-forties, he had not yet fathered a child. This was a scandal.

When a Basque lady of the harem named Subh (meaning Dawn) produced a royal son, there was great rejoicing at the palace but the snickers did not cease. It was like a twenty-year drought that is broken by an inconsequential drizzle.

To the Caliph, however, his son and heir was a monumental vindication of his manhood and his kinghood. He was everlastingly grateful to Subh, as if she had managed the trick by herself out of the goodness of her heart. She became the Caliph's favorite and could demand almost anything from her lord. When three years later she gave birth to yet another son the Caliph became her adoring slave, who would be forever blinded to any adultery she might have committed in the past or would be likely to commit in the future.

The fuss over two little boys did not redeem the image of the Caliph as a man of prowess. Political ambitions soar when the mighty are belittled by a leer or a pun. There must have been many who thought themselves more fit for the throne or the royal bed than was the reigning Caliph. Mohammed Abi

Amir was one of those dreamy and arrogant young men. He fancied himself a hero while he was still a student at the University of Cordoba. His family were originally Yemenite but an ancestor had crossed the straits to Andalusia with Tarik, and that pedigree set him a notch above the later immigrants.

Unfortunately, however, Abi Amir's ancestors chose to make their marks in society as judges, not as soldiers. A young man's heroes are likely to be brave and fierce rather than wise and virtuous. In his dreams he saw himself as a conqueror, but once he was out of school he had to make his living by the same dull means as those pursued by his pen-pushing predecessors. He set himself up at a palace gate as a public secretary, offering to draft elegant petitions to the Caliph for a small fee. He managed somehow to exhibit enough of his talents to be given a modest clerkship on the staff of the chief municipal judge of Cordoba.

Like most bright young men with heroic self-images, Abi Amir tended to be impatient with small-minded employers who seemed preoccupied with chaining his mind to day-to-day trivia. Finally the judge wearied of his clerk's disdain for the ordinary and used his connections at the palace to find another place for the young man.

It was the year 967. Abi Amir was twenty-nine years old and Subh's firstborn, Abd-er Rahman, had just turned five. A manager was needed for the young prince's property, which was rapidly accumulating in gifts from the Caliph or from courtiers. The Caliph was delighted to leave the selection of a suitable steward to Subh, who conscientiously interviewed all applicants.

Abi Amir was given a place in line and by all accounts made an instantaneous and powerful impression. He got the job of managing the prince's estate and in less than seven months he was managing Subh's estate and Subh herself. Shortly afterward he was made master of the mint and had his name engraved on the coins of Cordoba. He had become an official in the administration as well as the lover of the Caliph's favorite wife.

Actually he cuckolded his monarch wholesale. He strutted about the harem like the only rooster in a hen house. According to one chronicler the Caliph wondered aloud: "By what skills does this clever young man attract all my women and win their hearts?"

Abi Amir was acquiring a reputation as a potent lover, a politician who could work through Subh to gain and dispense royal favors, and as a man of lavish generosity. He bought courtiers and generals with loans and gifts. And he tightened his hold on the heart of Subh with extravagant playthings. For example, he had Cordoba's finest silversmiths create a miniature palace in silver, which was then paraded through the streets with appropriate fanfare. Thus he courted the Cordoban crowds while he courted Subh.

Some of the Caliph's advisers wondered where the money was coming from if not from the royal mint that Abi Amir was supervising. The Caliph summoned him one day to appear with all the accounts up to date. The situation threatened to undo him completely, but on his way to the palace he stopped off at the villa of one of the many highly placed politicians who had benefited from the generosity of the master of the mint. This friend obligingly made up the cash deficit so that when Abi Amir appeared before the Caliph he could show that the books balanced nicely. His accusers were confounded and Abi Amir continued to bestride the palace and the harem like the lord he was.

In 970 when Subh's first son, Abd-er Rahman, died, Abi Amir was given the post of managing the estate of the new crown prince, Hisham. He continued to manage Subh and also took command of a key regiment of the palace guard. He collected a number of other posts as well, not only because they paid salaries but also because they carried more opportunities to distribute patronage.

His villa at Rusafa on the hills above the Guadalquivir was always open to those who sought favors, for which they would cheerfully sing Abi Amir's praises to the Cordoban public. Aristocrats of the royal blood eagerly joined his staff as secretaries and administrators. So utterly bemused was the Caliph that he appointed Abi Amir governor of Mauritania. That kingdom south of the deserts of North Africa had been won in part by the sword, but mostly by bribing Berber chiefs with whatever the Caliph's generals could pilfer from the Cordoban treasury. Someone had to control the generals, and the Caliph, no doubt prompted by Subh, chose the ever more popular Abi Amir.

It was shortly after the Mauritanian adventure, which the generals and Abi Amir dressed up as a spectacular triumph, that Caliph Hakam II suffered an attack of apoplexy, which sharply reminded him of his mortality. He proceeded to wind up his wordly affairs like the scholar-saint he had longed to be. He slashed by at least fifteen percent the taxes that went to the central government; he emancipated one hundred of his slaves and decreed that henceforth all the rents of the saddlers' stalls in the Cordoba market (the Caliph's personal property) would be earmarked to pay the salaries of teachers in the public schools.

He forced the Cordoban nobles to acknowledge in writing the rights of his son Hisham as the heir. And he appointed Abi Amir as the royal chamberlain to protect the succession.

With his kingdom at peace, with the Christian kings in the north and the Fatimids in Africa held at bay, with his library the light of the Western world, with his people literate and well fed, with an heir born out of his own exploits with the peerless Subh, he was ready for his exit. On October 1, 976, he summoned the keeper of the wardrobe and the grand falconer— both eunuch slaves from the wilds of eastern Europe—sank into their arms and died.

The two eunuchs were technically slaves but actually owned as much property as many princes and commanded at least one thousand men—slave and free. These ran the palace and the harem to the profit of the eunuchs in command. They foresaw an uncertain future for themselves in a Cordoba nominally ruled by an eleven-year-old boy who would be a pawn in others' hands.

They considered withholding news of the death until they could prevail upon a pliable younger brother of the old Caliph to take the throne. They grew timid, though, and sought the advice of the grand vizier, Al-Mushafi, and of Abi Amir. These two quickly formed an alliance and nipped the conspiracy by dispatching assassins to strangle the innocent young man who was to have been the eunuchs' puppet. The keeper of the wardrobe and the grand falconer at once appreciated the mistake they had made and applauded the wisdom of the grand vizier and Abi Amir.

On the following day the eleven-year-old boy, the only surviving son of the dead Caliph, became Hisham II. Standing around his throne in the palace were the vizier, Al-Mushafi, a wily old Berber chieftain; Abi Amir; the grand falconer, and the keeper of the wardrobe. They came to the coronation fresh from the murder of the new Caliph's uncle. The ambitions of the men who grouped themselves around the boy presaged the doom of Cordoba, but it is unlikely that any of the lords assembled there sensed that fate as they touched the boy's hand and murmured the oath of fealty.

It is more likely that they commented only on how frail the boy Caliph appeared and how expensive were the robes of Abi Amir and how eunuchs inevitably put on weight and how taxes were certain to go up now that Abi Amir was free to indulge his and Subh's extravagant tastes.

Abi Amir played the game of politics cunningly. He was lavish to his friends, ruthless to his enemies, devout to the mullahs, a sound businessman to the merchants and a dazzling showman to the people.

From the beginning he and Subh groomed the Caliph Hisham II to assume a halo of sainthood, to perform acts of shining charity while he left the sordid business of government to others. Some say that they seduced him not only with a halo but with the private sensual pleasures of the harem, even when he was barely in his teens. In any case the boy quickly saw that such a course of life could be simple, and pleasant. Power and politics were not his dish, as they had not been his father's.

He watched the fortunes of courtiers rise when Abi Amir smiled and plummet when he frowned. The vizier Al-Mushafi was a pathetic case in point. Abi Amir had him arrested and tried for manifold acts of graft and treason. When he stood before judges he knew to be in fear of Abi Amir or in his pay he reportedly improvised a verse that included the line: "But lately lions were in fear of me, and now I tremble at a fox."

Abi Amir let the vizier eke out a miserable existence as a hanger-on in his retinue, starved and in rags. His function was to point a moral: He who opposes Abi Amir will wish he were dead. In time the humiliated old politician did die. Some say it was by poison, others say he was strangled. He was carried to his grave covered by an old cloak that a jailer had thrown away. No one dared to glance at the wreck of the once great vizier as it was trundled off the scene.

Abi Amir offered the sunny side of the coin as well. His favorites lived high. He threw fortunes away to the crowds who cheered him. He lavished great sums of money on mosques and on mullahs. Some of these were impressed by such laudable works but others required a greater demonstration of piety. They had chafed through one Omayyad ruler after another, each with a taste for the secular joys.

To enjoy women was not inconsistent with true piety and even a predilection for young boys was not likely to shock the clergy, but they had always detested the royal taste for profane literature, wordly beauty and worldly comforts. They had been scandalized by the magnificence of the Madinat al-Zahra and even more gravely disturbed by the poets, artists, singers, lute players and other "light people" who found favor with Abd-er Rahman III. Then there was the appalling absorption of Hakam II in infidel books by Christians, Jews, pagan Greeks and Romans, dealing in things alien to the Koran, unnecessary and distracting to the state.

Now they had another sort of ruler—not a Caliph but a Caliph's ruler. He could be more malleable than a Caliph, because he had the insecurity that comes from illegitimacy. He had to court the mullahs as he courted every class in Cordoban society. Therefore the mullahs could exact a price greater than architectural refinements on the grand mosque. Let him prove his devotion to Islam by repudiating the Omayyad tradition of tolerating false doctrine.

Abi Amir himself had been suspected of a fondness for philosophy, picked up at the University of Cordoba when he was a young student there. He tried now to expunge the stigma of rationalism by copying out the Koran in his own hand. He conspicuously displayed this copy as part of his baggage when he traveled. The mullahs were impressed by so patent a desire to please them, but still, they required some more decisive proof of doctrinal purity.

To satisfy them he invited a delegation of the most eminent clergymen in Andalusia to come to the palace of Cordoba. There he led them to the library of Hakam II, where the scholar had put together an enormous repository of the history, science and philosophy of a thousand years of Mediterranean civilization.

Abi Amir asked the defenders of Islamic orthodoxy to show him the works that they found offensive. They scurried about, picking from the shelves everything they could find on philosophy, ancient or modern, secular poetry, texts of astronomy and the natural sciences that seemed to exceed the limits set in the Koran.

As the clergymen ransacked the royal library, Abi Amir ordered guards to pile up the huge number of condemned scrolls in the central court. Then he had them set on fire. The clergy beamed at Abi Amir as he joined his guards in gathering up handfuls of scrolls and tossing them on to the flames. He smiled back in the certain knowledge that he had the godly in his pocket.

In order to have a wholly trustworthy army he knew, as other dictators before and since have known, that he would have to build one of his own, untroubled by previous loyalties and doubts. He found a fresh supply of soldiers among the Berbers in North Africa and brought them over in great numbers. They were fanatically Moslem, being relatively new to the religion. Having come up from poverty they loathed the easy-going Arab aristocracy for their effete ways and their wealth. They had no secure foothold in Andalusia and knew no star to follow but Abi Amir's.

Abi Amir wooed the Jews as well, seeking their skills and their money. Some of the wealthier Jews from North Africa came up in the wake of the Berbers, for the sheer excitement of Abi Amir's entourage sparked hopes. When things move quickly there is an illusion of progress.

True, corruption was visible everywhere; selected heads were rolling; books were no longer popular, and few poets read their works at the new palace, which Abi Amir called the Madina al-Zahira (a name meaning "shining city"). It was meant to belittle the old Madinat al-Zahra. It was quiet now at that old seat of royalty, where Sancho the Fat and Ordoño the Wicked were once awed, where Sudanese cavalry galloped on parade, and where a court wit could pick up a pretty piece of change for a good line.

The Caliph Hisham II was growing up there as in a cloister. He held no court and was accorded no pomp. He had been brought up to be powerless and so he was—a young man without hope and without ambition. His mother, Subh, had come to regret the deal she had made and belatedly tried to put some iron into the soul of her son. The Caliph's title still had a magic in Cordoba, and if Hisham could be emboldened to speak up, the public, romantically in love with kingship, might rally to him.

He tried occasionally, but when confronted by Abi Amir, he crumbled. He signed a document giving all state power to his minister Abi Amir. After that all harem conspiracies ended. Abi Amir allowed his Caliph one triumphal parade through the streets of Cordoba, with the crowds cheering the young Hisham, who wore the caliphal regalia and carried the caliphal scepter. Behind him rode Abi Amir, making it obvious that the pretty young Caliph was no more than an ornament of power. If the people were well-behaved, there might be other shows where they would see royalty rendered tame but pretty. Meanwhile the Caliph would spend his time in spiritual uplift, a model to the nation.

Subh rode behind Abi Amir, and it was reported that she too would devote the rest of her days to modest thought and deeds of charity in the quiet gardens of the Madinat al-Zahra.

By contrast Abi Amir's new palace, Madina al-Zahira, was the hub of Cordoban politics and society. Commerce, too, followed the new politics. Merchants set up shops to catch the crowds that thronged around the new court. Eventually whole new areas were developed, stretching out until they merged with the alleys and soukhs of the old city.

Abi Amir played the regent with consummate efficiency. He knew how to sniff out conspiracies, and how to assuage the injured feelings of those he could not intimidate, but he also fulfilled the royal obligation to build public works, improve agricultural production and, above all, conduct the defense of the realm against the old twin enemies, the Christian north and the Moslem rivals of Africa.

When his military exploits were sufficiently publicized he took the name al-Mansur—"the Victorious"—and thereafter lived the part of a hero. He sedulously cultivated the image of a Caesar or an Alexander. He was not the greatest of military geniuses but he was skillful enough to bedevil the Christians with his semiannual forays. He hammered relentlessly at his objectives and was successful year after year, but it must be admitted that the still disunited, back-biting Christian kings were rarely formidable.

They were usually intimidated, for al-Mansur carried a terrifying reputation. He was reported on one occasion to have decapitated his prisoners of war and used their bodies as ramparts. When he reviewed his troops, it was said, not a horse would neigh. Once he caught the gleam of a sword moving when all was to have been motionless in the ranks. He called the offending guardsman front-and-center and heard him explain that his scabbard had fallen. The man was at once decapitated. His head was mounted on a spear and paraded up and down the silent ranks of the assembled soldiers while a proclamation was read detailing the man's unpardonable breach of discipline.

Aside from the general panic caused by the very name of their leader, al-Mansur's army heading north must have carried the sounds, smells and colors of implacable doom. Over the olive-crested hills would thunder some forty-six thousand horsemen, dressed in leather or coats of mail, their faces masked by helmets with closed visors. They carried shields on their arms and in their hands they swung double-bladed axes. Swords, straight or curved, hung at their sides. Each horseman would be followed by a squire carrying a lance or perhaps a bow and arrows. He would have in tow a sumpter mule loaded with weapons and with tents to accommodate his master and himself on the march.

Then would come the infantrymen kicking up the dust. There might be as many as twenty-six thousand of them, carrying a bristling assortment of pikes, maces, scimitars, bows and arrows, javelins and slings. Heavy artillery, such as catapults, might be towed or carried by a string of camels, usually some thirty-nine hundred of them. Up in the van of the column would be 130 or more drummers.

At the tail end of the march would come the quartermaster corps carrying pots and pans for cooking, extra clothes, tents and cushions. The women—wives, camp followers, cooks—would be carried in palanquins. Some eight hundred horsemen would fan out around the line of march as outriders to guard against surprise.

When al-Mansur stopped for the night he was in a city of soldiers. Tents would sprout over the plain. The countryside would be scoured for food. His own pavilion would be set up where he could recline on cushions, receive local dignitaries and confer with his commanders. His women might amuse him. His musicians might play.

Although every soldier was promised loot, perhaps prisoners to ransom, perhaps a slave to keep, perhaps women to rape, al-Mansur always stressed the holy nature of his expeditions. It was a characteristic of Spanish wars that both sides felt the bloodshed to be sanctified, because on whichever side one fought it was always against the infidel.

As he grew older al-Mansur seemed to brood over his Islamic faith and to embroider it occasionally with bright threads of superstition. On all his campaigns in the latter part of his career "the Conqueror" carried his own linen shroud, lovingly prepared by his daughters. And at the end of each day's march he would carefully gather into a box the dust from his clothes and shoes. Certain that he was destined to die in heroic battle, he left orders that in such an eventuality he was to be wrapped in the shroud, and the dust of his marches was to be sprinkled on him so that those who judged him in the hereafter would know that he died in the midst of a holy war. That, he thought, might make up for a life that had not been free of sin.

On July 3, 997, al-Mansur packed his shroud and his dust box and took his place at the head of his cavalry, which stretched for miles over the dusty roads running northward from the gates of Cordoba. He had loaded most of the infantry, the women and supplies aboard a fleet of warships, which was to sail down the Guadalquivir to the Gulf of Cadiz, around the Algarve coast, and up the Atlantic to Oporto, where it would rendezvous with the cavalry.

There the ships were lined up prow to stern across the Douro so that horsemen could cross as on a bridge. Then they traveled uneventfully through the quiet valleys of the north, where the Christian rulers were friendly, terrorized or impotent. On the far side of the Miño River they came to the trackless passes of the Cordillera Cantábrica. There al-Mansur set his men to work clearing a road for the cavalry and artillery.

Eventually they poured down on the other side onto the plains of Galicia. They swept through villages, castles and monasteries, looting and burning, until they came to within sight of the church of Santiago de Compostela. On these plains, the name of which was corrupted from the Latin for "Field of Stars," stood the supposed tomb of Saint James, or Santiago.

The Apostle, who had been given Spain as his special province in which to spread the Gospel, had been hymned in the eighth century as "Spain's golden and shining head." James was known as a gentle saint who would respond to prayers to stave off crop failures or disease. In the ninth century, however, the Christians, with their backs to the wall of the Pyrenees, needed a saint of sterner stuff. Santiago proved capable of heroic transformation.

Soon he was seen by the devout to be riding a white horse above the battle against the infidel. He acquired a sword, shield and banners. He had become a warrior saint and was nicknamed Matamoros, the Killer of Moors. He was regarded by pious Christians not only as an apostle but also as a brother of Christ. They were seen as celestial twins confused with Castor and Pollux in the night sky.

When Santiago's body was reputed to have been buried at Compostela, the spot became the greatest site of Christian veneration in Europe. The monks of Cluny crossed the Pyrenees not only to venerate the saint but also to rebuild Christian morale and influence under his banners.

The pilgrimages, destined to draw millions over many centuries, had been started by the Cluniacs. In later years these processions of the pious would run straight from Paris—where the point of departure was named, appropriately, the rue Saint-Jacques—southward across the mountains to Santiago de Compostela. Here was the soul of Christian resistance to Moslem rule. This church was the fountainhead for streams of Christian warriors.

Al-Mansur knew well the power of mythology, for he had manipulated it and been manipulated by it. Al-Mansur had humiliated Christian kings by the dozen. He had seen them beg him to take their daughters—as concubines if not as wives—so that they might hold their lands or seize their Christian neighbors' lands. Now he would humiliate their most potent saint—the brother of their Christ.

When al-Mansur entered the town of Compostela it was deserted. In the quiet streets not a soul was found. The houses had been abandoned as if a plague had struck. The only man they found that day was a monk praying at the tomb of Santiago.

Al-Mansur set up a guard around the tomb and the praying monk, forbidding anyone to touch either. Then he ordered the systematic destruction of every building in sight. Every fortification, every house and the church itself was dismantled, stone from stone, until nothing was left but the tomb of Santiago. Why did al-Mansur spare that Christian relic? Was it some lingering remnant of Arab gallantry, which kept him from mutilating the body of a conquered foe? Or was it because when stones are endowed with holiness by the devotees of any religion, they acquire a fearful magic? A man who carried his own shroud and saved the dust, stirred by a holy mission, would be most susceptible to the dread of sacrilege.

In any case he left standing that tomb of Santiago, and generations of Moslems would hear the saint's name as a blood-curdling battle cry in savage crusades to come.

Al-Mansur stayed a week in Galicia, his forces completing the devastation of nearby convents and monasteries. Then he loaded the bells and the great metal gates of the cathedral onto the backs of Christian captives for the march home to Cordoba, some four hundred miles south.

The gates of the church were melted down to make lamps for the mosque of Cordoba. The bells were kept intact as trophies of the war between the warrior saints. A few centuries later the Christians would reclaim those bells and load them onto the backs of Moslem captives who would take them back to Compostela.

Al-Mansur carried on his uneasy regime for five years. Then, on a campaign against Castile, he began to suffer pain from an illness that is not diagnosed in the historical records. He sent his physicians back to their tents, but he consented to be carried in a litter rather than ride his horse.

At night he called in his sons. He told the younger to take command of the army and instructed the older to race back to Cordoba, for he feared a revolt that would snuff out the dynasty he had hoped to found. Then al-Mansur died, uncertain of his illegitimate power to the very end. A Christian monk noted in his running chronicle of the times: "Al-Mansur died in

1002; he was buried in Hell." Actually he was entombed in Medinaceli.

Throughout the dictatorship of al-Mansur, the Caliph of Cordoba, Hisham II, had grown from a cloistered boy into a very cynical young man. His only shield was his political impotence, which he used whenever the world came knocking at the door of his Madinat al-Zahra. He would proclaim to everyone the merits of his own weakness. When al-Mansur's son came racing back to Cordoba the people gathered in the streets to shout for a return to legitimacy, a return to the Omayyad family that had once made them the envy of the world. Hisham sent word to the leaders of delegations that waited upon him to the effect that he would reign but never rule, that he was raised in retirement and would remain there.

Thereupon the eldest son of al-Mansur, Abd-al Malik, who had taken the name of "the Triumphant," sent out troops to break up the crowd.

The years that followed were uneasy. Al-Mansur's troops, mainly Berbers up from North Africa or mercenaries recruited from Eastern Europe, saw themselves as strong men kept from the seats of power by fat eunuchs and effeminate pen-pushers lolling on silken cushions. The clergy preached a return to simple dogma. There is a natural affinity between warriors and the preachers of a simple faith, a simple science, a simple truth that mocks the questioner, the scholar, the artist and all who savor the complexities of life.

Intellectuals—Arab, Jew and Christian—seemed to take a fresh delight in those complexities as the forces of simplicity swaggered in the streets or thundered in the mosques. Agnostics now wondered aloud whether the will of Allah, or indeed even His existence, was demonstrable to reasonable people. There was a small movement to which some Arab and Jewish writers rallied, calling for one universal religion concerned not only with theology but with moral precepts that might hold society together.

Such talk disturbed the orthodox of all faiths and seemed to mock the literal creed of the Berber soldiers. For a hideous example of the end-product of complicated thinking and too wide a toleration they pointed to the spectacle at the Madinat al-Zahra.

There the Caliph Hisham II, according to popular talk, lived in a perpetual round of drunken parties and sexual orgies of an indescribable sort with the man who had been sent to guide him—the younger son of the dictator. His name was the much-venerated Abd-er Rahman, but he was called Sanchuelo— "Little Sancho." This served to remind everyone that he was part Christian. Actually his mother was the daughter of either the king of Navarre or the count of Castile. (Historians differ on the point.)

Sanchuelo had the dash and vigor of youth but none of the sober competence of his brother, "the Triumphant," who was trying to manage the Caliphate with the same combination of shrewdness and ferocity exemplified by his father. Sanchuelo and the Caliph were seen slipping in and out of the palace on their way to other villas for other parties. Wherever they went there were the titter of concubines and the rustle of silks. Sometimes the Caliph himself, scion of the great Omayyads, would be glimpsed veiled like a woman. The gossips of Cordoba thrived on the goings-on between the Caliph and the youngest son of the Conqueror. The scandal grew ever more lurid.

It was a matter for laughter in the salons and in the market-place, for shock in the mosques, and for fury in the barracks. Whatever there was between this middle-aged Caliph and the younger officer took a more ominous turn in the summer of 1008 when the man in charge of the state, "the Triumphant," older son of al-Mansur, suddenly died. He had been on the usual campaign in Castile when he complained of sharp pains in his chest. He was put on a litter and carried back to Cordoba, but he succumbed en route after barely reaching the suburbs.

It was widely reported that he had been poisoned. The dead man's mother publicly put the blame on Sanchuelo, but there were no grounds for a charge of murder, and it was regarded as quite possible that "the Triumphant" had died of natural causes. He had been in sound health, his officers said, but a heart attack might have struck without warning. True, Sanchuelo had most to gain by his half-brother's death but, on the other hand, the young man had always been lucky.

Within months the crowds of Cordoba were calling upon the Caliph to leave his harem and take the world. Instead, in November of that year, Hisham II, strong only in his refusal to be strong, announced to his subjects that he was giving power to the second son of the late dictator, Sanchuelo, the laughing boy of the palace parties.

For a while Sanchuelo played at power. He put on a turban—a head-dress reserved for lawyers and scholars—and demanded that all the court do likewise, that no man come before him unturbaned. Furthermore, when he took the field in a military campaign he ordered all officers to wear turbans. Armies ordinarily do not have a lively sense of humor. They will tolerate occasional whims in a much-respected commander but they would not think it hilarious, for example, to be commanded to wear cooks' hats into battle.

In less than a year Sanchuelo's luck ran out. Mobs had sacked his father's palace, Madina al-Zahira, in the first of what were to be a series of devastating riots in the streets of Cordoba. These protests were followed by the customary arson and looting.

The Berber troops deserted en masse. In vain Sanchuelo licked the boots of the Berber chief who had stolen his soldiers. Then, complying with the shouts of the infantry, he kissed the shoe of the horse the new conqueror rode. In the end Sanchuelo tried to stab himself, but the guards would not allow him that dignity. They hacked him to death and decapitated his corpse.

Cordoba and all Andalusia then descended into chaos while one conqueror succeeded another as the guardian of that tarnished relic, Hisham II. The Berbers, coming from various and conflicting traditions of North Africa, frequently ran out of control. Sometimes they fought one another and sometimes they joined to challenge their ancient enemy, the Arab lords who still flaunted wealth, power and cosmopolitan airs.

The artisans who had flocked to Cordoba in the prosperous early days of the dictatorship now hankered after the luxuries of the middle class and the rich. The mullahs saw merit in the simplicities of the Berber rage and the outcry of the men in the workshops against the extravagance of their warlords. The Jews prayed for a miracle that would convert the spineless Hisham into an Abd-er Rahman, be it the first, second or third. Some Jews toyed with the idea of taking to the road again as in the nearly forgotten days of the Visigoths. Some joined with their Arab compeers to write satiric verse on these most pitiful and absurd times. And the middle class complained of high taxes and of the pathetic decline in poetry, the art of lute-playing and the skill and beauty of dancing girls. They sounded like the vestigial Roman patricians who saw their empire fade in the same vineyards where now the Arabs sighed.

Nothing was as it had been and there was a widespread feeling that nothing would ever be great again, that Cordoba was shrinking to the size of the little men who were mocking her.

Some of these were Berbers, some were Arabs who tried to use the Berbers. A Catalan army, commanded by bishops and nobles, swept down on Cordoba in 1010 and massacred every Berber they could find. In the course of the fighting the old Madinat al-Zahra, the glory of Abd-er Rahman III, was burned and looted.

In the same spirit of divine mission the Berbers besieged the city the following year when Slavonian chiefs had taken command of the administration. With theatrical timing, the waters of the Guadalquivir rose that spring and flooded the suburbs on the left bank. Disease, famine, homelessness and hopelessness now wracked Cordoba.

During the siege Arabs, Jews and Christians clung to one another in a desperate defense. The enemy at the gates was calling upon a fierce Allah who had little in common with the urbane Omayyad spirit in whose name Andalusia had been governed.

When in May 1013 the Slavonian chief realized the hopelessness of his cause and sent his message of surrender, the besieging forces understood that they had ended a holy war in a holy victory, that they had come to set the world on God's course. Accordingly, they burned and raped and butchered, mutilating the corpses in a carnival of blood.

Most of the houses were demolished, the palaces burned or stripped of all worldly beauty, as if such sensuous delights were in themselves sins. In the confusion the Caliph of Cordoba, Hisham II, quietly vanished. Some of the women in his harem later reported that he had slipped out of the palace disguised as a laborer. He was said to have sailed to Asia, where all trace of him was lost. In the years that followed impostors would turn up, creating sensations that might last a month or two. One warlord or another would claim to have him in safe-keeping, as if he were a flag or a sacred relic. Sometimes there would be corpses passed off as his.

Survivors came out of the rubble and took the road east toward the Sierra Nevada or north toward the border, where Christian kings waited impatiently for Andalusia to fall into their hands.

Though their victory, in retrospect, seems to have been inevitable, the Christian forces would have to wait more than 450 years to deliver the coup de grace, at Granada. That city had grown from a Jewish provincial town to a marvel of elegance. The paradise that had been lost at Cordoba seemed to have been regained at Granada. A poet, assuming the stance of a blind beggar, wrote:

> Give alms, lady,
> For the world has no pain
> Like that of being
> Blind in Granada.

In its latter days the city had been made glorious by refugee artists, poets, architects, teachers, engineers of water fountains, musicians and dancing masters. They would have to take to the road again before the end of Granada, for the shell of the city would hold together long after the heart was gone out of it.

The final moments of Granada were tinged with high irony. Ferdinand of Aragon, himself a descendant of Jews on his mother's side, was waiting outside the walls of the doomed city with his wiser and more forthright wife, Isabella of Castile. They were able to assemble and supply their formidable attack force only with the aid of two high-ranking Jews, Don Abraham Senior and Don Isaac Abravanel. (In little more than a year after the fall of Granada Don Abraham would be obliged to have himself baptized and Don Isaac, rejecting that alternative, would be on his way into exile.)

In the years before Granada fell the Catholic monarchs were still protecting Jews against the fury of fanatics, whether Moslem or Christian. And Jews were still Spanish grandees, serving as ambassadors, advisers and treasurers. True, they were no longer accepted as military leaders, although a few centuries earlier they might have been found among the officers of Christian and Moslem monarchs. A peculiarly Spanish notion had taken hold, according to which it was quite all right for Jews and Moslems to buy, sell, write and think because these activities were not regarded as in the proper domain of either the hidalgo or the true Iberian peasant. What was authentically Spanish, according to the prevailing mythology, was bravery in battle. That quality was therefore rigorously denied to Jews and Moslems.

After Cordoba fell Andalusia broke up into a succession of city-states, some flaring brilliantly for a spell, only to sink into corruption or founder in new waves of fanaticism. With each new collapse the surviving Jews had to flee. They traveled to all parts of Spain, Christian as well as Moslem. Rarely and only reluctantly did they leave the country where their ancient songs had blended with those of Arabs, Berbers and gypsies, where their scholars taught, and where, despite the best efforts of their rabbis, Jews had mingled their lives and their blood with all the other strains that had created the Spaniard.

Many came to Granada. Indeed, some experts argue persuasively that much of the Alhambra itself, that simulacrum of an oriental heaven, was planned by the Jewish grand vizier, general and poet-politician, Prince Samuel. The most romantic and lyrical of Jewish poets, Judah Halevi, walked the streets and gardens of Granada with the philosopher-poet Moses ibn Ezra and his three brothers, and with Solomon ibn Gabirol. All of them celebrated the beauties of Andalusia in a minor key, as at a deathbed. When they thought of home they yearned for Jerusalem.

It was during the administration of Prince Samuel's son Joseph that anti-Jewish mobs, scandalized by the genial tolerance of their rulers, outraged by the influence wielded by non-Moslems, loathing the easy-going secular approach in government, and envious of the Jews' wealth, killed, burned, raped and looted.

That disaster came in 1066, the year when William, Duke of Normandy, was crushing Anglo-Saxon resistance at Hastings. It was a century before the Jews of York were to kill themselves in an English Masada rather than surrender to crowds whipped to an anti-Jewish frenzy following the coronation of Richard the Lion-Hearted. The incident—for it was regarded as no more than that—was said to have grieved Richard, who no doubt was brave but is not generally regarded as having been very astute.

After the disaster of 1066 in Granada the Jews again took to the trail. It was a road that Maimonides of Cordoba would follow a century later, pausing only briefly at Lucena on his way to Fez and Cairo, where he fashioned a brilliant career as court physician to Saladin, the gallant sultan. Richard, in the course of crusading, reportedly tried in vain to buy the services of Maimonides, but he was interested only in his medical talents, not in his far greater philosophical achievements of trying to wed reason to faith. That was an effort at intellectual matchmaking that scandalized the scholiasts of all religions and would have baffled Richard.

Granada's ultimate fall to the Christians in 1492 marked the turn from twilight into night for Arabs as for Jews. It would be as long and as dark a night for the Berbers as well, who in their populist-fundamentalist rage had so disastrously undermined the power of the Caliphate.

The last ruler of Granada, called Boabdil, short for Abu-Abdullah, had subverted all resistance to the armies of Castile and Aragon. As the Christian monarchs pressed closer to his stronghold, he had wheedled, bargained and finally betrayed his allies for a few sad years of grace. Then, when the jig was plainly up, he slipped quietly out of a side gate of the city. After a brief time as a kept satrap of a minor principality in the south of Spain, he headed for exile in Africa.

Aisha, Boabdil's mother, thought her son had betrayed not only his city and his people but his gender as well. Clinging to the notion of male strength and female weakness, while belying it in practice, that grand dame of Moslem militancy sent her son off with a bitter farewell: "Weep like a woman for what you could not defend like a man."

With Granada leaderless and in despair Ferdinand and Isabella could mount their horses, wave their banners, and, to the chanting of a Te Deum, ride majestically into that magical city of alabaster and marble and murmuring fountains.

The Catholic monarchs offered the most generous terms. Ships would be provided for any who wished to leave Spain but no one would be forced to emigrate. The property of all would be safeguarded. No Christian would be permitted to force his way into a Moslem house. Christianity would not be spread by the sword. There would be no forced baptisms.

As a gesture of conciliation to Moslem prejudices it was promised that no Jew would retain a position of authority in the new Spain. (Moslem fanatics had already taken care of that in Granada.) In all other respects, however, Jews were to enjoy the same mild and beneficent rule promised to Moslems. Only those who chose to backslide after baptism would face expulsion. To a Moslem, for whom apostasy was a capital crime, this seemed singularly gentle.

For five years Christians seemed to be writing a sweet and smiling postlude to the Andalusia of Arabs and Jews. Priests even studied Arabic to woo converts. Then, with the inauguration of a new and fiercer primate of Spain, the climate changed abruptly. Stubborn Moslems who had resisted conversion were rounded up and made to see the light. Baptisms were performed en masse. Mosques were transformed into churches. Moslem books were heaped in the plazas and burned. The terror of Church and state, which had become one, led to rebellion and this in turn led to more terror. Soon Moslems and Jews alike had to choose between conversion and expulsion with an excellent chance of death as suspected heretics or apostates.

The banners that flew over Granada were very different from those the Berbers had raised over the ashes of Cordoba many years before but these, too, imposed on the smiling, capricious land of Andalusia the dread simplicity of an uncompromising, uncomplicated, unarguable Truth.

Bibliographical Note

Historians of Spain's Semitic period have tended to be parochial. Christian writers generally treat the interlude of Moslem
rule and Jewish influence as if it were an anomaly, serving
merely to show the mettle of Christian Spain, which presumably grew out of an indigenous Iberian civilization, unsullied
by extra-peninsular strains. Similarly, Moslems have written as
if none but Moslems were of much account. In their histories
Jews and Christians tend to be little more than foils for the
principals of the drama.

And Jewish historians, by and large, insist on seeing the rise
and fall of al-Andalus as only another episode in the tragedy of
the Diaspora—persecution relieved by an illusory peace and
prosperity, with the usual temptations to assimilation, followed
by frustration, terror and once again the open road.

Scholars with such particularized approaches leave to the
reading public—and the journalists of history—the task of as-
sembling the fragments into a coherent whole. What follows is
not a definitive bibliography but only a list of the sources I
found most helpful or most engaging.

One must begin with the classic on the period—*Histoire de
l'Espagne musulmane* by Évariste Lévi-Provençal (Paris, 1950–
1953), which unfortunately has not been translated into
English. It is, however, available in a splendid Spanish translation by Emilio Garcia Gomez. Much of that work is found in
Volume 5 of *Historia de España,* edited by Ramón Menéndez

Pidal (Madrid, 1973). That volume also includes an authoritative and detailed essay, *Arte Califal,* by Leopoldo Torres Balbás.

The three volumes in the French edition of Lévi-Provençal's masterly work tell the story from the conquest of the peninsula by the disinherited Omayyad prince who became known as Abd-er Rahman I, "the Immigrant," to the fall of Cordoba and the subsequent rise of the Spanish city-states. Lévi-Provençal not only describes the main events but also conveys in interesting detail the look and life of those times.

He deals rather cursorily with the Jews, however. That flaw is a bit ironic, because this most distinguished Arabist was himself a Jew, born in Algiers, who lost his teaching post when Nazism penetrated the Middle East.

Before Lévi-Provençal the standard for scholarship in the field was *Histoire des Musulmans d'Espagne jusqu'à la Conquête de l'Andalusie par les Almoravides* (Leiden, 1861) by Reinhart Dozy, a nineteenth-century Dutch historian who wrote in French to gain a wider readership. His countrymen took that bit of publishing acumen as a snub and responded coldly to his book. It won wide attention everywhere else, however. Though Lévi-Provençal has put him somewhat in the shade, Dozy has a rhapsodic charm that recommends him even now. His work, which has been translated into English and annotated by Francis Griffin Stokes under the title *Spanish Islam* (London, 1913, 1972) has the romantic dash of a Delacroix painting, though it seems to be far more sound historically.

The sober Lévi-Provençal has verified, updated and occasionally disputed Dozy. Certainly in his own work he substituted the straightforward historical approach for Dozy's venture into drama and melodrama. Dozy tends to make history read like the *Thousand and One Arabian Nights,* though it shuns the salacious charm of that work. Although Dozy, like Lévi-Provençal, suggests that the Jews played an important role in the politics and economy of Andalusia, he never brings them from the shadowy wings to center stage.

One must go, therefore, to the Jewish writers. There is, for example, Heinrich Graetz, author of the monumental *History of the Jews From the Earliest to the Present Day* (Philadelphia, 1898). The third volume of that work contains material most relevant to the Spanish episode. Eliyahu Ashtor, professor of Moslem history at the Hebrew University in Israel, has written a scholarly two-volume work that has been translated into English by Aaron Klein and Jenny Machlowitz Klein under the title *Jews of Moslem Spain* (Philadelphia, 1973). Though it tends to plod, the book nevertheless covers the ground. A long chapter on Hasdai ibn Shaprut is certainly the closest one can come to a full biography of that astonishing poet-scholar-diplomat. An earlier work on Hasdai, still worth a look, is the *Notice sur Abou Iousouf Hasdai ibn Schabrout,* by Philoxene Luzzato (Paris, 1852).

Ashtor has at his command a full array of both Moslem and Jewish sources, which tends to put him ahead of some of the learned Moslem Arabists who still neglect the Hebrew sources.

Particular aspects of the story not covered by Ashtor or Graetz and only touched on in Salo Baron's invaluable *Social and Religious History of the Jews* (New York, 1937) can be found in some exciting scholarship, as exemplified by Arthur J. Zuckerman's *A Jewish Princedom in Feudal France, 768–900* (Denver, 1972). In that work Zuckerman records the facts and enticing conjectures concerning the Jewish rule of Narbonne.

A splendid compilation of what is known of the Radanites, those romantic Jewish commercial travelers, can be found in *Jewish Merchant Adventurers,* by Louis I. Rabinowitz (London, 1948). Actual accounts by some of those adventurers are included in a most exotic collection entitled *Jewish Travelers,* by Elkan N. Adler (New York, 1931). Notable among these reports is the highly perceptive travelogue by Rabbi Petachia of Ratisbon. Some of the reasons for the Jews' enthusiasm at the coming of the Arabs may be found in *The Jews in the Visigothic and Frankish Kingdom of Spain and Gaul* by Solomon Katz (Cambridge, Mass., 1937).

It is enlightening, too, to read the famous letter of Hasdai summarizing, with the selectivity of a diplomat, the state of affairs at the height of Arab-Jewish glory and inquiring into the situation in the mysterious Jewish kingdom of Khazaria. The document is to be found in many places, including Adler's collection, under the title *Epistle of R. Chisdai, son of Isaac (of blessed memory) to the King of the Khazars.*

The letter can also be seen in a most thoroughgoing essay on the subject, D. M. Dunlop's *History of the Jewish Khazars* (New York, 1954).

An anthology of eminently useful and interesting essays—some in English, others in French or Spanish—is the *Sephardi Heritage,* by Richard Barnett (London, 1971). Particularly stimulating is the discussion of the interplay between Jewish and Arabic literary influences in the contribution of Federico Perez Castro, entitled *España y los Judios Españoles.* I also found valuable a short piece in the first volume of *Andalucia Medieval,* the proceedings of the Congreso de Historia de Andalucia in December 1976. Written by David Gonzalo Maeso, the article details the schooling in Jewish communities in Spain.

Works such as Abraham Aaron Neuman's *The Jews in Spain* (Philadelphia, 1948) and those of Ashtor have largely superseded the nineteenth-century classic, *Historia social, política y religiosa de los Judios de España* by José Amador de Los Rios (Madrid, 1960). Just as Lévi-Provençal has shown that a Jew can become the world's most celebrated Arabist, so in his time did Amador de Los Rios demonstrate that a faithful Catholic may become his country's greatest authority on Spanish Jews.

Some Jewish critics have diputed the scholarship of Amador de Los Rios and even suggested that he carried the seeds of his century's abiding prejudice. Others have hotly refuted such charges. In any case it was the contention of Amador de Los Rios that the Jews have left their mark on Spanish history and are in fact an inseparable element in the texture of the Spanish nation.

In the continuing debate on that question the issue is cleanly drawn between two eminent contemporary authorities. On the one hand, Claudio Sánchez Albornoz suggests that the Spanish character, of pure Iberian descent, has remained impervious to Semitic influences, whether Jewish or Arab. The chief target of his polemics is Americo Castro, author of *España en su Historia.*

The work has been translated into English by Willard F. King and Selma Margaretten under the title *The Spaniards—An Introduction to their History* (Berkeley, 1971). Castro has profoundly irritated the camp of Sánchez Albornoz by contending that if one subtracts the Jewish and Arabic factors, the Spanish soul, itself, becomes thin and vapory. In an eminently readable argument he traces the various elements of the quixotic, chivalric Spaniard in literature and life, in art, science and genetics. He finds in all this a strong Semitic heritage, which he implores his countrymen to acknowledge proudly. Incidentally—as if to needle his adversaries—he notes the Jewish lineage of such quintessential Spaniards as Saint Teresa de Avila, Cervantes, Torquemada, Ferdinand the Catholic and many others.

It is also essential to taste the flavor of traditional Moslem history. There is, for example, the *History of the Mohammedan Dynasties in Spain,* written in the seventeenth century by Ahmed ibn Mohammed al-Maqqari and translated with copious notes by Pascual de Gayangos (London, 1840–1843). Similarly, *The Geography of the Inhabited World,* by Idrisi, is an enchanting though not altogether reliable report on the twelfth century. S. M. Imamuddin has given us history from a more modern though unswervingly Moslem point of view in *A Political History of Muslim Spain* (Dacca, 1961).

For a quick overall view of the field one should turn to Jan Read's *The Moors in Spain and Portugal* (London, 1974). Bravely, the author tries to condense the entire history of medieval Spain and Portugal—Christian and Moslem, with a nod to the Jews—in barely 250 pages.

For particular aspects of the story I found it helpful and exciting to dip into Pierre Riché's *Daily Life in the World of Charlemagne,* translated by Jo Ann McNamara (Philadelphia, 1978). The book served to take me into the larger European scene. For reaching backward in time there were, in addition to the standard Gibbon, a fine text on *Roman Society in the Last Century of the Western Empire,* by Samuel Dill (London, 1925), and some fragments of *Life in Gaul,* by C. Sollius Apollinaris.

Seeking a look at Cordoba from the perspective of a puritan

who came soon after the fall of the city, I had the delight of reading *Le Traité d'ibn Abdun.* (It was ibn Abdun who expressed his horror at the sight of young men with long hair playing music at picnics.) Lévi-Provençal translated that essay into French from a manuscript he himself had unearthed in Morocco. It was published in *Journal Asiatique,* April–June 1934.

In Spain I had the inestimable help of a number of scholars. I was particularly privileged to be guided by Don Rafael Castejón, who has written profoundly on the Caliphate but also has not disdained to put out popularly written though nonetheless expert handbooks for tourists exploring the Mezquita and the Medina Azahara in Cordoba. It was a delight to walk the city in his illuminating company.

I also had the benefit of a personal exposition of many intricate questions by Professor Ocaña Jimenez. For steering me to such sources and for many other reasons, I must also thank the Instituto Benito Arias Montano and the Instituto Balmas in Madrid.

These scholars can be credited with whatever insights this book may contain but the author alone is responsible for any errors or misunderstandings that may bedevil it.

Index

ibn al-Abbas, Abdallah, 49–50
Abbasid dynasty, 50, 51, 60, 63, 66, 75–76, 78
ibn al-Abd, Tarafa, 45–46
Abd-Allah (son of Abd-er Rahman I), 77
ibn Abd Allah, Ghirbib, 79
Abdallah, emir of Cordoba, 138–39, 141–44
Abdallah, Prince, 122–23, 132–33
Abd-er Rahman, Crown Prince, 223, 224
Abd-er Rahman I, emir of Cordoba, 50–53, 55–63, 65, 75–77, 246
Abd-er Rahman II, emir of Cordoba, 80, 81, 84–92, 100, 101, 103, 116, 118, 121, 128–30, 132
Abd-er Rahman III, Caliph of Cordoba, 18, 22, 143, 147–55, 157, 160, 162, 167, 169, 176, 184, 186, 187, 190–202, 204, 206–8, 210, 212, 215, 217, 221, 227, 238
ibn 'Abdun, 162–64, 250
Abi Amir, Mohammed, 222–35
ibn Abitur, Joseph ben Isaac, 220–21
Abraham of Saragossa, 70

Abravanel, Don Isaac, 240
Abur Bakr, 46
Acre, Isaac de, 178
Adler, Elkan N., 247, 248
Agobard, bishop of Lyons, 64
Agriculture, 159–60
Ailo (Egilona), 42, 43
Aisha, 49, 242
Alhambra, 241
Ali, Caliph of Damascus, 49
Alvaro, 116–18, 127–28
Alvaro Cordobes, Paulus, 74
Amador de Los Rios, José, 248
Amalaric, king of Visigoths, 30
Amrus, 79–81
ibn Anas, Malik, 77–78
Andromachus, 189
Animal husbandry, 159
Anulo, 118
Apollinaris, Sidonius, 28, 249
Argentea, 151–52
Arian Christians, 29–30, 64
Artisans, Jewish, 170–71
Ashtor, Eliyahu, 247, 248
Augustine, St., 28
Avenzoar, 176
Averroes, 176
Aziz, Abdul, 40, 42–44

Badr, 51–53, 55–58
Baldegotho, 119
al-Balluk, Sa'id, 194–95

Barnett, Richard, 248
Baron, Salo, 247
Basques, 29, 57, 75, 88
Berbers, 21, 24, 25, 34, 36–39,
  41, 49, 50, 56, 62, 63, 75,
  100, 142, 170, 221,
  228–29, 235, 237, 243
Bertha of the Big Feet, Queen,
  67, 68
al-Bikri, Yahya ibn Hakam,
  90–91
Boabdil, 242
Bobastro
  fall of, 151–52
  siege of, 136–38
Bodo, 73–74
Bofilh, 70
Book of Interpretations (Saruq),
  214
Book of Lands, The (al Hama-
  dani), 101
*Book of the Roads and the King-
  doms, The* (Khordadbeh),
  99
Breton March, 75
Burton, Richard, 165

Cabala, 115
Caste system, Roman, 25–26
Castejón, Don Rafael, 250
Castro, Americo, 248–49
Catholicism, 29–30, 64
  See also Christian martyrs
Ceuta
  Arab capture of, 34
  captured by Abd-er Rahman
    III, 151
Charlemagne, 68–70, 72, 75,
  96, 100, 102, 114
Charles the Bald, 133
Childbirth, customs surround-
  ing, 166–67
Chilperic I, king of France,
  72–73
Christian martyrs, 16, 116–29,
  134–35, 151–52
Circumcision rituals, 167
Class structure, 16

Clothing
  markets for, 159
  Ziryab's influence on, 96
Clotilda, queen of Visigoths, 30
Cluniac monks, 233
Compostela, destruction of,
  233–34
Congreso de Historia de Andalucia, 248
Constantine, Emperor, 28
Constantine Porphyrogenitus,
  Emperor, 19, 191–93,
  195
Contraception, 175
Cordoba
  childbirth customs in, 166–67
  declared Caliphate, 150, 152
  decline of, under Abdallah,
    142
  economic prosperity of,
    156–60
  education in, 211–12
  fall of, 238–40, 243
  Jewish culture in, 169–83
  Mezquita of, 11–13
  modern, 14–15
  Moslem capture of, 39
  navy of, 103–4
  rioting in, 237
  role of eunuchs in, 131
  sexual practices in, 161–64
  sports in, 167–68
  trade and, 100, 101, 115
  under Visigoths, 37–38
  Ziryab's influence on culture
    of, 93–97
Cuisine, Ziryab's influence on,
  94–96

Damakis, 184
Day of the Ditch, 81, 85
De Materia Medica (Dioscorides),
  19, 194, 195
Death, ceremonies surround-
  ing, 168
Dill, Samuel, 249
Diocletian, Emperor, 25–26
Dioscorides, 19, 194, 195

Dome of the Rock, 49
Dozy, Reinhart, 120, 246
Dunlop, D. M., 248

Education, 208, 211–12
  Jewish, 181–82
Egica, king of Visigoths, 32
El'azar, Rabbi, 108, 109
Eldad, 178–79, 215
Erwig, king of Visigoths, 32
Ethiopian Jews, 178–79
Eulogius, St., 117–18, 120,
  126–28, 134–35
Eunuchs, social role of, 130–32
Executions, 18
  See also Christian martyrs
ibn Ezra, Moses, 241

Falashas, 179
Fatima, 63
Fatimids, 150, 151, 184, 192,
  195
Ferdinand of Aragon, 240, 242
al-Fihri, Yusuf, 55–59, 61–62
ibn Firnas, Abbas, 89–90, 159
First Crusade, 114
Flora, 119–20, 127–28
Florinda, 35–38
Foulfoul, 106
Franks, 21, 29–30, 63, 64,
  67–68, 154

Galen, 138, 189
Gallegos, 21
Garcia Gomez, Emilio, 245
Garcia of Navarre, 203, 205–6
Gayangos, Pascual de, 249
Germans, 28
Ghazzalan, 93
Gomez, 125–26
Gonzalo Maeso, David, 248
Goths, 65, 66
Graetz, Heinrich, 246–47
Granada, 239–43
Great Mosque, 76–77
Gregory, bishop of Tours, 73

Hafsun, Omar, 135–40, 142,
  151–52
ibn Hajjaj, Ibrahim, 138–39
Hakam I, emir of Cordoba,
  78–85, 91, 158
Hakam II, Caliph of Cordoba,
  208, 210–13, 221–28
Halevi, Judah, 216, 241
al Hamadani, ibn al-Fakih Abu
  Bakr Anmad ben Mu-
  hammed ben Ishak, 101
ben Hanoch, Moses, 184–86,
  220
Hindah, 93
Hippalos, 104–5
Hisham I, emir of Cordoba,
  77–79, 81, 142
Hisham II, Caliph of Cordoba,
  50, 224–26, 229, 235–39
Holal, 59

Iberi, 27
Idrisi, 249
Imamuddin, S. M., 249
Inquisition, Holy Office of, 10
Isaac (Christian militant), 124
Isabella of Castille, 240, 242
Ishaq (Radanite), 105–7
Isidore, archbishop of Seville,
  31, 32

Jaffa massacre, 50
James, St., 232–33
Jerome, St., 29
Jerusalem, Jewish rebellion in,
  27
Jewelry workshops, 159
Jimenez, Ocaña, 250
John of Gorze, 196–201
Joseph, king of Khazaria, 216
Judaeus, Isaac, 176
Julian, archbishop of Toledo,
  64
Julian, commander of Ceuta,
  34–38
Julian, Emperor, 27

Kaijites, 49

Kaisites, 49
Kalam, 88
Kalbites, 49
Kamar, 139
Karaites, 179–81, 218, 219
Kasim, 142
Katz, Solomon, 247
ibn Khaldun, 100
Khalid (apostle), 46
Khalid (royal secretary), 57
Khazars, 111–13, 215–17
ibn Khordadbeh, Abdul Kassim
    Obaid Allah, 98–99,
    101–2, 107
King, Willard F., 249
Klein, Aaron, 247
Klein, Jenny Machlowitz, 247
Koran, 18, 34, 49, 54, 227, 228

ben Labrat, Dunash Ha-Levi,
    176–77, 217–19, 221
Languedoc, 63–64
Laws, 23
Lévi-Provençal, Évariste, 245,
    246, 248, 250
Louis I, king of France, 70–71,
    73
Lucena
    battle of, 140–41
    emasculation center at,
        130–31
    fifteenth-century, 11
    modern, 9
    Talmudic scholars of, 108–9
Luzzato, Philoxene, 247

McNamara, Jo Ann, 249
Madina, al-Zahira, 230, 237
Madinat al-Zahra, 146–50,
    154–56, 230, 238
Maimonides, 176, 241
Makhir, Rabbi, 69, 70
Malik, Abd-al, 235, 236
Malikites, 78, 79, 81, 83
ibn Malluk, Tarif, 37
Mansur, Abu al-Nasr, 91–92,
    94
al-Mansur, *see* Abi Amir,
    Mohammed

al-Maqqari, Ahmed ibn
    Mohammed, 249
Margaretten, Selma, 249
Markets, 16–20, 159
    slave, 20–23, 111
Marriage
    Karaites strictures on, 180–81
    Moslem celebrations of, 165
Martel, Charles, 54, 65
Marthad, king of Yemen, 41
Martyrdom, *see* Christian mar-
    tyrs
Marwan II, Caliph of
    Damascus, 49
Masrur, 118
Matrand, ruler of Narbonne, 66
al-Mawsili, Ishak, 91
Medicine, 131, 171–76,
    189–90, 194, 195, 204,
    207
    women practicing, 166
Menéndez Pidal, Ramón,
    245–46
Merida, siege of, 40
Mezquita of Cordoba, 11–13
Mining, 158–59
Mints, establishment of, 85
Mithradates VI, king of Pontus,
    189
Mohammed, 41, 45–47, 121,
    122, 124
Mohammed, Crown Prince,
    142, 143
Mohammed, emir of Cordoba,
    122–23, 133–34
ben Moses, Hanoch, 184,
    220–21
Mozarabes, 135, 198
al-Mundhir, emir, 137–38, 142
al-Mushafi, 226, 227
al-Mutarif, 143
Muwalladun, 135

ibn Nafi, Abu al-Hasan'ali
    (Ziryab), 91
Narbonne, 64–72
    siege of, 65–66
al-Nasr, Abu al-Fath, 89, 118,
    121–23